Islam and Mammon

Islam and Mammon

THE ECONOMIC PREDICAMENTS OF ISLAMISM

Timur Kuran

PRINCETON UNIVERSITY PRESS

PRINCETON AND OXFORD

Copyright © 2004 by Princeton University Press
Published by Princeton University Press, 41 William Street, Princeton,
    New Jersey 08540
In the United Kingdom: Princeton University Press, 3 Market Place,
    Woodstock, Oxfordshire OX20 1SY

Third printing, and first paperback printing, 2006
Paperback ISBN-13: 978-0-691-12629-6
Paperback ISBN-10: 0-691-12629-1

THE LIBRARY OF CONGRESS HAS CATALOGED THE CLOTH EDITION OF
THIS BOOK AS FOLLOWS

Kuran, Timur.
    Islam and Mammon / the economic predicaments of Islamism /
Timur Kuran.
      p. cm.
Includes bibliographical references and index.
ISBN: 0-691-11510-9 (cl : alk. paper)
    1. Economics—Islamic countries. 2. Economics—Religious aspects—Islam.
3. Islam—Economic aspects. I. Title.
HB126.4K87 2004
330.917′67—dc22   2003060094

British Library Cataloging-in-Publication Data is available

This book has been composed in Sabon

Printed on acid-free paper. ∞

pup.princeton.edu

Printed in the United States of America

10 9 8 7 6 5 4 3

TO MY SISTERS

Suzan and Melisa
and our childhood memories
of growing up in Ankara and Istanbul

Contents

Preface

IF ANGER, RESENTMENT, FRUSTRATION, AND ENVY were four of the factors that sowed the horrors of September 11, 2001, another is the belief that Islam offers solutions to entrenched problems of human civilization. Militants who strike in the name of Islamism, like millions of peaceful Islamists, argue, some no doubt with conviction, that Islam holds the key to a social order capable of providing social justice along with economic prosperity. Islam harbors an economic vision, Islamists contend, whose superiority has already been proven. Its first few decades in the seventh century, they say, and to an extent also the subsequent few centuries, amply demonstrate the merits of Islamic economic values and institutions.

There exists a voluminous modern literature that purports to identify Islam's economic wisdom and to derive implications relevant to the present. Grounded in medieval Islamic thought, it is known as "Islamic economics." Notwithstanding the claims of its promoters, the significance of this literature does not lie in its substance. It does not describe the advantages of Islamic economic principles in a manner that would make sense to a well-trained economist. Nor has it produced solutions that more than a small minority of Muslims take seriously. The significance of this literature lies chiefly in the support it gives to the quest for a distinctly Islamic social order. Islamic economics has fueled the illusion that Muslims can solve a wide range of social problems simply by embracing Islam and resisting Mammon—the evils associated with immoral forms of economic gain. It has promoted the spread of antimodern, and in some respects deliberately anti-Western, currents of thought all across the Islamic world. It has also fostered an environment conducive to Islamist militancy.

The most conspicuous assertion of Islamic economics is that interest is patently un-Islamic. Given the central role that interest plays in any modern economy, this claim sanctifies opposition to global economic integration. Most Muslims, whether or not they favor a ban on interest, and regardless of how they interpret Islam, readily agree that avoiding interest is among the constraints Islam places on economic behavior, if not its most important economic requirement. Likewise, non-Muslim observers of the Islamic world generally take it for granted that to shun interest is a basic Islamic requirement. Few people question whether the traditional sources of Islam do, in fact, prohibit *all* forms of interest. Nor is it common to encounter inquiries into whether the belief in a categorical ban has always enjoyed currency. Whatever their own attitudes toward interest, most observers, regardless of faith, believe that Islam treats interest as the clearest embodiment of Mammon. Among other doubtful assertions of Islamic economics is that Islam harbors an unsurpassed institution for redistributing wealth to the poor. And another is that the Islamic heritage offers economic norms well suited to ridding a modern economy of opportunism and corruption. Like the claim that Islam prohibits all interest, these assertions are rarely challenged explicitly or directly. Writings critical of Islamic economics, especially scholarly publications, are uncommon in any language.

There are several reasons why Islamic economics has largely been spared the sort of critical analysis to which the typical economic doctrine or program is subjected routinely. The most basic is that its prescriptions are considered too unrealistic to threaten prevailing economic structures. Another is that evaluating an economic doctrine grounded in Islam requires familiarity with economic theory, Islamic history, and the contemporary Islamic world—realms of analysis that rarely intersect. Still another factor is cultural relativism. Promoted by certain influential strands of multiculturalism, this attitude discourages challenges to cultural products considered expressions of authenticity. Whatever the relative weights of these various factors, they all distort public discourses on the contributions that religion in general, and Islam in particular, may make to a society's economic well-being. Inflating the apparent popularity of Islamist economic goals, they also put a veneer of antiquity on practices and institutions that are actually recent constructs.

Islamic economics itself exemplifies what has been called an "invented tradition."[1] As several of the following essays document, not until the mid-twentieth century were campaigns launched to identify self-consciously, if not also exclusively, Islamic patterns of economic thought and behavior. Until that time the economic content of discourses grounded in Islam's traditional sources lacked systematization; they hardly formed a body of thought recognizable as a coherent or self-contained doctrine. Nor did promoters of an Islamic social order have an economic agenda drawn from Islam's intellectual heritage. When Muslim Arabs, Turks, Slavs, Iranians, Central Asians, or Indians of the early twentieth century expressed economic demands, they usually did so without invoking exclusively Islamic concepts or using identifiably Islamic terminology. Not even pan-Islamists intent on overthrowing colonial regimes put forth an economic agenda recognizable as Islamic.

Just as the interest ban became the most salient objective of Islamic economics, its most visible practical achievement has turned out to be Islamic banking, itself an invented tradition. Even the concept of Islamic banking is a product of the twentieth century. To be sure, early Islamic civilization developed impressive financial institutions. By the tenth century, Islamic law supported credit and investment instruments that were as advanced as their counterparts outside the Islamic world. In fact, they stimulated institutional advances elsewhere, including Western Europe.[2] Yet prior to the nineteenth century, the Islamic world did not generate durable financial organizations recognizable as banks; and when such organizations finally appeared, it was through Western initiatives. It is also significant that the first mainly Muslim-owned banks emerged in the 1920s.

As for the first "Islamic" banks, they made their appearance a half century later, in the 1970s. Although massive efforts have been made to portray them as analogous to an ancient financial organization, in truth they function more like conventional commercial banks than like the ephemeral and small-scale financial enterprises of the premodern Middle East. The first two essays document that Islamic banks do not even avoid interest, except in name. But the differences do not stop there. An Islamic bank enjoys standing before the law as a juristic person, which is a concept alien to traditional Islamic law. It can, and is expected to, outlive its founders, shareholders, and employees, as no financial enterprise could under Islamic law except a waqf, or pious foundation. Unlike a waqf, however, an Islamic bank is authorized to make and remake its own rules and objectives. Under Islamic law, a waqf had to remain frozen, bound in perpetuity by its founder's directives.[3]

If organized efforts to give economics an Islamic hue began no more than a few generations ago, and the practical results of these efforts present unmistakably modern features, are the links between Islamic history and Islamic economics merely symbolic? On the contrary, Islamic economics endeavors to situate its prescriptions in Islam's very rich legal, social, and intellectual heritage. As a case in point, it portrays Islamic banking as a reincarnation of the Islamic law of partnerships, developed a millennium ago. That law, it is said, gave humanity a timeless institutional basis for saving, investing, lending, and borrowing without using interest. Islamic economics is as much a return to the distant past, then, as it is an attempt to embrace modernity. It pursues contemporary economic objectives through institutions rooted in Islamic history. If an Islamic bank lived up to the theory of Islamic banking, not to mention its own charter, it would, in fact, form multitudes of partnerships every day, some with individual depositors and others with individual borrowers. Each of these partnerships would subject it to uncertainties evadable through interest.

It is not self-evident why the twentieth century spawned a movement committed to developing an Islamic variant of economics. After all, there is no distinctly Islamic way to build a ship, or defend a territory, or cure an epidemic, or forecast the weather. Nor are there constituencies for basing such tasks on Islamic teachings. Moreover, every period of Islamic history offers abundant examples of innovations with little, if any, basis in religion. Over the centuries Muslim achievements in diverse domains—science, art, governance, commerce—have involved doctrinal flexibility, openness to outside influences, and respect for creativity. Where we now observe a commitment to narrowly Islamic principles, traditions, or even imagery, there is a need, then, for an explanation.

A major reason for the existence of Islamic economics, documented in this book's fourth essay, lies in the objective to tighten communal bonds among Muslims, and in particular among those of the Indian subcontinent. In the course of the political struggles that resulted in the establishment of Pakistan as a homeland for India's Muslims, certain activists sought to strengthen Muslim communal ties by reinforcing personal identification with Islam. This campaign led to the resurrection or invention of numerous Islamic traditions in domains considered receptive to religion. Among these domains was economics. Since that time Muslims from the Indian subcontinent have stood at the forefront of efforts to develop recognizably Islamic economic theories, practices, policies, and institutions.

In certain predominantly Muslim countries, including Pakistan, these efforts have enjoyed at least the tacit support of politicians and intellectuals fearful of being stigmatized as insufficiently Islamic. The consequent reticence has muted questions concerning the viability and desirability of the Islamist economic agenda. Making people privately opposed to Islamic economics pay lip service to a vague ideal of economic Islamization, it has even emboldened Islamists. Ceding Islamists a monopoly over the interpretation of Islam's economic requirements, it has enabled them to determine which economic behaviors and approaches are properly Islamic and which are to be resisted as dangerously un-Islamic.

The resulting expressive imbalance is particularly striking in view of the limited support that economic Islamization enjoys in markets of the Islamic world. As the first two essays show, in heavily Muslim countries where ostensibly interest-free Islamic banks coexist with conventional banks, the market shares of the former have remained very low. It appears, therefore, that the constituency for economic Islamization is modest. This inference is consistent with the reluctance that Islamic banks have shown in purging interest from their operations. Significantly, the courts have done little to enforce anti-interest legislation. Under pressure from the business community, they have evaded that responsibility, first, by granting banks transition periods during which they could continue dealing in interest with impunity and, second, in the face of imminent deadlines, by revoking previous decisions to allow more time for reflection and consensus building. Most recently, in 2002, the Supreme Court of Pakistan rescinded a 1999 judgment of the Federal

Sharia Court, under which all interest-based banking was to be strictly illegal as of mid-2002.[4]

The economic Islamization campaign had received a second wind during the Arab oil boom of the 1970s, when Saudi Arabia and other wealthy monarchies of the Arabian peninsula felt compelled to demonstrate a commitment to Islamic causes. The oil revenues of these states had grown tenfold in inflation-adjusted terms between 1970 and 1974. The consequent enrichment of Arab oil exporters reinforced already potent images of decadent sheiks squandering Arab and Muslim resources. It also drew attention to huge inequalities within the Islamic world, within the Arab world, and even within the oil-rich monarchies themselves. These monarchies felt threatened by diverse groups, including antiroyalists, foreign workers living in shantytowns, and religious conservatives appalled by moral laxity.[5] To pacify these groups, they took to enlarging their already substantial aid programs to various Arab and Muslim constituencies. They also established, or began supporting, organizations that served Arab or Islamic causes.[6] Among the beneficiaries of this drive for global legitimacy were schools and research organizations dedicated to the bourgeoning doctrine of Islamic economics.

At the time that Islamic economics got reenergized by oil wealth, it stood on the fringes of global economic discourse. Notwithstanding its rejection of capitalism and socialism, it contributed minimally to major policy debates of the era. This is consistent, of course, with its emergence as a tool for identity preservation as opposed to economic improvement. Little changed on this count after Saudi Arabia assumed a leading role in its development. Islamic economics hardly participated in the headline-grabbing economic debates of the 1970s and 1980s: trade liberalization, privatization, and environmental regulation. Most remarkably, it did not even take a stand on the recycling of oil revenues—widely championed as an instrument for alleviating the massive trade deficits that oil importers, including ones with largely Muslim populations, were enduring because of skyrocketing oil prices.

The founding of the Islamic Development Bank in the mid-1970s might have provided an occasion for developing distinctly Islamic policy positions on the recycling of petrodollars. Though modeled after the World Bank, the Islamic Development Bank enjoyed immediate identification with Islamic economics because, at least on paper, it committed itself to interest-free financial methods. However, Islamic economics refrained from critiquing the Islamic Development Bank's operations or priorities. One reason, no doubt, lay in the enormous support that Islamic economics was receiving from Saudi Arabia, the bank's host country. The Saudi regime was, and remains, notoriously sensitive to feedback liable to prompt questions about its Islamic correctness.

This sensitivity has helped to limit the substantive range of Islamic economics. The consequent narrowness is evident in the scope of the essays that follow. If my critiques focus mainly on just three matters—the interest ban, wealth redistribution through the zakat system, and Islamic norms of economic behavior—the reason is that these constitute the central topics of Islamic economics itself. The limitations of Islamic economics become obvious when one thinks of what the literature generally ignores. A list of omitted topics might include the economic effects of gender discrimination, the productivity implications of replacing secular schools by Islamic schools, the role of Islamic law in the emerging global economy, and the institutional determinants of scientific creativity. Broadening the scope of Islamic economics to include such topics might have undermined the Saudi quest for political legitimacy. For one thing, by encouraging intellectual creativity it might have diluted the traditionalist character of the enterprise. For another, it might have spawned criticism of Saudi policies, the Arab social order, even Islam itself. The narrowness of Islamic economics, not to mention the infeasibility of its prescriptions, must have suited the Saudi Arabian government, which was pursuing an ambitious economic modernization program behind a protective façade of Islamic traditionalism.

To one degree or another, most of today's fifty-six predominantly Muslim countries are economically underdeveloped. Therefore, it is natural to wonder about how Islam has affected economic evolution. Unlike many secular schools of thought, Islamic economics does not deny the existence of links between religion and economic performance. In highlighting early Islamic policies and institutions that helped the Middle East register impressive economic advances, it asserts that the links were mainly favorable. Thus, it offers the zakat system of seventh-century Arabia as evidence of Islam's capacity for poverty alleviation, and the Islamic law of partnerships as an example of the support early Muslim authorities gave to commerce. Yet, institutions initially favorable to one economic objective or another might eventually have become dysfunctional, even counterproductive.[7] Islamic economics avoids such possibilities by claiming that whatever may have slowed the economic development of Muslim-governed states, or prevented them from keeping pace with global economic modernization, must have had foreign origins. But what made the economic systems of the Islamic world vulnerable to harmful external influences?

The last essay of the volume explores the possibilities. Drawing attention to a variety of social mechanisms through which Islamic institutions, practices, beliefs, and attitudes may have helped or hindered economic development, it also identifies a series of unresolved historical puzzles.

The essays make clear that there is no simple answer to the question—asked with increasing frequency in the wake of September 11—of whether Islam has been, or turned into, an obstacle to economic progress. As we shall see, the claim that "Islam is hostile to commerce" is refuted as easily as the opposite assertion. Like any great religion with a long history, Islam has stood for many things, and its effects have varied according to time and place. Identifying why the members of the Organization of Islamic States do not top the World Bank's current per capita income roster requires fine-combed, patient, and dispassionate analysis.

To observe that Islamic economics has received support from parties with one political agenda or another does not imply that its individual practitioners and followers are themselves political operatives. The motives of an expositor of Islamic banking need not match those of his financial supporters. Nor must a saver who opens an account at an Islamic bank have a political goal. By the same token, the effects of Islamic economics may transcend those pursued by its principal financial supporters. Among the themes of this book is that Islamic economics fosters an intellectual climate unconducive to open-ended discourse on policies and practices that have achieved identification with Islam.

Among the by-products of the resulting expressive reticence is the paucity and shallowness of debates on the sources of underdevelopment highlighted by the first *Arab Human Development Report*, prepared entirely by Arabs and issued in 2002. If this report received enormous attention in the global media, one reason is that it articulates diagnoses and proposals that Arabs rarely defend publicly. Observing that the Arab world suffers from "capability and opportunity poverty," the *Report* draws attention to three deficits responsible for economic backwardness—none noted by Islamic economics. The first is a "freedom deficit" caused by limits on political participation, the second a "women's empowerment deficit" rooted in laws and norms that allow, if not require, gender discrimination, and the third a shocking "knowledge deficit" that stems chiefly from inadequate schooling.[8] In view of these undeniable deficits, the significance of Islamic economics may lie less in what it preaches than in topics it avoids. However peaceful and well intentioned the Islamic economists themselves, their works may also contribute to global economic instability. In hindering institutional reforms necessary for healthy economic development, they contribute to social despair. As important, they allow Islamic militants to rationalize crimes as serving a sacred cause.

The complexities and silences of Islamic economics have contributed to its many contradictions and inconsistencies, which are discussed in several of the essays, most directly the fifth. To be sure, any movement serving as a conduit for diverse agendas may suffer from incoherence.

Think of the antiglobalization movement that has made headlines since the late 1990s. Mass protests organized in the name of antiglobalization unite people with agendas as diverse as wildlife preservation, sustainable development, economic protectionism, AIDS research, marijuana legalization, and gay rights. Such agendas are not necessarily mutually compatible; there may exist trade-offs, for instance, between assisting endangered species and promoting industrialization.

Islamic economics, which is scrutinized in each of the first five essays, is easily confused with the economic activities of organizations that claim an Islamic identity. Such organizations include retail outlets as well as giant corporations, charities as well as profit-seeking banks. A subset of them—most conspicuously, Islamic banks—assert a commitment to the global struggle for economic Islamization. But others show no desire to restructure the world economy. There are Islamic charities that have a religious identity not because they follow distinctly Islamic fundraising principles but because they draw resources from Muslim congregations. Likewise, there are clinics, schools, and relief organizations that are considered Islamic simply because they are run by devout Muslims expressly for the benefit of Muslims. Some of these organizations are highly effective—measurably more successful, in fact, than their counterparts operated by governments or secular private establishments. Whatever their successes, in various places they collectively form Islamic subeconomies. The composition and operation of Islamic subeconomies are discussed in the second and third essays.

The entire volume bears on Samuel Huntington's controversial claim that we are in the throes of a "clash of civilizations."[9] The leading luminaries of Islamic economics could have stressed the resemblances of, and mutual influences among, the world's great religions. They could have emphasized the Judaic and Christian roots of Islamic social thought, the high esteem that ancient Hellenic philosophy enjoyed among early Muslim writers, and the commonalities of the partnership forms once in use along the Mediterranean coastline. Instead, and as we shall see, they have treated economics as a vehicle for accentuating the uniqueness of Islamic civilization and its incompatibility with other civilizations, even the emerging global civilization. To this day, Islamic economics insists that living as a good Muslim requires adherence to distinctly Islamic norms. Consequently, it requires practicing Muslims to limit, if not shun, economic relations with non-Muslims, even with nonconformist Muslims.

Huntington's clash-of-civilizations thesis falters, however, when one turns from ideology to practice. The cultural separatism preached by Islamic economists has had little practical impact. More than a half century after the birth of Islamic economics, nowhere has interest been purged from economic transactions, and nowhere does economic Islamization enjoy mass support. Although there exist Muslims who consider Islamic civilization at war with other civilizations, the economic manifestations of their divisive measures remain exceptional and superficial.

Looking back at the essays grouped in this book, I am struck by how well they have stood the test of time. None of my assessments of Islamic economics has required substantive revision in the face of later developments. My claims as to the infeasibility of Islamic banking and the inadequacy of Islam's traditional redistribution instrument carry as much truth today as they did when first articulated. Editing has been limited to stylistic standardization and minor cuts to avoid repetition.

I am indebted to the publishers of the original essays for granting permission to reproduce them here. In order of appearance in this volume, the six essays and their publishers are: "The Economic Impact of Islamic Fundamentalism," in *Fundamentalisms and the State: Remaking Polities, Economies, and Militance*, edited by Martin E. Marty and R. Scott Appleby (Chicago: University of Chicago Press, 1993), pp. 302–41; "Islamic Economics and the Islamic Subeconomy," *Journal of Economic Perspectives* 9 (Fall 1995): 155–73 (© American Economic Association); "Islamism and Economics: Policy Prescriptions for a Free Society," *International Review of Comparative Public Policy* 9 (1997): 71–102 (© Elsevier Science); "The Genesis of Islamic Economics: A Chapter in the Politics of Muslim Identity," *Social Research* 64 (Summer 1997): 301–38; "On the Notion of Economic Justice in Contemporary Islamic Thought," *International Journal of Middle East Studies* 21 (May 1989): 171–91 (© Cambridge University Press); and "Islam and Underdevelopment," *Journal of Institutional and Theoretical Economics* 153 (March 1997): 41–71 (© J.C.B. Mohr [Paul Siebeck] Tübingen).

In conducting the early research on which this book rests, I had the support of the Faculty Research and Innovation Fund of my university, the University of Southern California, and from 1993 onward, of its King Faisal Chair in Islamic Thought and Culture. During the academic year 2002–3, while this book was in preparation, I was a fellow of the Center for Interdisciplinary Research, University of Southern California. Some of the work displayed in the book was conducted in 1989–90, which I spent at the Institute for Advanced Study at Princeton, supported by a fellowship of the National Endowment of the Humanities. Two of the essays were written or completed in 1996–97 at the University of Chicago, where I held the John Olin Visiting Professorship at the George J. Stigler Center for the Study of the Economy and the State, Graduate School of Business. Along the way, numerous individuals—far too many to name here—provided data, drew attention to references, helped clarify ideas, corrected errors, and critiqued drafts. I benefited especially from Anjum Altaf, Muhammad Anwar, Sohrab Behdad, R. Scott Appleby, Murat Çizakça, Faisal Devji, Laurence Iannaccone, Jomo K. S., Eric Jones, Seyyed Vali Reza Nasr, Jeffrey Nugent, Şevket Pamuk, Frederic Pryor, D. M. Qureshi, Fazlur Rahman, Yusuf Rahme, Ekkehart Schlicht, Murat Somer, Timothy Taylor, Bruce Thompson, and Shahid Zahid. At Princeton University Press, Peter Dougherty, Margaret Case, and many others helped to improve this book; to each, I owe a debt of gratitude.

Finally, I wish to thank my wife, Wendy Kuran, who heard various arguments in this volume in their infancy and contributed more to their development than she realizes. Over the years our children, Kent and Fiona, have lived with a father who has a habit of letting article drafts, self-imposed reading deadlines, conferences, and other such academic quirks interrupt weekends and even dictate vacation plans. I am grateful to both for their patience and understanding.

Islam and Mammon

CHAPTER ONE

The Economic Impact of Islamism

IN 1979 PAKISTAN TOOK SOME MAJOR STEPS to give its economy an Islamic character. To satisfy the presumed Qur'anic ban on interest, banks were ordered to offer an interest-free alternative to the conventional savings account and to purge interest from all their operations within five years. Although the wider objective has not yet been met, the interest-bearing savings account is no longer an option for new depositors. Another highlight of the 1979 program was zakat, Islam's tax on wealth and income. Voluntary until then, zakat was made a legal obligation. The Pakistani government now collects zakat from several sources, notably bank deposits and farm output. Every year thousands of local committees distribute the proceeds to designated groups.[1]

Pakistan has not been alone in trying to restructure its economy according to ostensibly Islamic stipulations. Zakat is now compulsory for certain groups in Malaysia, Saudi Arabia, and the Sudan. In some other predominantly Muslim countries, the establishment of a state-run zakat system is under consideration. The impact of Islamization is especially widespread in banking. Banks claiming an Islamic identity are in operation in most countries of North Africa, the Middle East, and South Asia. In some of these they hold more than 10 percent of the commercial deposits.[2] The leading Islamic banks have also established a presence in countries where Muslims form a small minority. New Zealand now has an "Islamic Finance Corporation," and Pasadena, California, an "Al Baraka Bankcorp."

These developments are not occurring in an intellectual vacuum. A rapidly growing literature known as "Islamic economics" seeks to guide and justify the ongoing reforms.[3] The prescriptions in this literature rest partly on economic logic and partly on the Qur'an and the Sunna, the latter consisting of recollections of the words and deeds of Prophet Muhammad and his companions. Several research centers have been established to promote Islamic economics. Some of these, including the International Center for Research in Islamic Economics at King Abdulaziz University in Jeddah, the International Association for Islamic Economics in Leicester, and the Kulliyah of Economics at the International Islamic University in Kuala Lumpur, publish journals devoted to the discipline. There are also several specialized periodicals, such as the *Journal of Islamic Banking and Finance*, a quarterly published in Karachi.

The exponents of this discipline, who call themselves "Islamic economists," emphasize that it covers far more than zakat and interest-free banking. The discipline aims, they say, to provide a comprehensive blueprint for all economic activity. Accordingly, a list of suggested research topics published by the International Center for Research in Islamic Economics covers every major category of research recognized by the American Economic Association, including consumer behavior, market structure, central planning, industrial relations, international trade, and economic development.[4] Some Islamic economists are quick to admit that in most of these realms the nascent discipline has yet to make a significant contribution. But they generally agree that the fundamental sources of Islam harbor clear and definitive solutions to every conceivable economic problem. To find these, they suggest, we must turn to the Qur'an and to the wisdom of the earliest Islamic community in seventh-century Arabia, drawing wherever necessary on modern tools and concepts.

ISLAMIC ECONOMICS AS FUNDAMENTALIST DOCTRINE

The classical sources of Islam contain numerous prescriptions that lend themselves to the construction of economic norms, and the religion's early history offers an array of lessons concerning economic behavior and institutions. But the notion of an economics discipline that is distinctly and self-consciously Islamic is very new. The great philosophers of medieval Islam wandered freely beyond the intellectual confines of the Islamic scriptures. And none of their works, not even the celebrated *Prolegomena* of Ibn Khaldun (1332–1406 C.E.), gave rise to an independent discipline of economics.[5] The origins of Islamic economics lie in the works of Savyid Abul-Ala Mawdudi (1903–79), a Pakistani social thinker who sought to turn Islam into a "complete way of life." In his voluminous writings, Mawdudi exhorted that Islam is much more than a set of rituals. It encompasses, he argued, all domains of human existence, including education, medicine, art, law, politics, and economics. To support this assertion, he laid the foundations of several Islamic disciplines, among them Islamic economics.[6] Other seminal contributions to Islamic economies were made by Sayyid Qutb (1906–66), an Egyptian, and Muhammad Baqir al-Sadr (1931–80), an Iraqi.[7]

The teachings of these pioneers differ in major respects. Mawdudi is sympathetic to the market process, though he insists that market behavior must be constrained by behavioral norms found in the classical sources of Islam. Generally distrustful of the market, Qutb and al-Sadr favor supplementing norm-guided self-regulation by state-enforced controls. A related difference is that the latter two thinkers are relatively less tolerant of economic inequality. These variations among the pioneers of Islamic economics are reflected in the writings of their followers, which offer a wide spectrum of views concerning government, markets, and property rights. But they have not given rise to sharply differentiated subschools. The substantive divisions within Islamic economics are more amorphous than, say, those between neoclassical economics and Marxian economics. Thus, the followers of Mawdudi tend to hold the works of Qutb and al-Sadr in high esteem. Moreover, their key positions often bear the influence of these other pioneers.

Whatever its internal divisions, Islamic economics has always presented a united front in justifying its own existence. The dominant economic systems of our time, virtually every major text asserts, are responsible for severe injustices, inefficiencies, and moral failures. In capitalism, interest promotes callousness and exploitation; in socialism, the suppression of trade breeds tyranny and monstrous disequilibria.[8] The fundamental sources of Islam prohibit interest but allow trade; hence, a properly Islamic economy would possess the virtues of these two systems without their defects. Typically, this claim is supported by references to Islam's canonical Golden Age—the period 622–61, spanning the last decade of Prophet Muhammad's life and the tenure of the "rightly guided" caliphs.[9] During this period, it is suggested, the Islamic code of economic behavior enjoyed widespread adherence, the prevailing spirit being one of brotherly cooperation. With everyone "subject to the same laws" and "burdened with the same obligations," injustices were minimized.[10] Resources were allocated very efficiently, ensuring a rapid rise in living standards. After the Golden Age, so the belief goes, the Muslim community's attachment to Islamic precepts weakened, setting the stage for a painful and protracted decline in Islam's global economic standing.

The case for restructuring economies according to Islamic principles thus rests on two claims. First, the prevailing systems have failed us. Second, the history of early Islam proves the Islamic system's unrivaled superiority over its alternatives.

To put the latter claim in perspective, we must recognize that by modern standards the seventh-century economy of the Arabian peninsula was very primitive. It produced few commodities, using uniformly simple technologies. It was essentially free of the major physical externalities that afflict modern economies, like air and water pollution. Moreover, it featured only the most rudimentary division of labor. The specific economic injunctions found in the Islamic scriptures—mostly in the Sunna—are responses to problems that arose in this ancient setting. Some of these injunctions were perceived as eternally valid. But many others were seen as changeable. Thus, rules and regulations were altered openly and unabashedly in response to new conditions. As a case in point, the scope and rates of zakat underwent many modifications during the Golden Age.

The historical record also calls into question certain virtues attributed to the Golden Age. The notion that the early Islamic community was a paragon of brotherly unity conflicts with evidence that it was plagued by disagreements and that force played an important role in its governance. Significantly, three of the four "rightly guided" caliphs met their ends at the hands of fellow Muslims. Nor was the Golden Age free of the corrupt practices attributed to contemporary capitalism and socialism. Officials of the Islamic state, including the caliphs themselves, were often accused of nepotism and misjudgment.[11] During part of this period the state did indeed enforce the collection of zakat, and a substantial portion of the proceeds must have accrued to various disadvantaged groups. We possess no reliable evidence, however, on whether this redistribution brought about a major reduction in inequality.

Still, the literature is replete with calls for the immediate implementation of the holy laws of Islam (*Shariᶜa*) in the form they ostensibly took almost a millennium and a half ago, in one locality. In issuing such calls, Islamic economics denies that certain economic problems of the modern age had no counterparts in the past. It also denies that once-beneficial institutions might now be dysfunctional, even harmful. Some of the rhetoric of Islamic economics thus conveys the impression that it seeks to rediscover and restore the economy of a distant past.

At the same time, it draws heavily on modern concepts and methods, including many that originated outside the Islamic world. And it pursues such modern objectives as growth, employment creation, and efficiency.[12] It would be wrong, therefore, to characterize the doctrine's intense preoccupation with the economy of seventh-century Arabia merely as a scholastic search for ancient solutions to ancient problems, although this representation does fit certain writings. Islamic economics applies ancient solutions to perceived problems of the present; and where such solutions are lacking, it seeks scriptural justification for its favored reforms. Accordingly, Islamic economics shows interest in only some features of the seventh-century Arabian economic order. Having identified the prohibition of interest as the sine qua non of Islamic reform, it is engrossed in Qur'anic verses concerning lending and borrowing. It devotes comparatively little effort to exploring whether the Golden Age offers useful prescriptions against environmental pollution, having chosen, if only by default, to refrain from making the environment a major issue.

So Islamic economics is as much a response to contemporary grievances as it is a nostalgic escape into the imagined simplicity, harmony, and prosperity of an ancient social order. Notwithstanding much of its rhetoric, in its applications it seeks to revive only bits and pieces of the seventh-century Arabian economy, not to restore it in toto. In practice it thus exhibits more willingness to accept economic realities than it does in theory.

Islamic economics is appropriately categorized as a "fundamentalist" doctrine, because it claims to be based on a set of immutable principles drawn from the traditional sources of Islam. By no means does its flexibility in practice negate this label's descriptive power. All doctrines labeled "fundamentalist" claim to rest on fundamentals set in stone, yet in application these prove remarkably malleable. Moreover, such doctrines assert a monopoly over knowledge and good judgment, even as they show receptivity to outside influences.[13]

Having billed itself as a superior alternative to all other economic traditions, Islamic economics has drawn sharp criticism from two quarters. A number of scholars, including this writer, have drawn attention to the literature's empirical and logical flaws, arguing that the proposed institutions are either unworkable or inherently inefficient.[14] Other scholars, notably Seyyed Vali Reza Nasr, have observed that Islamic economics has invited all this criticism by presenting itself not as a faith or philosophy to be understood on its own terms but as a positive science that lives up to established scientific standards. In this view, Islamic economics has been drawn into the game of utilitarian social science, and it is trying to prove its worth by beating the materialistic economic traditions of the West on Western turf. The mission of Islamic economics, maintains Nasr, should be to create a worldview that brings material goals into harmony with spiritual yearnings. It should get on with this mission without apology—without offering excuses, that is, for pursuing nonutilitarian objectives. By concentrating on its own agenda, it will eventually prove its superiority, but according to its own standards as opposed to those of the non-Muslim West.[15]

Nasr would thus have Islamic economics withdraw into its own shell in order to avoid being sidetracked by Western priorities. The logic behind this call to self-imposed isolation parallels Mawdudi's apparent motivation for founding the discipline. What propelled Mawdudi to establish Islamic economics along with other distinctly Islamic disciplines was a desire to defend Islam "against the inroads of foreign political and intellectual domination." He wanted to bolster Islam's authority in domains where Muslims had come to rely on the West's guidance, in order to restore the Islamic community's self-confidence and enable it to face the world proudly, as in the days before the economic and military rise of the West.[16] Thus, for Mawdudi Islamic economics was primarily a vehicle for reasserting the primacy of Islam and secondarily an instrument for radical economic change. Like Mawdudi, many other supporters of Islamic economics have subordinated it to wider objectives. For example, the Ayatollah Khomeini made a point of denying that Iran's Islamic Revolution was motivated by economics. It was not made, he once quipped, to make watermelons more plentiful.[17] He meant that the uprising was spawned primarily by noneconomic factors—most important, the threat to Islam's role in providing cultural identity, social cohesion, and moral guidance—so it should not be judged by its economic impact. Khomeini repeatedly spoke out, of course, against poverty and exploitation, and he supported certain economic reforms, including the ostensible elimination of interest. But he always subordinated economic objectives to the general goal of restoring the centrality of Islam in private and public life, even to particular objectives such as eliminating the consumption of alcohol and ensuring feminine modesty.

Just as Khomeini's aides included activists for whom economic concerns were paramount, the expositors, practitioners, and sympathizers of Islamic economics include people drawn to the discipline's substantive goals. Many undoubtedly see it as an antidote to exploitation and expect it to bring prosperity. For some, the attraction of Islamic economics lies in its promise to solve heretofore intractable economic problems. The raison d'être of Islamic economics, they say, is its ability to improve economic performance, defined in materialistic terms. But the point remains that Islamic economics also serves, and is perceived as serving, as an instrument of legitimation and power. In proposing that an Islamic economy will promote harmony, growth, and justice simultaneously, Islamic economics enhances the appeal of an Islamic political order. It also bolsters the case for a pan-Islamic union within which Muslims can enjoy the benefits of cross-continental trade without having to compromise their religious principles.[18]

Each of the two principal institutions engendered by Islamic economics, zakat and Islamic banking, provides sources of funding for Islamic fundamentalist, or simply Islamist, causes. Islamic banks channel a portion of their profits into religious education, publishing, networking, and other activities that foster the spread of Islamism. Likewise, in countries with obligatory zakat, a significant portion of the proceeds are allocated to religious schools dedicated to the dissemination of Islamist views. Islamic institutions also constitute a channel of upward mobility for Islamists and potential Islamists. In Turkey, for example, Islamic banks provide career opportunities to relatively religious youths whose cultural backgrounds might otherwise handicap them in the corporate world.[19] Another attraction of Islamic economics, then, is the economic basis it provides for expanding the influence of Islamism.

Not everyone who voices support for Islamic economics is at heart an Islamist. Both the discipline and its applications enjoy the public support of intellectuals, politicians, and laymen who are committed neither to

Islamization in general nor to Islamic economics in particular. Their motivation for preference falsification lies in the identification of Islamic economics with core Islamic values. Because of this identification, it has become prudent in some societies to be known as sympathetic to its objectives. In Pakistan, for instance, a politician who fails to endorse Islamic banking may find his aspirations thwarted. Significantly, Islamic banking is on the platform of every major political party.[20] Yet it is known to seasoned observers of Pakistani politics that many politicians have a low opinion of Islamic economics. Indeed, politicians who lend public support to its goals are apt to do little of practical significance to promote it, once in power.[21]

All this goes to show that Islamic economics owes its support only in part to the real and imagined successes of its past and present applications. Although one would hardly know this from studying theoretical expositions, there exist diverse reasons why people find Islamic economics appealing. The merits of Islamic economics lie for some Islamists primarily in its Islamic character but for others mostly in the substance of its economics. For still others, it is an instrument for advancing the political agenda of Islamism. Finally, there are non-Islamists who lend it support simply to avoid being stigmatized as bad Muslims.

It is important to keep this diversity of motivations in mind as we turn to an analysis of the discipline's practical accomplishments. There are vast incongruities, I argue below, between the rhetoric of Islamic economics and its practice. Specifically, I demonstrate that the impact of Islamic banking has been anything but revolutionary, that obligatory zakat has nowhere become a significant vehicle for reducing inequality, and, last, that the renewed emphasis on economic morality has had no appreciable effect on economic behavior. By its own lofty yardstick, then, Islamic economics is a failure. This assessment needs to be qualified by the fact that the strictly economic impact of Islamic economics is not the only measure of its achievements. Some of its promoters may well consider the shortcomings I describe to be outstripped, from the standpoint of the wider Islamist cause, by political and cultural consequences beyond this essay's purview.

BANKING AND FINANCE

Islamic Banking

Suppose you lend $100 to an industrialist, at 5 percent interest for a period of one year. Since you stand to receive exactly $105 at the end of the year, your return is predetermined. But the industrialist's return depends on the success of his business. If his revenue exceeds $105, he will make a profit. If it falls short of $105, he will incur a loss. An interest-based loan thus places the risk of loss entirely on the borrower. Under one interpretation of Islam, this is prohibited as unfair.

The literature is replete with additional reasons why interest is best avoided. "Interest," writes one Islamic economist, "inculcates love for money and the desire to accumulate wealth for its own sake. It makes men selfish, miserly, narrow-minded and stone-hearted."[22] Another evil attributed to interest is that it "transfers wealth from the poor to the rich, increasing the inequality in the distribution of wealth."[23] And yet another: it turns people away from productive enterprise.[24]

The purpose of Islamic banking is to prevent such inefficiencies, moral failures, and injustices by allowing people to borrow and lend without having to deal in interest. In theory, an Islamic bank accepts only two types of deposits: transaction deposits, which are risk free but yield no return, and investment deposits, which carry the risk of capital loss for the promise of a variable return. Deliberately ruled out are the insured savings deposits of conventional banks, which provide a predetermined return. An Islamic bank's lending operations are based on the same principle of risk sharing. In lending money to a firm, it agrees to share in the losses of the underwritten business activities in return for a share of any profits.

Since Islamic banks and their depositors are allowed to profit from their monetary assets only by carrying some risk of loss, Islamic economics treats the mechanics of profit and loss sharing as a topic of paramount importance. Two profit and loss sharing techniques, each utilized in early Islam and discussed in classical Islamic jurisprudence, receive the bulk of attention: *mudaraba* and *musharaka*. Under mudaraba, an investor or group of investors entrusts capital to an entrepreneur, who puts this into production or trade, and then returns to the investor(s) a prespecified share of the resulting profits, along with their principal. The remaining share accrues to the entrepreneur as a reward for his time and effort. If the business fails, the capital loss is borne entirely by the investor(s), the entrepreneur's loss being his expended labor. Under musharaka, the entrepreneur adds some of his own capital to that supplied by the investor(s), exposing himself to a risk of capital loss. The key difference between the two techniques lies in the entrepreneur's own financial commitment.

Mudaraba and musharaka have been likened to the financing techniques used by the venture capital industries of today's advanced economies.[25] Three factors differentiate a venture capitalist from a conventional bank. First, whereas the bank bases its loan decisions primarily on the creditworthiness of its applicants, the venture capitalist focuses on the potential profitability of the proposed projects. Thus, an applicant with no collateral but an economically promising project may fail to secure an ordinary bank loan yet succeed in obtaining venture capital.

Second, the conventional bank earns interest on its loans, whereas the venture capitalist receives shares of profits. Third, unlike the bank, the venture capitalist often participates in the execution of the projects he underwrites, sometimes by supplying managerial know-how. The second and third differences are obviously linked. The venture capitalist's closer involvement in project execution reflects his greater stake in the project's profitability.

In advanced economies the venture capital industry has fostered the rise of many new enterprises, most recently the high-technology sector. Islamic banking, say its proponents, can make an equally significant contribution to the Islamic world's economic development. The logic of this claim is simple. A banking system that bases its loan decisions on project profitability does not turn down projects with excellent long-term prospects but lengthy gestation periods. Nor does it deny support to entrepreneurs merely for lack of a track record. It thus allocates credit more efficiently than one that insists on demonstrated creditworthiness. The result is faster development, with everyone benefiting: entrepreneurs, who find it easier to finance their projects; owners of banks, who share in the profits of the projects they underwrite; and depositors, whose investment accounts earn greater returns.

The first Islamic bank offering a range of commercial services opened in Dubai in 1975, and Islamic banks are now in operation in more than sixty countries.[26] Many of these banks have been secretive about the composition of their assets. Knowledgeable observers generally agree, however, that neither mudaraba nor musharaka has ever absorbed a dominant share of the Islamic banks' assets. According to figures supplied by the Central Bank of Iran, in 1986 mudaraba and musharaka accounted for 38 percent of the assets of Iranian banks.[27] Two years earlier, when the Islamization of Pakistan's state-owned banking system was ostensibly nearing completion, only 14 percent of that country's bank assets were in mudaraba or musharaka, according to official reports.[28] Moreover, most of the contracts categorized as mudaraba or musharaka were actually based on thinly disguised interest. In violation of the spirit of profit and loss sharing, the bank would set a target return on its loans, agreeing in advance to reimburse the entrepreneur for any "excess profit."[29] In the Pakistani banking community it is widely believed that the share of legitimate mudaraba and musharaka never rose above a few percentage points and that it quickly fell to under 1 percent. In Turkey, where, in contrast to Pakistan and Iran, the banking sector remains heavily dominated by conventional banks, profit and loss sharing is similarly unpopular. Privately owned Islamic "finance houses" place at most 8 percent of their funds in mudaraba and musharaka.[30]

By far the most popular financing mode of the Islamic banks is *murabaha*, which works as follows.[31] A producer or trader submits to his Islamic bank a list of goods that he wishes to purchase, let us say a ton of steel. The bank buys the steel, marks up its price as compensation for this service, and then transfers ownership to the client. Along with his steel, the client receives a bill at the inflated price, to be paid at some jointly determined date in the future. What makes this transaction legitimate from an Islamic standpoint is that the bank takes ownership of the steel for some time, exposing itself to risk. Indeed, if the steel were stolen while under the bank's ownership, the loss would fall on the bank rather than the client. But the risk could be negligible, because there is no minimum to the duration of the bank's ownership; a millisecond suffices to make the transaction legitimate. From an economic standpoint, of course, an infinitesimal ownership period makes murabaha equivalent to an interest-based loan: the bank bears no risk, and the client pays for the time-value of money. There remains merely a semantic difference, which is that the client's payment is called a "service charge" or "markup" in one case and "interest" in the other.

In their applications of murabaha, the Islamic banks are keeping their ownership periods very short. Banks whose declared mission is to stamp out interest are thus making extensive use of a technique that is nothing but interest concealed in Islamic garb. In defense of Islamic banking it could be said that under murabaha there is no penalty for late payment, as there is under interest. This is true in principle, but in practice the Islamic banks have devised an ingenious method for penalizing accounts past due. They simply charge in advance for late payment, offering the client a rebate for payment on time.[32] In implementation, therefore, murabaha differs only cosmetically from the interest-based financing practices of the merchant banks and trading firms of the West. Not surprisingly, Pakistani bankers routinely tell their clients that murabaha is equivalent to interest.[33] There is actually a precedent for treating the two terms as synonymous: an Ottoman ruling of 1887 that pegged interest rates at 9 percent was named the "murabaha ordinance."[34]

The second most popular financing instrument is lease financing, known in some countries as *ijara*. Through this instrument, the bank rents some asset, let us say a truck, to an end user for a specified period of time, at a mutually agreed upon rental rate that reflects the truck's cost as well as the time-value of money. The end user may have the option of purchasing the truck. In theory, at least, lease financing satisfies the requirement of risk sharing, since the bank owns the asset for some period. If the truck suffers damage during the leasing period, the resulting loss would be borne by the bank.[35] In practice, however, the bank shifts such risk onto others by requiring the user to put up collateral and to pay for insuring the asset.[36] From an economic standpoint, therefore, the lease-financing practices of the Islamic banks do not differ from those of the interest-laden, risk-averse leasing firms long common throughout the world, including predominantly Muslim countries.

Murabaha and lease financing are well suited to trade and commodity financing, but neither is applicable to the provision of working capital. A start-up firm that needs to finance its day-to-day operations will receive no help from an Islamic bank that has chosen to specialize in murabaha and lease financing. Nor are these financing instruments of use to a firm with a cash-flow problem: a company facing a pile of unpaid bills needs not merchandise but money. So, at least in its current form, Islamic banking does not qualify as a full-fledged substitute for conventional banking, if only because it offers a limited range of financing services.

On the whole, the sectoral composition of the Islamic banks' investments does not differ significantly from that of conventional commercial banks. Their clients tend to be established producers and merchants, as opposed to newcomers. They generally favor urbanites, as opposed to villagers, who in many parts of the Islamic world remain dependent on moneylenders charging notoriously high rates. The banks have shown no inclination to favor labor-intensive firms. Many have invested in real estate, and a few have speculated in international currency and commodity markets. With few exceptions, they have preferred trade financing to project financing. Insofar as they have engaged in project financing, they have favored safe short-term projects over long-term projects fraught with uncertainty.

Even the Islamic Development Bank, an intergovernmental organization established in 1975 to promote economic development using Islamic financial instruments, has evolved into an export-import bank. It uses funds at its disposal largely to finance international trade, in particular, oil exports to poor countries of the Islamic world. Revealingly, from 1975 to 1986 the portion of profit and loss sharing in the Islamic Development Bank's portfolio fell from 55 percent to 1 percent, while that of murabaha rose from nil to over 80 percent. Lease financing has also increased sharply, although this mode of business is not even mentioned in the bank's charter.[37] Like its commercial counterparts, the Islamic Development Bank now goes to great lengths to avoid risk. Through governmental guarantees and client-financed private insurance, it absolves itself of risk, in violation of its own principles. If a machine purchased on behalf of a Bangladeshi company is damaged in transit, the loss falls on the company, or some insurance agency, or the government of Bangladesh, but never on the bank itself.[38]

None of this implies that the financing operations of the Islamic banks are harmful to social welfare. They do no damage by refraining from carrying bona fide risk. The promotion of international trade is an economically valuable service, especially in countries plagued by allocational distortions rooted in protectionism. Lease and commodity financing stimulate economic production. At least with respect to countries where the Islamic banks compete with conventional commercial banks, they would probably not have survived were they not meeting some previously unfulfilled need. My basic point is simply that the lending practices of the Islamic banks do not conform to the stipulations of Islamic economics.

The Resilience of Interest

Why, it behooves us to ask, does the practice of Islamic banking diverge so critically from the underlying theory? Why, specifically, are banks intended to revolutionize the world of finance sticking so closely to the techniques of conventional banks?

One reason has to do with the ongoing presence of conventional banks in all countries with Islamic banks, except Iran and Pakistan. By allowing entrepreneurs to choose between interest and profit and loss sharing, conventional banks create an "adverse selection" problem for the Islamic banks: entrepreneurs with below-average profit expectations prefer profit and loss sharing in order to minimize their losses in the likely event of failure, while those with above-average expectations prefer interest in order to maximize their gains in the likely event of success. The upshot is that the Islamic banks receive a disproportionately large share of the bad risks.[39] Implicit in this observation are the following two points. First, an entrepreneur who considers his project very risky is likely to conceal this knowledge from the Islamic banking community. Second, no bank possesses a reliable method for determining a project's riskiness.

Through training, of course, bankers can become reasonably adept at identifying bad deals. Were such skills unattainable there would be no venture capitalism in the West. But the required skills are in short supply, which is a factor in the Islamic banks' reluctance to engage in genuine profit and loss sharing. To remedy this recognized deficiency, an institute was established in 1982 in northern Cyprus for the training of personnel to screen projects. But it closed in 1984, leaving the Islamic banking system without a training center.[40] If one factor in this closing was the curriculum's shortcomings, another was a lack of enthusiasm on the part of the Islamic banks for genuine profit and loss sharing. As we saw above, even the banks of Iran and Pakistan, which are shielded by law from having to compete with conventional banks, have been reluctant to commit substantial funds to mudaraba or musharaka.

So the adverse selection problem caused by conventional banking cannot be the only reason why the Islamic banks are extremely reticent to abide by their own principles. A more fundamental factor is the widespread practice of double bookkeeping. Firms habitually understate their revenues and overstate their costs to conceal their profits from the tax collector, generally getting away with it because of inadequate government audits.[41] Under the circumstances, bankers are reluctant to lend on the basis of profit and loss sharing, unless they can sit on the recipient's board. By the same token, the typical firm will let no banker monitor its operations, for fear that information about its true profitability will find its way to the government. In sum, there is a mutual distrust between the providers and users of funds. This makes interest, a compensation mechanism that requires no monitoring, mutually preferable to profit and loss sharing. Some Islamic economists are beginning to realize that profit and loss sharing is unworkable in the presence of rampant dishonesty.[42] They continue to believe, however, that it is possible to lower dishonesty to a level where all borrowers and lenders will happily substitute profit and loss sharing for interest.

An additional reason why the practice of Islamic banking conflicts with the underlying theory has to do with the profitability and relative risklessness of trade and commodity financing. In many parts of the Muslim world, certain goods are routinely in short supply due to production controls, import restrictions, and price ceilings. The firms that acquire these scarce goods for resale or production tend to profit handsomely, which makes financing their operations ordinarily quite safe. Understandably, many Islamic banks would rather finance such commercial ventures than sink funds into long-term development projects with highly uncertain outcomes. In so doing they seek, like the typical business enterprise, to avoid unnecessary risks. What needs recognition here is that the abundance of low-risk yet lucrative opportunities in trade and commodity financing reduces the appeal of long-term development financing.

A Historical Perspective

To put in perspective all these incongruities between theory and practice, it may be noted that Islamic banking is a very recent creation. Neither classical nor medieval Islamic civilization featured banks in the modern sense, let alone "Islamic" banks. Classical Islamic jurisprudence produced elaborate rules to regulate financial transactions among individuals. Yet, as Murat Çizakça notes, these rules did not give rise to a system of banking.[43] Medieval Islamic civilization produced no organizations that could pool thousands of people's funds, administer them collectively, and then survive the death of their managers. The financial rules of Islam remained frozen up to modern times, precluding the formation, except outside Islamic law, of durable partnerships involving large numbers of individuals. It was the Europeans who, possibly starting from Middle Eastern financial practices, developed a complex financial system centered on banks.[44] So it is not surprising that the banks now operating in the name of Islam look more like other modern financial institutions than like anything in Islam's heritage.

In the 1930s there were some abortive attempts in India to establish interest-free banks. But the first successful forerunner of Islamic banking was a savings bank established in 1963 in the Egyptian town of Mit Ghamr. This bank was modeled after some of West Germany's local savings banks. It paid no interest on deposits and charged no interest on loans, borrowing and lending on the basis of profit and loss sharing. On account of these features, the bank claimed an Islamic identity, partly to distinguish itself from government banks and partly to enhance its attractiveness in the eyes of pious Egyptian peasants. The Mit Ghamr Savings Bank rapidly gained popularity and began making a substantial contribution to the local economy. Nonetheless, it was closed in 1968 by a government hostile to private initiative and suspicious of religion, under the pretext that it violated the country's banking laws.[45] Significantly, Mit Ghamr was not modeled after some Islamic enterprise of the past. Although it assumed a religious identity as a public relations ploy, its essential features were transplanted from a non-Islamic source, with no attempt to disguise this appropriation.[46] A fundamentally different claim is made on behalf of the commercial banks chartered as Islamic organizations since 1975, under the watchful eyes of clerics. They have all been billed as inherently Islamic creations. Yet, as we have seen, there is nothing distinctly Islamic about their operations. The contrast could not be more striking. Mit Ghamr shunned interest and actively promoted long-term development; today's Islamic banks pay and receive interest as a matter of course, and their primary activity is the promotion of trade.

Not that it is particularly Islamic to favor profit and loss sharing over interest. Profit and loss sharing predates Islam, and since the seventh century it has been practiced continually by diverse non-Muslim societies. Like the venture capital industry, the world's stock markets operate on the basis of profit and loss sharing. In any case, it is unclear that the Qur'anic prohibition of interest was originally understood to encompass the institution of interest as we know it today. What the Qur'an bans unambiguously is the pre-Islamic Arabian institution of *riba*, whereby a borrower saw his debt double following a default and redouble if he defaulted again. Because it tended to push defaulters into enslavement, riba had long been a source of communal friction. The purpose of the ban was undoubtedly to forestall communal disharmony by curbing, in the spirit of a modern bankruptcy law, the penalty for default. Accordingly, Qur'anic verses banning riba tend to be accompanied by calls for charity. The Qur'an enjoins lenders to show compassion toward borrowers in distress and to refrain from taking advantage of their misfortunes. The ban on riba may be interpreted, then, as an injunction against kicking a person who is down.[47]

Many early Muslims subscribed to this interpretation, and they clashed with their contemporaries who read into the ban not an injunction against exploitation but a general prohibition of interest.[48] While the broader interpretation eventually gained dominance, this did not deter Muslims from continuing to borrow and lend at interest.[49] They went on doing so through various ruses, such as the following practice that leading jurists endowed with legitimacy: A wants to lend B $100 at 5 percent interest, but without violating the ban. So he buys a chair from B in return for $100 and then promptly returns it for $105, payable in one year. The chair's ownership remains unchanged; B receives $100 now; and A stands to receive $105 in a year. Although the individual transactions involve no interest, together they are equivalent to a single transaction whereby A lends $100 to B at 5 percent per annum.

Murabaha, the most popular lending mechanism of the Islamic banks, is a similarly ancient ruse. It consists of several interest-free transactions that together amount to interest. Not surprisingly, murabaha was a source of controversy in the early days of Islamic banking. In 1980 Pakistan's Council of Islamic Ideology took a cautious view on its legitimacy, stating that although it was "permissible under the Shari'a, it would not be advisable to use it widely or indiscriminately."[50] Another common ruse takes the form of redefining as Y what everyone knows to be X. In Iran, for instance, the government has decreed that when a financial transaction between two public agencies takes place at a fixed rate of return, the charge involved is not called interest, as it would be if one party were a private citizen. So agencies freely borrow from each other at interest, liberated by the twist of a definition from having to acknowledge their violation of what passes as a sacred Islamic tenet.[51]

While a consensus exists among both theorists and practitioners of Islamic economics that interest is sinful, there is no agreement on what is meant by an "interest-free" loan. Under inflation, is it the nominal rate of return that must be zero, or the real? In other words, must loans be indexed to the rate of inflation to protect their purchasing power? A few writers argue that indexation is not only legitimate but a requirement of justice, although the dominant view is that indexation is un-Islamic.[52] Two international conferences on indexation, one held in Islamabad in 1986 and the other in Jeddah in 1987, concluded that indexation is incompatible with Islam.[53] Nonetheless, the Islamic banks index their markups, commissions, and service charges to inflation. In Turkey, where in the mid-1980s the rate of inflation was about five times higher than in Pakistan, the murabaha markup was also about five times higher.

Denunciations of the Anti-Interest Campaign and the Islamist Defense

The controversy over interest rages on. Expositors without practical experience in banking tend to insist on the necessity of eliminating interest, but they are divided as to whether Islamic banking, as it exists, is genuinely Islamic. While many are comfortable with the ruses that provide ways around the prohibition, others see these as a manifestation of the Muslim community's moral degradation.[54]

Each of these positions draws fire from Süleyman Uludağ in a 1988 treatise that employs an Islamic form of expression and draws heavily on Islamic classics. Those who insist on banning interest are ignorant, he says, of Islamic history and guilty of misinterpreting the Qur'an, which bans not interest but usury, or exorbitant interest. And those who appreciate the impossibility of doing business without interest and who, for this reason, tolerate various ruses are guilty, in addition, of promoting dishonesty and hypocrisy. This, he says, is a serious crime against Islam, a religion that stands for truthfulness. It is also a grave offense against God: even if interest were unlawful, it would be a lesser sin to deal in interest openly than to cloak it in practices aimed at deception.[55] Uludağ's suggestion that Islamic banking promotes dishonesty is highly significant in view of the argument, mentioned earlier, that the diffusion of veritable profit and loss sharing must await the improvement of business morality. If so, Islamic banking is its own worst enemy: by fostering trickery and duplicity, it hinders the task of imbuing businessmen with norms of truthfulness and trustworthiness.

Another broad attack on the prevalent opinion concerning the legitimacy of interest came in 1989 through a legal opinion (*fatwā*) of Muhammad Sayyid Tantawi, mufti of Egypt. Interest-based banking instruments are not necessarily corrupt, says Tantawi, because they may benefit everyone involved, including third parties. Generally beneficial and, hence, legitimate instruments include, he says, high-yielding government bonds and interest-bearing savings accounts.[56] But Tantawi's position is a minority position within the Islamic establishment. The dominant position remains that all interest, regardless of the benefits it confers to borrowers, lenders, and third parties, violates both the spirit and the letter of Islam.

If the proceedings of recent conferences on Islamic banking and statements by leading Islamists provide any indication, now Islamists generally accept that the Islamic banks in existence are not quite the intended interest-free enterprises. Khurshid Ahmad, a prolific writer who has held influential positions on key governmental commissions charged with steering the Islamization of Pakistan's economy, has publicly criticized his country's Islamic banks, saying that "99 percent" of their business is still based on interest.[57] Many Islamic economists believe nonetheless that for all their identified shortcomings the Islamic banks are superior to conventional banks.

For one thing, they say, even if Islamic banks lend at interest, they generally avoid paying interest to their depositors. Indeed, the dividends paid to depositors are not predetermined, in that they fluctuate. But the same can be said of the bond funds in operation throughout the Western world. A bond fund holds interest-bearing assets, its yield on any given day being the day's average interest income, minus a managerial commission. This average may vary from one day to the next because of changes in the fund's holdings. Yet the dividends paid to the fund's depositors are financed by pure interest. Similarly, the dividends the Islamic banks pay to their depositors originate, as we saw earlier, in thinly disguised forms of interest. The variability of these dividends makes an Islamic bank no more "Islamic" than an ordinary bond fund in Korea or Switzerland.

The second line of defense against the shortcomings of Islamic banking hinges on its allegedly superior profitability. Independent observers have found, in fact, that in the late 1970s and early 1980s Islamic banks made huge profits. But their profit rates have subsequently fallen below the domestic norms. Clement Henry Moore finds that between 1984 and 1986 Islamic banks in Bahrain, Tunisia, and Turkey earned higher returns on total assets than their conventional competitors, while those in Egypt, Jordan, Kuwait, Qatar, and the Sudan achieved substantially lower returns. Outside of Bahrain, only the younger Islamic banks seem to be enjoying returns above the norm. The star performers in this period were two Islamic banks in Turkey, the Al Baraka Turkish Finance House and the Faisal Finance Institution, both established in the mid-1980s.[58]

It is not surprising that certain Islamic banks have done very well, because they enjoy some special advantages. The existence of a small but significant group of savers who feel uncomfortable with interest has furnished a ready-made source of deposits. Thus, with a handful of branches Turkey's Islamic banks managed in a few months to attract about 1 percent of the country's total bank deposits. After this initial surge, however, they found that to expand further they must open more branches. The resulting rise in their overhead will most likely reduce their profitability. Still, they could remain more profitable than their conventional rivals because, like many of their counterparts elsewhere, the Turkish Islamic banks enjoy some important legal privileges. They enjoy tax breaks. They have lower-than-usual reserve requirements, which means that, relative to their rivals, they transfer a smaller fraction of their deposits to the

Central Bank. Moreover, unlike ordinary banks, they are allowed to engage in real estate transactions and in foreign trade.[59]

In view of all this, what is surprising is that the older Islamic banks have tended to suffer a fall in profitability. A major reason is that they made careless loans during the oil boom of the 1970s, which are now taking a toll on their profits. The fact that some of these bad loans were made under profit and loss sharing helps explain why the Islamic banks are now lending almost exclusively on the basis of interest. It also supports my contention that these banks face a shortage of the skills required to make profit and loss sharing viable.[60] Interestingly, in terms of profitability Turkey's spectacular performers of the mid-1980s had by the late 1980s fallen below the Turkish norm.[61] While this slip is attributable partly to the expenses of establishing new branches, it calls for added caution in accepting the claim that Islamic banking is inherently more profitable.

Yet another defense of Islamic banking is that it enhances economic stability. In an interest-based system, macroeconomic shocks may lower bank revenues, thus aggravating the crisis by causing defaults. This source of instability allegedly disappears when returns to depositors are variable, because any decline in bank revenues is then matched by a fall in bank obligations.[62] There is a flaw in this argument, which stems from the implicit assumption that an Islamic bank whose revenues fall will not suffer a withdrawal of deposits. One would expect, on the contrary, deposits to move away from banks performing poorly and into those performing relatively well. In fact, the depositors of Islamic financial intermediaries are just as fickle as their counterparts in conventional banks. In Egypt, news in 1986 that the al-Rayan Islamic investment company lost $100 million speculating in gold provoked massive withdrawals. Depositors who were happy to hold al-Rayan's shares when high returns seemed assured were apparently unwilling to do so once the downside risk became appreciable.[63]

As Volker Nienhaus observes, Islamic banks losing funds must reduce the credit they supply to their clients.[64] So it is unclear that replacing interest by profit and loss sharing enhances macroeconomic stability. The opposite may well be true, and the Iranian and Pakistani governments take this danger seriously. Iran requires banks to share a single rate of return, while Pakistan forces rates to stay within a narrow band.[65] Consequently, there is no necessary relationship in either Iran or Pakistan between a depositor's rate of return and the actual profitability of his own bank's operations. Since a common rate of return effectively precludes profit and loss sharing, one may infer that the Iranian and Pakistani authorities consider genuinely Islamic banking destabilizing.

Responses of Conventional Banks

Attempts to establish interest-free banks or banking systems have failed, then, to replace interest by its much heralded alternative, profit and loss sharing. In no country and in no sense has the anti-interest movement revolutionized banking, let alone the entire economic system. Perhaps this is why the secular financial community shows no sign of alarm. On the contrary, secular banks see the anti-interest campaign as having created an exploitable opportunity. In Egypt and elsewhere many conventional banks, even those under non-Muslim ownership, have established interest-free branches or windows, and some investment companies have begun touting their operations as "Islamic." Even Wall Street has become a player: Citicorp and other large American banks have devised financial instruments acceptable to their customers troubled by interest. And where interest is illegal, European, American, and Far Eastern banks have had no trouble abiding formally by this ban. The Pakistani branches of Chase Manhattan and Deutsche Bank now claim to do only interest-free business, although it is widely recognized that their operations have not changed in any fundamental sense.

REDISTRIBUTION

Zakat

Like other religions, Islam stands opposed to great inequalities in the distribution of resources. From the very beginning, therefore, it has featured instruments aimed at reducing, though not necessarily eliminating, social inequalities. These include an inheritance law that specifies in intricate detail how a person's estate is to be divided among his or her relatives.[66] A more celebrated instrument is zakat, an annual tax on wealth and income generally understood to incorporate certain levies that have been collected under other names, like the agricultural tax ushr. The proceeds of zakat are earmarked mostly for assistance to specific categories of impoverished and disadvantaged individuals. Mentioned explicitly in the Qur'an, zakat is viewed as one of the five pillars of Islam, along with belief in the unity of God, obligatory prayers, fasting during Ramadan, and pilgrimage to Mecca for those who can afford the trip.

The Qur'an provides only the broadest guidelines on zakat's coverage, and it leaves open the issue of rates. By tradition, it is levied on agricultural output, livestock, minerals, and precious metals—the major sources of income and wealth in seventh-century Arabia. The rate varies between 2.5 and 20 percent, depending on the source and conditions of production, although there are various exclusions and exemptions. Wealth held in the form of precious metals is subject to a 2.5 percent levy, whereas mining income is subject to the highest rate, 20 percent. For another illustration, the rate on agricultural output is 5 percent if the land is irrigated by the owner, 10 percent if it is irrigated naturally. Again by tradition, the beneficiaries of zakat include the poor, the handicapped, travelers in difficulty, debtors, dependents of prisoners, and the zakat collectors themselves. The proceeds are also used to free slaves and to assist people serving the cause of Islam.[67]

Little is known on how zakat affected inequality in the Arabian economy of early Islam. It has been claimed that the scheme was progressive in collection, which is to say that its burden fell disproportionately on the rich.[68] This is plausible, but to determine the scheme's overall impact we would need to know not just the intended collection pattern but also the actual collection and disbursement practices. If evasion was especially prevalent with respect to certain sources of income or if the proceeds went primarily to the affluent, the overall effect might have been unequalizing. In any case, the purpose of zakat was not only to reduce inequality but also to raise revenue for the Islamic state. The state was empowered, as already noted, to channel funds to "people serving the cause of Islam," which allowed it to spend zakat revenue on public works and territorial expansion. Such objectives need not have been compatible with the goal of inequality reduction.

But whatever the impact of zakat in seventh-century Arabia, in a modern economy the effect of a traditional zakat scheme is unlikely to be equalizing. For one thing, the involved rates are generally lower than those of the prevailing secular taxation systems; even the 20 percent levy on mining income falls short of the marginal income tax in most modern economies. For another, the commodities covered by the traditional scheme play a considerably less important role today than they did more than a millennium ago. In any economy, even a highly underdeveloped economy like that of the Sudan, a substantial portion of income originates in industry and the services, sectors the traditional scheme exempts by default. And a major share of wealth assumes forms not covered by the traditional scheme, such as oil wells and corporate equity.

Yet some expositors of Islamic economics consider the forms and rates used in the seventh century to be applicable, with similarly beneficial results, to any modern economy. They believe, moreover, that a restructuring of zakat would violate Islam's spirit.[69] This attachment to ancient specifics has drawn fire from the modernist school of Islamic thought. A luminary of this school, the late Fazlur Rahman, wrote: "It is surely this kind of attitude which gives point to the communist maxim, 'religion is the opium of the poor people,' since it effectively throws dust in their eyes."[70] The modernists want the sources of collection to include new commodities and activities, and they favor varying the rates according to society's changing needs. They also wish to redefine the categories of expenditure.

The modernist position now has the support of most Islamic economists.[71] But among the reformists there is yet no consensus on what reform should entail. There are disagreements on rates, exemption limits, and disbursements. Another source of controversy is the seventh-century principle that property is taxable if it is apparent (*zāhir*) but not if it is hidden (*bātin*). On the basis of this principle, some would exempt bank deposits, equities, and other financial assets. Others hold that because of advances in accounting and record keeping the distinction between apparent and hidden property is obsolete.[72]

Voluntary versus Obligatory Zakat

Two of the zakat systems in operation, those of Pakistan and Saudi Arabia, feature major innovations concerning coverage and rates. Whereas traditionally zakat was levied only on individuals, these countries have extended the obligation to companies, on the ground that companies are juristic persons. In addition, they have imposed a flat levy on certain types of bank deposits. Saudi Arabia levies zakat on imports, at rates varying from commodity to commodity. Pakistan allows farmers to deduct their expenses on fertilizers and insecticides, items for which classical Islamic law makes no allowance. Another Pakistani innovation is that the levy is 5 percent on all farm output, regardless of irrigation mode.[73] In contrast to Pakistan and Saudi Arabia, Malaysia has in place a collection system that departs minimally from traditional stipulations. Thus, each farmer is granted a fixed exemption, but no deductions are allowed for modern production costs. Another striking aspect of the Malaysian system is that it effectively exempts industrial workers, bureaucrats, businessmen, and shopkeepers, along with growers of rubber, coconuts, and other tropical cash crops, none of whom are mentioned explicitly in classical texts.[74]

As one might expect, these systems vary greatly in terms of yield and incidence. Pakistani figures for 1987–88 show that revenue stood at 0.35 percent of Gross Domestic Product. A mere 8 percent of the total came from agriculture, which is explained partly by the difficulty of making rich and powerful landlords pay their dues.[75] Saudi Arabian figures for the 1970s show that revenue hovered between 0.01 and 0.04 percent of Gross Domestic Product.[76] Given that per capita income in Saudi Arabia is much higher than in Pakistan, this is prima facie evidence of restrictive coverage and extensive loopholes. In fact, certain commodities of great economic importance, like housing, are exempt from zakat. There is also evidence of widespread evasion.[77] In Malaysia, too, extremely restrictive coverage and substantial evasion constrain the yield. As of 1988, the rate of compliance was just 8 percent.[78] More interesting is the fact that the zakat burden falls almost exclusively on rice growers, most of whom lie below the country's poverty line. In the state of Perlis, for instance, rice growers accounted for 93 percent of the zakat collection in 1985.[79] If nothing else, this finding shows that zakat does not necessarily transfer resources to the poor; it may transfer resources *away* from them. It is also significant that in sharp contrast to Pakistan, the agricultural sector carries a huge share of the burden. Within the agricultural sector, zakat is progressive at the lower end of the income scale because of the traditional exemptions. But it is regressive at the upper end, apparently because wealthy farmers are particularly prone to evasion.[80] In one village in the state of Kedah, for which we have a detailed study by the political scientist James Scott, the rate of compliance between 1977 and 1979 was merely 15 percent, which means that the farmers evaded 85 percent of their obligations. Evasion took a variety of forms: disguising or underdeclaring one's cultivated acreage, underreporting one's crops, and handing over to the zakat collector spoiled or adulterated grain.[81]

Malaysia, Saudi Arabia, and Pakistan are among a handful of countries where zakat is administered by the state. In most of the Muslim world individuals have discretion over whether and how to pay zakat.[82] The Qur'an itself is mute on issues of administration and enforcement, ruling out neither the centralized, obligatory mode nor the decentralized, voluntary mode. Yet each mode has a basis in historical precedent. In the earliest years of Islam, when the Muslim community lived in Mecca, assistance to the poor was unregulated and strictly voluntary. Zakat became a formal and compulsory transfer system shortly after the community's relocation to Medina (*hijra*), at a time when it was expanding very rapidly. Thus, during Prophet Muhammad's last few years zakat came to be administered by state-appointed agents and enforced, as necessary, by military might.[83] Barely two decades after his death, however, the Islamic state's ability to administer zakat crumbled in the course of violent leadership struggles.[84] From then on, zakat was up to the individual Muslim's discretion, although in certain times and places local bodies played a role in collection and disbursement. In sum, while zakat formed a centrally administered, obligatory system during a brief but important segment of early Islamic history, for most of the religion's life it has been administered in a decentralized manner, the agents of enforcement being peer pressure, fear of God, and the individual's own conscience.

Distressingly little research has been conducted on the voluntary system in operation. But the available studies suggest that only a fraction of the nonimpoverished population pays regularly. A 1978 survey of educated middle-class Muslims in Karachi showed that while almost all had heard of zakat, fewer than a quarter made regular payments themselves.[85] Under the present Pakistani system, Muslim citizens must assess the dues on their precious metals by themselves and deposit these voluntarily into a national zakat fund. According to an internal document of the Permanent Commission on Islamisation of Economy, such deposits have been negligible.[86] Revealingly, the zakat tables in the *Pakistan Statistical Yearbook* contain no entry for precious metals. Yet a study on the zakat potential of another country, Turkey, suggests that the dues on precious metals may be substantial. On gold and diamonds alone, the study found, this potential is around 5.5 percent of Turkey's annual savings.[87] But it would be very difficult to enforce payments on precious metals, since they are easily hidden. In any case, an enforcement campaign would most certainly cause people to shift wealth from precious metals into assets exempt from zakat, like real estate.

Another important finding is that charity is not the only impetus for making voluntary payments. Other common motives are the encouragement of worker loyalty and the promotion of social conformity. In the Kedah village studied by Scott, where payment was essentially voluntary until 1955, it was customary for landowners to make, under the rubric of zakat, a small gift to their workers, over and above wages. This gift, which the workers came to expect, helped ensure the loyalty of the landowner's work force during times of peak labor demand. Typically, the size of a worker's gift depended on his "respectability" in the eyes of the landowner. A worker whose comportment, manners, or political views gave him an unfavorable reputation received a relatively small gift. In addition to reputable workers, the major beneficiaries appear to have been the village's religious functionaries, such as the teacher of religion and the caretaker of the local mosque.[88]

Kedah's system shows that the voluntary mode does not treat the needy equitably. Apart from the religious establishment, it benefits primarily those with connections, tending to pass over the truly destitute, the unemployed, and the handicapped. This observation is bolstered by the common fact that the Islamic world has long featured, even in relatively prosperous localities, many desperately poor people who receive little, if any, charity. Against this background, the ongoing fundamentalist campaign to recentralize the administration of zakat is, if not reasonable, at least understandable. The proponents of obligatory zakat argue that this mode will augment the funds available for distribution and prevent their disbursement on the basis of personal ties. They remind us that the Prophet himself made zakat obligatory and also that the currently dominant voluntary mode took hold after the Prophet's death.

State-Administered Zakat in Operation

How, then, are the recently instituted state-administered systems performing? Relative to their decentralized counterparts, are they more successful at channeling resources to the poor? Have they overcome the role of personal connections? Although pertinent documentation and research are inadequate, clearly the high hopes of Islamists have not materialized.

In Pakistan, the Zakat Administration channels revenues into thousands of local committees that make lists of community members eligible for support. Funds are allocated among the committees roughly according to the populations they represent, which means that relatively poor communities generally receive more than their contributions to the national fund.[89] According to official records, during the 1980–88 period, 58 percent of the zakat funds went as subsistence allowances to people unable to work, including widows, orphans, and the handicapped.[90] But the grants involved were much too small to make a significant difference in the living standards of such groups. In the 1980s, when an individual needed an estimated $22 a month just to survive, most zakat payments varied between $4 and $8 per individual, and in some regions the typical payment was as low as $1.[91] The system has one million beneficiaries, which represents about 10 percent of the Pakistanis situated below the country's poverty line. An official report notes in this connection that in its eight years of operation Pakistan's state-administered zakat system has had little visible impact on inequality. There has been no noticeable decline, it says, in the number of beggars and no discernible alleviation of poverty. Under the circumstances, "people are losing faith not only in the system, but also in the belief that Islam offers a better economic order."[92]

It would be a gross error, the report goes on to say, to attribute the system's failure merely to a shortage of resources. The funds set aside for subsistence aid and rehabilitation should have been enough to provide around $8 per month to every person below the poverty line. Although the assumptions behind this assertion are open to question, the figure is suggestive, as the report itself indicates, of serious mismanagement and corruption.[93] In fact, ever since the system's inception Pakistan has been awash in rumors and newspaper reports of arbitrariness, favoritism, nepotism, and embezzlement. Zakat recipients apparently include "orphans" with two living parents, "impoverished women" wearing rows of gold bracelets, and "old people" long under the ground. Influential people have used zakat resources as a slush fund for programs benefiting primarily the rich.[94]

Ever since the beginning, Pakistan's Zakat Administration has been allocating about 20 percent of its funds to rehabilitation. Under this program, many poor women have received a sewing machine. Unfortunately, inadequate training and materials hamper the earning ability of these women.[95] Still, in official circles there is a growing feeling that properly managed rehabilitation and public works programs would constitute more effective antidotes to poverty than subsistence allowances. Accordingly, the Zakat Administration is now building 75,000 houses for the poor, and various public works schemes are under discussion.[96] Ironically, it was a modernist, Fazlur Rahman, who launched the debate on whether zakat funds could be used on public health, housing, and education. When in the 1960s he pushed for a program-oriented expenditure pattern, Islamists denounced him for promoting a scheme alien to traditional Islam. Since then the widely recognized failures of the subsistence-oriented expenditure pattern have made many Islamists increasingly receptive to innovative alternatives.

Malaysia's federal structure assigns the administration of zakat to an office at the state level. In each state, collected funds are forwarded to the zakat office for disbursement. Here is how the zakat office in Alor Setar, the capital of Kedah, allocated its proceeds in 1970, according to its own official report: of the total, 53 percent went toward "commendable measures" (which generally means religious education), 6 percent to people making a pilgrimage to Mecca, 2 percent to converts, and 22 percent as commissions to the zakat collectors and central administration, leaving a mere 15 percent for the poor.[97] Figures from the early 1980s show that disbursements to the poor ranged between 11 and 13 percent, with zakat officials and various religious causes claiming much of the rest.[98] In Perlis, likewise, about 12 percent of the annual zakat revenue was going to the poor, the lion's share being set aside for zakat officials, the faculty and students of Islamic schools, and pilgrims.[99] The amounts given to the indigent were minuscule. Those included in the list of recipients received between U.S. $3 and $19 a year—for many, less than the cost of traveling to the zakat office to collect the money.[100]

As in Pakistan, funds collected in one locality are often spent in another. Thus, an impoverished rice-growing village that contributes to the system will not necessarily receive anything in return. In the village studied by Scott, in fact, not a single poor peasant had ever received aid through the zakat office, at least as of 1980. Apparently, the only recipient of official aid was a university student whose father was the zakat collector, among the wealthiest men in the village.[101] Many Malaysian Islamic economists now consider the established system an embarrassment to those who have touted zakat as a supremely effective measure against poverty. Some are now advocating a drastic reorientation of expenditures toward rehabilitation. One proposal is to use zakat funds for providing the very poor with resources to start their own businesses. Another is to divert some of the funds into a program to help urban prostitutes find new jobs.[102]

As we saw earlier, decentralized, voluntary zakat was criticized for its bias against poor people without proper connections and its failure to alleviate poverty. The Pakistani and Malaysian records suggest that the same flaws may also afflict obligatory zakat administered by the state. The two modes do differ, of course, in their effects, but the essential difference lies neither in fairness nor in ability to reduce poverty. It lies, rather, in the connections to which they confer value. Decentralized zakat confers value to economic connections, especially ones based on employment; state-administered zakat confers value to political connections, particularly ones touching on religion. Thus, under Malaysia's old decentralized system the surest way to obtain regular zakat payments was to work loyally for a wealthy landlord; under the current centralized system it is to enroll in a religious school or work for the zakat office.

A major difference between the current Pakistani and Malaysian systems lies in the source of compensation for officials of the zakat administration. In Malaysia officials are paid out of zakat revenues, in accordance with scripture. In Pakistan they are paid out of general government funds, apparently to foster the illusion that the system is costless, thereby enhancing its appeal.[103] Even in Pakistan, of course, the religious establishment benefits from the system. Some religious functionaries receive compensation for collection and administration; in addition, a portion of zakat revenue is channeled into religious education.[104] But the religious establishment's stake in zakat has been far greater in Malaysia, where helping the poor appears as a convenient pretext for advancing broad Islamic objectives and for lining the pockets of religious officials. To make matters worse, the official Malaysian figures underestimate the actual take of the officials. There are various irregularities in collection that benefit the collectors personally. For instance, collectors are known to under-invoice their collections, presumably embezzling the differences.[105]

Malaysia's state-administered zakat system has generated resentment among the peasantry, which tends to view it as just another tax. What may be surprising is that many ordinary Pakistanis harbor similar feelings. One cause of their resentment is the impression of widespread corruption. As in Malaysia, another factor is that the payer does not see, much less determine, how his personal contribution is spent.[106] Not only does this deny him the satisfaction of observing his contribution's impact but it facilitates disagreement over spending priorities and decisions. A zakat payer whose needy acquaintances are passed over by a fund known to support distant students may well consider the system inequitable, as apparently many contributors do. Some telling evidence on people's dislike of governmental involvement is that almost no contributions were made to a voluntary zakat fund established by the Pakistani government in the 1950s.[107] More recent evidence comes from a Malaysian survey conducted in 1987 by Aidit bin Ghazali. About 60 percent of this survey's participants indicated that they prefer to choose the beneficiaries of their zakat payments on their own, as opposed to leaving the decision to the government.[108]

A significant source of friction in Pakistan has been the Shiite minority's unwillingness to pay zakat to a Sunni-dominated government.[109] In its original form, the zakat law obliged all Muslims to contribute to the government-administered fund, but when the Shiites took to the street in protest, the law was amended to give members of minority sects the option of exemption. To exercise this option a Shiite would simply have to submit an affidavit to his bank or the rural zakat collector.[110] Many Shiite depositors have opted to exempt themselves, and it is known that a small number of Sunni depositors are passing as Shiites simply to avoid automatic annual deductions.

Yet another cause of frustration lies in the compulsory nature of the payments. In each of these countries some individual Muslims feel that obligatory payments leave their religious obligations unmet. Consequently they make additional payments to people of their own choice.[111] In Malaysia there is even a terminological distinction between the two types of zakat. Payments to the government are designated by a pejorative term, *zakat raja*, literally "ruler's zakat," while voluntary payments made as acts of charity are called *zakat peribadi*, or "personal zakat." Because some Pakistanis and Malaysians make zakat payments over and above their obligatory payments, zakat transfers more wealth to the poor than official records show. However, while no systematic research exists on the additional transfers, they appear small. In neither Pakistan nor Malaysia can the typical indigent count on significant support from prosperous groups.

Evaluation

Underlying all the problems of the recently established zakat systems—public opposition to government involvement, widespread evasion, nepotism, and the diversion of extensive resources to the religious establishment—are two basic characteristics of human nature. People's personal experiences and circumstances color their perceptions of justice and efficiency. And they seek to influence the allocation of resources as a means of promoting their own priorities. Thus, no society is without citizens opposed to government spending patterns; charges of favoritism, fraud, and misuse are as ubiquitous as government itself. In general, moreover, government officials are more sympathetic than ordinary citizens to centralized redistribution and relatively suspicious of private decision making. In view of these observations, the recorded frictions over zakat are merely another manifestation of the universal struggle to control resource allocation. Neither Islam nor any other religion has overcome the human impulse to control economic outcomes.

Earlier I concluded that Islamic banking has not revolutionized the way Muslims save and invest. Now I can add that zakat has not made a major dent in Muslim poverty and inequality. While it has obviously redistributed some income and wealth, it has not conferred substantial benefits on the poor as a group. One must recognize in this connection that in its Islamist interpretation zakat constitutes a rather conservative means of redistribution. Touching neither on productive assets like land and physical capital nor on consumption goods like housing and furniture, it allows limited transfers involving a restricted menu of goods and assets. Even in the best of circumstances the distributional impact of such a scheme would be modest. Poor management has compounded the disappointment.

It is worth reiterating that by extending its coverage to new forms of income and wealth zakat may be turned into a highly significant instrument of redistribution. The potential yield is indeed considerable. Islamic economists have shown that it can exceed 3 percent of Gross National Product.[112] But this estimate overlooks the huge problem of evasion. In any case, turning zakat into a major equalizer requires more than raising its yield. It is necessary also to increase the share of the proceeds channeled to the poor. The latter objective requires the development of auditing systems as well as the establishment of social and legal sanctions for diverting funds away from the poor.

The existing state-administered systems might be defended on the grounds that similar problems afflict many other official transfer programs. But remember that Islamic economics aspires to vastly superior standards. It promises not that zakat will do as well as other systems of redistribution but that it will do markedly better.

Economic Development: The Role of Islamic Morality

Islamic economics claims, as mentioned, that Islamic scripture harbors solutions to every conceivable economic problem. Many problems are to be solved by curbing selfishness through injunctions concerning consumption, production, and exchange. If these injunctions are followed, the pace of economic development will allegedly quicken, while taking on a fairer, more balanced, and less disruptive form. This assertion turns on its head the long-standing Western suspicion that Islam hinders modernization.[113] Rejecting the notion that Islam is inimical to economic development, Islamic economics affirms it to be a principal source of growth and harmony.

In their most general form, the advocated economic injunctions consist of moral guidelines common to many value systems, both religious and secular. The individual is encouraged to enjoy the bounties of civilization, but he must be willing to share his possessions with others, particularly with the less fortunate. He must refrain from abusing goods at his disposal and from keeping them unutilized. As a producer or trader, he is free to seek personal profit. But in exercising this freedom he must avoid harming others. Nor must he earn more than his efforts justify; he must pay "fair" wages to his employees and charge "just" prices to his customers. Remaining honest in his economic dealings, he must admit his mistakes and avoid false advertising. He must work hard and strive to fulfill his commitments.[114]

In the early centuries of Islam these general injunctions were applied to a panoply of situations, generating multitudes of specific injunctions. For example, the requirement to earn no more than one's fair share was taken to imply that Islam prohibits the sale or purchase of a fruit tree in blossom. The logic: since the traders cannot predict the tree's yield with certainty, the selected price could confer an unearned gain to one party while burdening the other with an undeserved loss.[115] Some Islamic economists consider such ancient interpretations to retain validity in the modern world, even though some are contradictory, and classical Islamic jurisprudence provides several different interpretations of many individual cases.[116] Feeling less constrained by classical applications, other Islamic economists call for fresh interpretations.[117]

But regardless of where they stand on the applicability of ancient interpretations, Islamic economists generally agree that if the moral guidelines of Islam are observed and enforced, the economic performance of Muslim societies will improve dramatically. People will readily sacrifice their own material pleasures for society's interests. They will find their economic activities more fulfilling. Even their jobs will become more satisfying, as they take on the character of worship. Some writers observe such changes already in countries that have committed themselves to Islamization. Here is a striking statement by a Turkish writer in a 1987 volume on economic development and Islam:

> In February 1982, I was in a bus on the way to Tehran airport, at dawn, during the time of morning prayers. We passed a middle aged, bearded street sweeper, who was cleaning the sidewalk on one of the main avenues. That one glimpse gave me the impression that in this hour of prayer he was sweeping with devotion and ecstasy. The glow on his face affected me deeply, and I conveyed my feelings to the young Iranian sitting beside me. He explained: "At various levels of our society there are Muslims for whom diligent, effective work is like worship, like a

service to religion and community. This street sweeper must know that to devote oneself to cleaning the streets of an Islamic state is a form of worship."[118]

The central point of the article to which this quote belongs is that successful development requires imbuing society with a communitarian morality of self-sacrifice, altruism, and brotherhood. This is not an isolated view. Here is a supporting statement from the literature: "[Islam] deals with all aspects of economic development but always in the framework of total human development and never in a form divorced from this perspective."[119]

In accordance with this view, a major, if not the primary, source of the Muslim world's underdevelopment is held to be its moral degeneration. The standard of morality began falling when a string of increasingly corrupt leaders succeeded the "rightly guided" caliphs of the seventh century. But this degeneration has taken a calamitous form only in recent centuries, through the influence of the West. Declining morality, say Islamic economists, has sapped productivity and reduced the effectiveness of government. Moreover, by weakening the ties of Islamic brotherhood, it has made Muslims oblivious to one another's needs. As a sad consequence, Muslims are divided on key issues, and their rivalries are keeping them from cooperating toward common objectives. Low morality is also held responsible for the practical shortcomings of zakat and Islamic banking. The misuse of zakat funds is attributed to the moral deficiencies of local officials. Likewise, the continuing prevalence of interest-based lending is ascribed, as we saw, to rampant dishonesty in business.

All these problems are taken to mean that moral education must be accorded a crucial role in economic development. Through family and school instruction, people must be molded to fit the requirements of a just, harmonious, and efficient society. They must be imbued with the notion that they belong to a community of Muslims, the umma, whose interest takes precedence over their interests as individuals. Yet one could reform, rather than individuals, the institutions that direct, shape, and constrain their choices. Many students of development would argue that the roots of underdevelopment lie primarily in institutional inefficiencies. As far as I know, no Islamic economist denies that social institutions matter; after all, they attach great importance to zakat. The distinctiveness of their position lies in the primacy it gives to the restructuring of individuals. Throughout the Muslim world, of course, massive efforts have been made since the beginnings of Islam to instill in individuals an Islamic morality. Have these efforts influenced work effort, generosity, and market behavior? If so, how? Islamic economics has undertaken no serious investigation of such matters, treating it as self-evident that Islamic education furthers growth and justice simultaneously.

Much of Islamic economics conveys the impression that a communitarian ethic is a prerequisite for economic development. But certain writers hold that such an ethic is an objective in its own right. This objective takes precedence, they say, over economic development, recognizing explicitly that in certain contexts moral imperatives conflict with growth.[120] But the two camps are united in the belief that Islamic morality is a crucial ingredient of healthy economic development. Accordingly, they agree that Muslim societies have been held back by an individualistic ethic that keeps them from working together toward common objectives.

A striking aspect of this emphasis on the inculcation of a communitarian ethic is that it draws no distinction between numerically small and large groups. The Islamic morality of self-sacrifice, altruism, and brotherhood is expected to work with equal effectiveness and beneficence in a populous modern nation as among Prophet Muhammad's first group of companions. Let us be clear about what this means. The development of a country committed to an Islamic way of life is expected to be driven substantially by Muslims' efforts to meet one another's observable needs and by their mutual cooperation toward jointly held and commonly perceived goals.

There are two serious flaws in this thinking. First, it implicitly attributes to the individual an infinite ability to receive, store, retrieve, and process information. In fact, even in a small city no individual can handle more than a minuscule fraction of the information relevant to local interests. Consequently, no member of a modern nation can be aware of the wants of more than a tiny fraction of his fellow citizens. He may understand the needs of his acquaintances and have some feel for the wants of strangers. But in general not even a pure altruist can identify the socially optimal course of action. The argument's second flaw is that it overlooks the difficulty of generating common goals. In a large society environmental heterogeneities and the division of labor make individuals experience different joys and frustrations and develop different conceptions of reality. Consequently they tend to form different judgments concerning justice and efficiency. A common Islamic education might mitigate these differences but never eliminate them.

This argument is supported by recent applications of Islamic economics. Islamic banks are supposed to commit a portion of their assets to making interest-free loans to the needy (*qard hasana*). By and large they make such loans only to their own employees, as advances on their salaries. Evidently, Islamic bankers are more sensitive to the needs of their acquaintances than to those of strangers. The same can be said about officials charged with distributing society's zakat funds. The pervasive irregularities in their operations indicate that they are inclined to differentiate among the needs of their fellow Muslims.

In an isolated group numbering at most in the low hundreds and whose members perform similar tasks, the range of experiences may be sufficiently narrow and the volume of relevant information sufficiently small to enable a veritable agreement on objectives. Moreover, the members of such a group may possess adequate knowledge of one another's needs. But it is sheer romanticism to expect such traits to characterize a population running into the millions. In a large society sustained cooperation toward jointly held and commonly understood ends is possible only in small subgroups like the family, the work team, and tightly knit partnerships.

If economics has taught us anything over the past two centuries, it is that the institution of the market allows traders pursuing *different*, rather than *similar*, ends to achieve mutually satisfying outcomes. As an unrivaled economizer of information, the market permits traders to serve the needs of others while pursuing nothing but their own selfish objectives. True, the viability of the market mechanism depends on the existence of certain constraints on people's actions, such as property rights, sanctions against dishonesty, regulations to curb harmful externalities, and contracting rules. And cooperative production in firms is a source of immense social gain. Still, a large society's economic viability is ensured not simply, or even mainly, by altruism or jointness of purpose. A crucial role is played by institutions that induce traders to serve society as a by-product of personal pursuits based on personal knowledge. Put differently, prosperity does not require the commonality of all knowledge, in the sense of each person knowing the needs of every other. Nor does it require general conformity to joint objectives. Given people's very limited informational abilities, it always requires some division of knowledge and labor.

Friedrich Hayek, the most forceful modern exponent of these insights, traces the common misperception that the economic viability of a large society depends on jointness of both knowledge and purpose to Aristotle's teachings on household management and individual enterprise. These teachings showed no comprehension of the market order in which Aristotle lived, yet they set the pattern over the following two millennia for religious and philosophical thinking on the social order. Generalizing erroneously from the household to the wider economy, later thinkers such as Thomas Aquinas held that only actions aiming at known benefits to others are morally justified and, hence, economically desirable. Not until the eighteenth century would it be recognized that the market makes it possible "to do a service to another without bearing him a real kindness," or even knowing him.[121]

But habits of thought do not die easily. Socialism, arguably the most influential social doctrine of the twentieth century, promotes the notion that a classless society is possible, even inevitable, where selfish greed has given way to benevolence. Hayek calls this the "fatal conceit" of our time, the fundamental error that led dozens of countries to appalling inefficiency and tyranny. The supremely efficient, just, and harmonious society promised by socialism has existed nowhere but in murals of blissful workers resolutely serving socialism.

This brings us back to the Iranian street sweeper. The apparent glow on his face was taken to imply that Islam can generate widespread benevolence and, further, that this benevolence can propel a large and complex economy. Such thinking obviously betrays the Aristotelian influences on Islamic philosophy. Like other derivatives of Aristotelian thought, such as socialism, this philosophy rests on empirically untenable assumptions concerning human inclinations and capabilities.[122]

Given the preeminence of morality in Islamic thinking on economic development, one might expect a consensus on the proper domain of government and the need for central planning. In fact, there is none. The literature harbors various arguments in favor of government ownership and central planning, and many others in favor of private property and the market mechanism, all supported by revelation and tradition.[123] Significantly, the term "Islamic" has been juxtaposed both with "socialism" and with "capitalism." And however tolerant or intolerant of market processes, regimes have had no trouble finding an Islamic basis for their policies. The exponents of Islamic economics seldom appreciate this point. On the contrary, they claim routinely that their own particular positions are rooted in a well-articulated divine law admitting a single, unambiguous meaning.

The point was not lost on Hashemi Rafsanjani, who as speaker of the Iranian Parliament observed during a heated debate that some of his colleagues favored more government control over the economy, others less. Describing the disagreements as "differences among experts, not over matters of religion," he said that "Islam can accommodate all these views." It is desirable, he went on, that the rival camps reach a consensus. But if a consensus cannot be reached, then the majority view will have to prevail, and "if in practice the majority view yields no results, then the community will obviously revert to the other view."[124] As Shaul Bakhash observes, "to say that the government will try one policy and, if it fails, it will go back and try another is . . . very different from asserting that Islam requires that economic and property relations be ordered on the basis of divine law."[125]

Islamic economics features divisions on numerous other concerns of the field we call "development economics," including trade protection and industrial promotion. Many such issues have no counterparts in early Islam. In seventh-century Arabia central planning was not a possibility, industrialization not an issue. As the economy was mostly nonmonetized, there was no monetary policy in the modern sense. It is even doubtful that the notion of economic development was present. Early Muslims had a sense of the ideal economy: one that treats its participants fairly and minimizes inequality. Clearly, they felt that the attainment of this ideal depends on curbing selfishness and dishonesty. There is no evidence, however, that they conceived of self-sustaining economic growth, let alone that they reflected and agreed on how best to attain it. In view of all this, it is unsurprising that Islamic economics is as divided on the institutional context of development as it is united on the primacy of morality.

PROGNOSIS

It is time to pull together the threads of a long argument. In practice, not to mention doctrine, Islamic economics is hardly as comprehensive as its proponents apparently believe. Its concrete applications have been limited essentially to redistribution and banking. Not even in Pakistan, which has undertaken the most carefully planned attempt to reorder an economy according to Islamic precepts, and which has a population exceptionally committed to the concept of an "Islamic way of life," has the scope of reform gone much beyond these two areas. Like the underlying theory, the implemented modifications lack coherence. Islamic redistribution and banking have involved two separate agendas, and neither has been reconciled with other institutions and practices serving related or similar goals. As a case in point, the Pakistani zakat scheme coexists with a plethora of price controls and indirect taxes that counteract, if not offset, the intended redistribution. Nor have the specific reforms been revolutionary in their consequences. The advent of Islamic banking has altered only the cosmetics of banking and finance, and zakat has nowhere led to a perceptible reduction in poverty or inequality. Finally, the Islamic economic agenda remains poorly defined. It remains unclear, for instance, whether the ban on interest precludes the indexation of monetary transactions. And although there is agreement on the desirability of imbuing Muslims with an Islamic morality, no consensus has emerged on the implications for governance.

In trying to explain why Islamic economics has had no major impact, one identifies several classes of causes. First, its many ambiguities allow the prevailing political forces to give it whatever meaning seems least threatening to the status quo. Second, certain elements of the Islamic economic agenda conflict with human nature. Thus, Muslims are required to accept financial risk, whereas they prefer security. And they are supposed to pay zakat on their precious metals, but they resist. Third, the Islamic reforms have been impeded by social realities that their promoters have expected religious sentiment to overcome. We saw, for instance, how the continuing prevalence of tax evasion has made it imprudent for bankers to engage in profit and loss sharing. Finally, Islamic reforms have suffered from poor organization and a shortage of skills. While there is some demand in every society for profit and loss sharing, the Islamic banks do not yet possess the skills necessary to make this financing method viable. Likewise, the established zakat systems lack effective monitoring.

What does the future hold for Islamic economics, and what of its continuing impact? The myth that reforms undertaken in the name of Islam represent radical departures from preexisting practices is unlikely to be sustained much longer. Yet they can be recognized as ineffective without causing the abandonment of basic objectives such as the elimination of interest. People do not modify their ideologies at the first sign of conflict with reality. As Albert Hirschman suggests, mental resistance is especially pronounced where the fit between ideology and reality was poor to begin with. Given the initial disparity, new facts that contradict the ideology do not worsen the fit appreciably and are therefore disregarded or else easily rationalized.[126] In any case, even when an individual becomes disillusioned with the prevailing ideology, real or imagined social pressures might make him refrain from publicizing his doubts.

Yet, as long as some individuals have the will to voice misgivings, there is reason to expect the eventual mobilization of an organized opposition, even in countries where the wisdom of Islamization is now seldom questioned in public. How long, then, will it take for the emergence of widespread dissent? And what will be the response of committed Islamists? Forecasting is a difficult task, especially, it has been said, when it is about the future. A social scientist can detect instabilities but not predict when these will give way to order, recognize sources of conflict but not specify how these will be resolved, and identify ranges of future possibilities but not provide a definitive account of impending evolution. While historical circumstances delimit the possible evolutionary paths, historical accidents determine the paths actually followed.

One possible scenario is for the ongoing quest for a moral order to become an obsession that makes power holders try earnestly to perfect the individual Muslim. Since there is vast room for disagreement on the nature of moral perfection, a consensus that the human impulses of Muslims need no further organizing would prove elusive. But if the history of socialism is any indication, it could take decades for a broad segment of society to wonder why the desired benevolence is so difficult to elicit. Failures along the way could easily be taken to mean that educational efforts need to be redoubled and non-Islamic influences curbed further. In this vain search for the Islamic utopia the political establishment would become increasingly repressive, making it treacherous to suggest that

Islam does not offer clear and definitive answers to economic problems. Meanwhile, the discipline of Islamic economics could feed on itself for decades, mistaking apologetics for serious reflection and cosmetics for genuine reform. The twenty-first century could thus become for Islam what the twentieth was for socialism: a period of infinite hope and promise, followed by disappointment, repression, disillusionment, and despair. Identified with failed policies, Islam would lose its authority as a wellspring of sound economic policy. The sequence could end with a flight from Islam into other sources of spiritual and moral inspiration.

An alternative scenario is for Islamic economics, which emerged as a movement to restore idealized economic relationships of the past, to turn into a major innovative force. After all, the Protestant Reformation started as a backward-looking movement, only gradually assuming a forward-looking character. As R. H. Tawney has documented, Luther and other leaders of the Reformation fought for the restoration of virtues they thought had been abandoned; yet, paradoxically, their attacks on ecclesiastical corruption weakened Church authority, thereby accelerating the developments they tried to reverse. The Reformation thus set the stage for the Industrial Revolution.[127] Such a scenario could be replayed within the Islamic world. Here is a possible sequence of events. The current preoccupation with economic morality turns the spotlight on incumbent political establishments, discrediting them further. Progressively delegitimized and weakened, existing regimes are replaced by Islamist regimes. The new regimes promise to rid society of its major social and economic problems by restoring properly Islamic values and practices. Alas, problems do not just yield to fresh policies. Disillusionment sets in, the Islamist regimes split into discordant factions, and the ensuing power struggles force the traditionally interventionist governments of the Islamic world to loosen their controls on private economic activity. By the time central governments regain their lost authority, market institutions are firmly entrenched and private enterprise very influential. These developments leave the promoters of an Aristotelian morality with no significant base of support.

Just as the rise of European capitalism coincided with the emergence of new social philosophies, so, too, political and economic liberalization in the Islamic world could be accompanied by a complete transformation of Islamic economics. The Islamic banks become genuine venture capital organizations, and zakat evolves into a bona fide social security system. Meanwhile, it becomes commonplace that feelings of altruism and solidarity carry less significance in a large, complex economy than in a small, simple one. And the notion that the Qur'an offers limited help in the realm of economic policy gains increasing recognition. There are, in fact, Islamic precedents for accepting the limitations of the traditional sources.

As a case in point, clerics eventually released army commanders from the requirement to abide by Islam's rules of warfare, permitting Muslim armies to act as their commanders saw fit.

In a less tumultuous and less circuitous variant of the second scenario, the key players are the practitioners of Islamic economics. Endeavoring to implement Islamic economics, they recognize its unrealism. As we have seen, this stage has already been reached in Islamic banking, where bankers instructed to lend on the basis of profit and loss sharing have discovered that under current circumstances this lending instrument yields more loss than profit. Sensing that it may never be practical to eliminate interest, that zakat requires new thinking to become an effective instrument of redistribution, and that the envisaged moral transformation is a mirage, onetime believers in Islamic economics begin chipping away at its edifice. At first they transform only the practice, resorting to many ruses. Then they begin altering the theory openly—for example, by redefining interest and reformulating the mechanics of zakat. Their endeavors gain the approval of individuals with a stake in common practices, including Islamists who have prospered doing "interest-laden" business. In this scenario the practitioners of Islamic economics serve as hidden agents of secularization, arbiters between the doctrine's goals and the secular practices it still condemns.

Stp

CHAPTER TWO

Islamic Economics and the Islamic Subeconomy

THE MID-TWENTIETH CENTURY SAW the emergence of a literature characterized as Islamic economics. The declared goal of this literature has been to identify and promote an economic order that conforms to Islamic scripture and traditions. Now featuring thousands of books, articles, and pamphlets in dozens of languages, it asserts that an Islamic economy would unite the strengths of capitalism with those of socialism, while overcoming their weaknesses.[1]

For several decades, Islamic economics remained almost exclusively an intellectual exercise. Since the 1970s, however, steps have been taken to put its ideals into practice. Dozens of countries now have Islamic banks—financial intermediaries that claim to offer an interest-free, and thus morally superior, alternative to conventional banking. Many Islamic banks have proven profitable, and some are expanding rapidly. Several countries, notably Pakistan, have gone so far as to outlaw every form of interest, thus forcing all banks, including foreign subsidiaries, to adopt ostensibly Islamic methods of deposit and loan management. Pakistan, Saudi Arabia, Malaysia, and a few other countries have instituted official redistribution systems to collect an ancient religious tax and disburse the proceeds to causes endorsed by religious councils. And numerous economies now contain distinctly Islamic enterprises, including retailers, publishers, investment companies, factories, construction firms, and even conglomerates. Especially in the fastest growing metropolises of the Islamic world, these enterprises, along with the Islamic banks and redistribution systems, have formed vibrant subeconomies.

The purpose of this essay is to analyze and link these developments. How, I ask, does Islamic economics differ from secular economic traditions? Does it amount to a coherent body of scientific thought, and how comprehensive is it? What practical innovations has it stimulated? What social groups are involved in Islamic economic activities, and what are their aims? Finally, what social benefits have flowed, and what social costs have arisen, from economic activities undertaken in the name of Islam?

DISTINGUISHING ELEMENTS OF ISLAMIC ECONOMICS

Islamic economics did not emerge from a drive to correct economic imbalances, injustices, or inequalities. The Indian Muslims who launched it in the 1940s were motivated by a desire to defend Islamic civilization against foreign cultural influences. For Sayyid Abul-Ala Mawdudi, the Pakistani ideologist whose voluminous writings popularized the term "Islamic economics" and set the tone for later contributions, this new approach to economics was to be a vehicle for establishing, or reestablishing, Islamic authority in a domain where Muslims were falling increasingly under the influence of Western ideas. By replacing Western economic approaches with an Islamic one, he hoped to restore the Islamic community's self-respect and improve its cohesion.[2]

Because Islamic economics was developed to serve cultural and political ends, it did not have to meet scientific standards of coherence, precision, or realism. It needed only to differentiate itself from the intellectual traditions that it was aiming to displace. Accordingly, contributions to Islamic economics typically begin by identifying the distinguishing characteristics of an Islamic economy. From Mawdudi to the present, the most fundamental of these characteristics has been the prohibition of interest. Two others have been zakat, which is an ancient redistribution system, and the requirement that economic decisions pass through an Islamic moral filter.

The Prohibition of Interest

The hostility to interest is based on the belief that the Qur'an bans all interest, regardless of its rate or form. In fact, what the Qur'an bans is riba, the pre-Islamic Arabian practice of doubling the debt of a borrower unable to make restitution on schedule, including both the principal and the accumulated interest. Riba tended to push defaulters into enslavement, so it was an acute source of social friction. From the earliest days of Islam to the present, various interpreters of the Qur'an have held, accordingly, that the purpose of the ban on riba was simply to block socially harmful financial practices. In particular, they have suggested that the ban was intended, like the bankruptcy laws of a modern state, to make creditors deal charitably with debtors unable to make timely payment.[3]

Nevertheless, for the past half century opposition to interest has been treated as the sine qua non of being an *Islamic* economist. To be recognized as an Islamic economist it is not sufficient to be a learned Muslim who contributes to economic debates. One must be opposed in principle to all interest, including not only the monopolistic returns of rural moneylenders in financially underdeveloped countries but also the competitive returns of commercial banks in the industrialized world. Thus, the focus of Islamic economics is neither on ways to keep interest rates within bounds nor on keeping financial markets competitive. Rather, it is on the eradication of interest.

There exists no ancient or modern example of a country that has disposed of interest. Although there have always been groups hostile to interest—especially in economically primitive communities—in no large community have interest-based financial deals ever become uncommon.[4] Islamic economists have made great efforts, therefore, to justify a ban in terms that go beyond the simple claim that the Qur'an demands it. A common argument, found in all popular texts on Islamic economics, is that it is unjust to earn money without assuming risk.[5] By the logic of this argument, it is unjust for a bank to earn interest on an industrial loan, for the arrangement places the risk of the financed venture entirely on the industrialist, allowing the bank to earn a return even if the venture fails. Likewise, it is unjust for a saver to earn interest on her savings deposits; the investments financed through her savings could go sour, in which case her bank would lose money while she, the deposit holder, still earns the predetermined return. Whatever the merits of the notion of risk-free returns, the crux of the argument is that profit is legitimate only as a reward for risk. Accordingly, banking must be based on the sharing of both risk and profit, which rules out interest. It is permissible, of course, for an individual to put money in a bank for safekeeping, provided no interest payments are involved.

The literature on Islamic banking does not specify how a depositor and his bank, or the bank and a borrower, are to apportion risk. It insists only that each party to a financial contract must bear some share of the risk. In principle, one party could carry just one-twentieth of the risk, although some writers caution that the apportionment must conform to customary notions of fairness. Always left unclear is why it would be unjust for one side to accept most, or even all, of the risk if, as is common, the parties differ in their capacity to bear risk. Consider a bank and one of its 50,000 depositors, a retired widow whose sole source of income consists of her modest savings. The widow is likely to be averse to risking her capital, for a sufficiently large loss would leave her destitute. By contrast, the bank may easily pay her a fixed return, and thus bear the full risk of investing her savings, for it is able to minimize its overall risk exposure through diversification.

In any modern economy, one will encounter bank depositors prepared to put their capital at risk for the promise of a greater return. Also, one will find banks that are happy to earn a variable return on some, even all, of their assets in order to raise their expected earnings. So where financial intermediaries are free to choose their preferred mixes of fixed and variable earnings, and likewise for their lending commitments, competitive pressures will provide people averse to interest opportunities to make contracts of the kind Islamic economists characterize as profit and loss sharing.[6] The relative popularity of profit and loss sharing arrangements will depend on factors such as informational asymmetries between the providers and users of funds, the costs of managing variable-commitment contracts, the efficiency of the legal system, and, of course, the pattern of risk preferences.

In an unregulated economy, then, nothing would block the emergence of banks that Islamic economics defines as "Islamic." And if banking based on profit and loss sharing is in practice not as common as one might want or expect, the probable reason is that the contracting options available to financial intermediaries are restricted. That is the case in, for instance, the United States, where banking regulations have long limited the risks banks may accept or impose on their depositors. Yet, what Islamic economists demand is not just financial deregulation aimed at generating more profit and loss sharing. They desire new regulations that would force *all* banks to limit themselves to variable earnings and commitments. And they want interest-based banking outlawed, on the ground that recipients of interest income achieve gains without assuming any risk whatsoever.

This justification rests, as Abdul Halim Ismail notes, on a serious misunderstanding concerning the sources of financial risk.[7] Contrary to the perceptions of Islamic economists, a bank that earns interest on its assets is not engaged in risk-free business. It might fail to collect on some of its loans; an unanticipated economic slump might leave it with an inordinately large workforce; and, after the terms of a long-term loan have been set, macroeconomic conditions might force it to raise its payments to depositors, reducing its profitability. Similarly, an interest-earning depositor carries some risk, if only because his bank may fail. True, as a practical matter deposit insurance will eliminate the depositor's risk. But most Islamic economists reject such insurance as un-Islamic. On the ground that existing economic systems suffer from excessive risk avoidance, they wish to expose individuals to more risk—precisely the opposite of what deposit insurance achieves.

Islamic Redistribution

According to the promoters of Islamic economics, the second identifying characteristic of an Islamic economy is its redistribution system known as zakat. The system levies a tax on sufficiently wealthy Muslims to finance eight causes, including poor relief, the emancipation of slaves, and assistance to individuals serving Islam. Both collection and disbursement are matters of potent controversy.[8] With regard to collection, some Islamic economists hold that the rates and scope should be those that prevailed in the preindustrial desert economy of seventh-century Arabia. But a growing number propose modernizing the collection process, partly to ensure the coverage of assets still unknown fourteen centuries ago. On the disbursement side, some want expenditures divided equally among the eight original categories; others, by now a large majority, allow spending ratios to be varied in accordance with evolving social needs. Thus, where the former want exactly an eighth of a community's zakat resources spent on freeing slaves, the latter recognize that such spending would be meaningless in a society without slavery.

Notwithstanding such disagreements over the form of zakat, the Islamic economists are convinced that zakat can be a more effective weapon against poverty and inequality than the redistribution instruments used by modern states. Because of its religious significance, they argue, zakat would be paid willingly. Muslims who evade their tax obligations to secular governments would gladly pay zakat to an Islamic government even in the absence of coercion.

Islamic Economic Norms

The final distinguishing element of an Islamic economy, according to Islamic economists, is that its agents act under the guidance of norms drawn from the traditional sources of Islam.[9] These norms "command good" and "forbid evil." They promote the avoidance of waste, extravagance, and ostentation. They discourage activities with harmful externalities. They stimulate generosity. They encourage individuals to work hard, charge fair prices, and pay others their due. The intended effect of the norms is to transform selfish and acquisitive homo economicus into a paragon of virtue, homo Islamicus. Homo Islamicus acquires property freely, but never through speculation, gambling, hoarding, or destructive competition. And although he may bargain for a better price, he always respects his trading partner's right to a fair deal.

The agents that populate the ideal Islamic economy thus exercise many liberties, yet they pass all their claims through a normative filter. On this basis, the Islamic economy is said to differ from both capitalism and socialism. From the standpoint of Islamic economics, economic freedoms are too broad under capitalism and too narrow under socialism. The Islamic economy constitutes a "third way" that constrains economic liberties optimally.

Many Islamic economists believe that Islamic norms provide clear guidance in every conceivable economic arena. They are convinced, too, that the norms would be equally effective in all Muslim societies, regardless of size, history, level of development, and institutional framework. In an Islamic economy, they believe, disagreements over economic matters will be rare, for individuals will deal with one another fairly and honestly, and conceptions of economic justice will be homogeneous. These views are overly optimistic. For one thing, the proposed norms leave abundant room for individual judgment. For another, norms of altruism and responsibility are generally more effective within small networks than in large nations.[10]

Expositions of Islamic economics typically give the impression that the Islamic economy is a static structure consisting of fixed norms, an invariable zakat system, and a financial system equipped with unchanging instruments. However, the most sophisticated writers recognize that evolving opportunities generate pressures for institutional adaptation. They incorporate processes of change into their accounts of the Islamic economy by asserting that the holy laws of Islam accommodate the necessary flexibility.[11] This position is based, of course, on the empirically problematic view that changing social needs are knowable centuries in advance. It also reflects undue optimism regarding an Islamic society's capacity to keep vested interests from blocking socially desirable changes.

Islamic Economics in Practice

Although efforts to restructure the entire economy according to Islamic criteria have been limited to a handful of countries, there is one domain, banking, where the influence of Islamic economics has spread widely. There now exist Islamic banks, or branches of such banks, in more than sixty countries. All claim that their operations are free of interest, and also that their decisions rest on considerations that transcend profit maximization. As of the late 1980s, those based in the Arab world, which include the two largest groups of Islamic banks,[12] were capitalized at around $2.6 billion, and they held assets worth $22.9 billion. During the entire decade of the 1980s, the assets of these banks grew by 18.8 percent a year, although the subsequent growth has been considerably slower.[13] In some of the countries where the Islamic banks compete with conventional banks, notably Egypt and Kuwait, the banks have managed to attract around 20 percent of all the bank deposits; in most other countries, their shares, though rising, remain much smaller.[14]

These banks offer accounts said to involve profit and loss sharing. The holders of these accounts receive not interest but "profit shares" that tend to fluctuate. But the fluctuations closely follow the movements of ordinary interest rates. This is because the banks channel their deposits mostly into bonds and other interest-bearing instruments. The returns on individual

TABLE 2.1
Nominal Returns on Saving Deposits at Turkish Banks

	Term					
	3 months		*6 months*		*1 year*	
Month	*Conventional banks*	*Islamic banks*	*Conventional banks*	*Islamic banks*	*Conventional banks*	*Islamic banks*
June 1990	11.64	11.68	25.38	24.90	69.47	69.42
January 1991	12.34	12.02	25.51	24.61	56.25	57.12
June 1991	15.25	15.20	26.92	26.60	58.79	58.83
January 1992	15.68	15.58	30.51	30.46	65.11	64.30
June 1992	13.91	16.01	30.00	30.39	66.84	66.16
January 1993	14.72	15.65	29.88	30.43	66.96	64.51

Source: Köfteoğlu (1994), p. 28.
Note: Each figure represents the weighted average of returns to depositors over the designated period.

investments can vary, and they may come due at different times, which is why the "profit shares" of depositors are observed to differ from one period to the next. That these "profit shares" are supported by interest-based investments is evident from the fact that employees of Islamic banks unofficially promise potential depositors returns no lower than the prevailing interest rate. In fact, in countries where Islamic banks compete with conventional banks, the ostensibly interest-free returns of the former essentially match the explicitly interest-based returns of the latter.

Some evidence from Turkey appears in Table 2.1. For each term to maturity running from three months to one year, the first column provides the weighted average of the returns received by the depositors of conventional banks in the form of interest. The second column shows the average returns achieved by the depositors of the country's four Islamic banks under the rubric of "profit shares."[15] Even a cursory examination of the table suggests that the average "profit shares" earned by the depositors of Islamic banks were more or less identical to the interest rates of conventional banks. Nor were the profit shares appreciably more volatile. Though never fixed in advance, at least not officially, they rarely turned out substantially different from the average interest rate for the relevant period. In view of the rhetoric of Islamic banks, this is quite striking. But it is hardly surprising once one recognizes that, like the interest payments of conventional banks, "profit shares" are supported by interest-bearing assets.

Even some prominent Islamic economists now acknowledge that Islamic banks are avoiding the risky investments their charters require them to make. Ahmed al-Naggar, an Egyptian banker whom Islamic economists credit with founding the first Islamic bank, characterizes the existing Islamic banks as terrible failures. Their operations differ only cosmetically, he says, from those of conventional banks. Indeed, only a minuscule portion—generally well under 5 percent—of the assets of Islamic banks consist of loans based on genuine profit and loss sharing.

By far their most common financing method is murabaha, which is formally equivalent to the resale contracts used in various parts of the world, even in places where interest avoidance is not an issue, to take advantage of differences in tax rates. Let us say a cash-poor industrialist needs a new computer. His Islamic bank buys the computer, marks up its price, and then transfers to him the computer's ownership; in return, our industrialist agrees to pay the bank the marked-up price in a year's time. Ordinarily, then, murabaha serves as a cumbersome form of interest. Why have the Islamic banks been using a financing method equivalent to interest? Recognizing that they lack the skills to distinguish among good and bad investment opportunities, they fear that if they lend on the basis of profit and loss sharing they will make many bad choices, possibly ending up with more losses than profits. They fear, moreover, that industrialists with high expected returns will borrow from conventional banks (to maximize their returns in the likely event of success), while those with low expected returns will favor profit and loss sharing (to minimize their losses in the likely event of failure).

In addition to this adverse selection problem, the Islamic banks face a serious information problem. In countries where Islamic banks have achieved the greatest prominence, firms that would be natural candidates for profit and loss sharing are ordinarily highly secretive about their costs and revenues, lest information about their actual profits reach the government's tax department. But without access to the borrower's true accounts, as opposed to those concocted for tax purposes, the Islamic banks fear that under profit and loss sharing they will experience unsustainably high losses. The information problem becomes all the more serious insofar as the borrowing firm pursues numerous activities within a multidivisional structure. If the division that uses the computer purchased on credit incurs heavy losses, while during the same period the firm's other divisions enjoy huge profits, what is the bank's appropriate return under a profit and loss sharing contract? In principle, the method for determining the return could be negotiated in advance, but even in the absence of double bookkeeping the firm will be tempted to apportion its costs and revenues among its divisions to minimize repayments to the bank. If the firm keeps two sets of accounts, the scope for such opportunism is all the wider.

Remarkably, the Islamic banks are shunning profit and loss sharing even in the presence of huge tax incentives. In Turkey, the government taxes interest income, including income from murabaha, at 48 percent. By contrast, equity income, including income from profit and loss sharing, is tax-free.[16] Evidently, even such a large incentive fails to compensate for the drawbacks of profit and loss sharing.

Even though the Islamic banks pay and receive interest as a matter of course, certain ones have shown some creativity. For example, several of those located in the United States now offer interest-free mortgage opportunities. Under an interest-free mortgage contract the homeowner pays rent to the Islamic bank that helped finance his home. As with a conventional mortgage, the rent has two components, one that transfers equity from the bank to the homeowner and another that yields the bank income. The difference is that the home's value is reassessed periodically and, if necessary, rental payments adjusted. The homeowner's rent increases when the real estate market is booming, decreasing when the market is depressed. Consequently, the risk of a home loan is shared by the owner and the mortgage lender, rather than falling essentially on the former. If the owner defaults, the Islamic bank will sell the home, and the proceeds will be split according to the prevailing ownership shares. The homeowner will thus lose none of his accumulated equity, as he might under a standard mortgage plan.[17]

Next to Islamic banking, the most salient practical achievement of Islamic economics has been the establishment of government-run zakat systems in six countries: the Yemen Arab Republic, Saudi Arabia, Malaysia, Libya, Pakistan, and the Sudan. These systems vary greatly in both collection and disbursement, even though their architects all claim to have abided by the principles of the original zakat system in seventh-century Arabia. Whereas zakat was levied originally only on individuals, some modern systems extend the obligation to firms. In some countries, various modern financial assets, including bank deposits, are subject to zakat. Some systems allow producers to take deductions for costs, like those on synthetic fertilizers, for which classical Islamic law makes no allowance. The burden of zakat falls primarily on farmers in some places, mainly on urban residents in others. A notable consequence of the various innovations is that no established system resembles any other.[18]

Although some Islamic economists have touted zakat as an unmatched instrument for inequality reduction, none of the official zakat systems has put a significant dent in poverty.[19] There are three reasons why the equalizing effect of zakat has been disappointing. First, zakat revenue is limited everywhere by low rates, vast loopholes, and widespread evasion. Second, the costs of administering the system, including losses due to official corruption, have been high. Finally, much zakat revenue is spent on causes other than poverty reduction, including religious education and pilgrimages to Mecca.[20]

Zakat itself is not a novelty. Wherever Muslims live, including places currently without an official zakat system, there exist pious individuals making voluntary annual payments to persons, private collection agencies, or causes of their choosing.[21] Where the above-mentioned six countries stand out is in their efforts to turn zakat into a state-administered redistribution system under which people make obligatory payments. Studies of the recently established obligatory systems show that the beneficiaries of state-sponsored zakat are not always, or even mainly, the poor.[22] In fact, there exist places where the recipients of zakat assistance tend to be wealthier than the typical contributor, and even entire impoverished regions where no one gets any support. It appears, furthermore, that the essential difference between the voluntary and obligatory systems lies in the connections to which zakat confers value. Where voluntary zakat enhances the value of economic connections, obligatory zakat favors political connections, particularly ones related to religion. Under the voluntary system, the surest way to benefit from zakat is to have a wealthy employer. Under the obligatory system, it is to live in a politically sensitive city, work for the zakat administration, or enroll in a religious school.[23]

The obligatory zakat systems established in recent decades have bred resentment, partly because of their widely recognized inequities, and partly because payers like to have some say in how their contributions are spent. This observation is borne out by findings that most zakat payers would rather make their donations to private charities, if not directly to individuals of their own choice.[24]

The third major objective of Islamic economics, the reader will recall, has been to inculcate Muslims with behavioral norms drawn from the classical sources of Islam. In most countries, efforts to implement this objective have been limited to publications, educational programs in the mass media, and the incorporation of Islamic economics into school curricula. Only in Iran have efforts gone much further. Following the revolution of 1978–79, Islamic councils (shūrās) were set up at Iranian factories and offices, partly to monitor the atmosphere for violations of Islamic morality. The councils have been promoting public prayers, enforcing gender segregation, and serving as watchdog agencies to suppress opposition to the Islamic regime. There is no evidence that such measures have brought about the behavioral changes envisioned in Islamic texts. Nor is there evidence from any other country that the promotion of Islamic morality has altered work patterns or business relations. To be sure, variations in such factors as honesty, generosity, and work effort are notoriously difficult to measure. However, if the incessant complaints found in textbooks of Islamic economics provide any indication, the Islamic moral agenda has not made business relations palpably more honest or improved trust among traders.

One reason for the apparent ineffectiveness of this moral campaign is that the practical implications of Islamic economics are often ambiguous. Because fairness is a relative concept, business partners committed to the Islamic principle of fairness may differ sharply over the just division of their joint profits. Another important factor is that the fundamental sources of Islam are silent on many dimensions of a modern economy. The Qur'an contains verses that address issues such as distribution and pricing, but it is not, after all, a treatise in economics. The traditions of early Islam (*Sunna*), rich as they are in commentary concerning such matters as contracting, taxation, property rights, and inheritance, do not speak to every contemporary issue. Finally, the early Muslims whose words and deeds turned into sacred traditions were not economic theorists; they were gifted leaders trying to cope with the problems of a rapidly expanding community. A practical consequence of basing the normative framework of Islamic economics on the Qur'an and the Islamic traditions is that contemporary Muslims, even the devout, are liable to reach sharply different conclusions regarding the properly Islamic solution to any given economic problem.[25]

Even within Islamic economics itself, controversies abound. There exist two Islamic views on loan repayments under inflation, one that prescribes indexation and another that prohibits it. Significantly, the rival views rest on the same justification, namely, that interest is unjust. Supporters of indexation want society to abide by what they consider the spirit of the ban on interest; opponents want society to implement the letter of the ban. For another example, although there is near-agreement that Islamic economics stands for limited private property rights, Islamic economists differ greatly in regard to the specific limits that they favor. On the ground that Islam prohibits extravagance, ostentation, and extreme inequality, some Islamic economists advocate measures aimed at radical equalization. Others argue that it is legitimate to accumulate great wealth, provided the requisite zakat payments are made faithfully, and the means of accumulation are honest and just. Yet another area of disagreement involves pricing. While many Islamic economists favor leaving price determination to market forces, there exist Islamic approaches that advocate some form of bureaucratic control. For example, in the Just Order (*Adil Düzen*) advocated by Turkey's Islamist opposition party, sellers of a product would have to charge the same price throughout the country, regardless of variations in delivery cost and local demand. Moreover, wage and profit rates would be determined "scientifically" by scholars steeped in Islamic tradition.[26]

Nowhere are the divisions within Islamic economics clearer than in Iran, where advocates of Islamization have differed greatly on such matters as private property, profits, wages, labor laws, trade, and development strategy.[27] At one extreme, leaders of the Mojahedin Khalq Iran have advocated vast redistribution to achieve a classless social order—one that would depart from socialism only in its rejection of atheism. At the other extreme, an Islamic research center in Qum has maintained that all property acquired legitimately should enjoy the full protection of the law. One of the center's publications, *Introduction to Islamic Economics*, holds that social conflicts and inequalities are unavoidable. Notwithstanding its biting criticisms of capitalism, it proposes sharp restrictions on state activism, including limitations on workplace and child labor regulations. In a move that libertarians would applaud, the book even argues that the Islamic injunction against excessive consumption puts no limit on wealth accumulation. Citing examples of revered early Muslims who wore fine clothes and ornaments, it argues that luxurious consumption is often a sign of good economic judgment.

The fact that Islamic economics features divisions over basic economic matters like property rights and state regulation practically guarantees the existence of groups that will consider the prevailing economic structures un-Islamic. Compounding the problem is the fact that the economic structures imposed in the name of Islam have exhibited substantial variation over both time and space. Almost two decades after the Libyan leader Muammar Qaddafi began implementing the version of "Islamic socialism" described in his *Green Book*,[28] he took measures that rescinded his most critical directives. For example, having pursued economic self-sufficiency and abolished private property, he abrogated the state monopoly on foreign trade and started privatizing state enterprises. Both the original reforms and the subsequent U-turns have galvanized popular discontent.[29]

THE EMERGING ISLAMIC SUBECONOMY

Nothing so far explains why Mawdudi's call for economic Islamization has been heeded. His following among academics is attributable, perhaps, to the readiness with which intellectuals embrace reformist causes. But what is one to make of the practical achievements of Islamic economics? It is one thing to promote the idea of an Islamic bank, another to raise the capital to implement the idea, yet another to find depositors and borrowers who will keep the bank in business. Likewise, it is one thing to propose making zakat obligatory but quite another to organize thousands of local committees to carry out a redistribution program encompassing millions of households. If institutions promoted by Islamic economists have not brought about palpable improvements in living standards, what explains why they have generated excitement and participation?

Certain Islamic reforms have been pursued by politicians eager to demonstrate a commitment to Islamic ideals. In Pakistan and Iran, among other countries, politicians known to have reservations about Islamic economics have contributed to the adoption, and then the retention, of an interest ban. Yet Islamic banking spread also in countries where conventional banking remains legal. What explains this achievement? Banks are not the only firms that claim an Islamic identity. Many places now feature nonfinancial enterprises that advertise their operations as Islamic. One finds, for example, Islamic grocery stores that avoid dealing in liquor; Islamic boutiques that carry neither miniskirts nor bikinis; and Islamic theaters that make a point of conforming to religious sensibilities. There also exist diverse other firms, including some conglomerates, that consider themselves Islamic on the grounds that they shun interest, abide by Islamic norms, and make conscious efforts to support and promote Islamic causes.[30] Such companies are partial to other Islamic firms. Thus, an Islamic manufacturer of plastics will keep accounts at an Islamic bank and turn to an Islamic builder for its remodeling needs. In addition, the manufacturer will channel some of its profits to Islamic charities, schools, and political organizations.

Linked as they are by special relationships, Islamic enterprises collectively form a subeconomy within the broader national economy. Research on the Islamic subeconomy is in its infancy. It appears, however, that its constituent firms operate much like their secular counterparts. Islamic firms seem to seek profits as aggressively as firms without a religious identity, to enjoy no advantages or disadvantages in regard to quality control, and to be as productive.

Two factors, each rooted in rapid socioeconomic change, have contributed to the emergence of an Islamic subeconomy in various predominantly Muslim countries. The first has to do with the feelings of guilt experienced by industrialists, shopkeepers, and professionals trying to get ahead in societies where the prevailing social standards of honesty and dependability fall short of their own personal standards. The Islamic world has been urbanizing rapidly against the backdrop of inefficient legal systems that hinder the enforcement of private contracts. Explosive population growth has aggravated the enforcement problem, both by making it increasingly difficult to control official corruption and by turning traders into mutual strangers. Business relations thus suffer from widespread mistrust. Under the circumstances, it has become a growing challenge to succeed in business, industry, or the professions without bribing government officials, breaking laws, and deceiving business partners. To stay afloat, individuals are reluctantly making themselves part of the moral rot they find offensive. Especially for those who grew up in small communities enjoying high standards of honesty and dependability, these compromises give rise to guilt.

Various psychological experiments show that guilt-ridden people will take actions aimed at guilt alleviation.[31] In one set of experiments, randomly selected shoppers who were led to believe that they broke a camera showed a much greater eagerness than shoppers in the control group to help the victim of a staged accident. These experiments suggest that Muslims who behave in ways they consider un-Islamic will strive to rehabilitate themselves by going out of their way to bring religion into their daily routines. To such guilt-ridden Muslims an Islamic subeconomy offers an array of opportunities for relief. By holding an Islamic bank account, shopping whenever possible at Islamic stores, and donating to Islamic causes, an industrialist can achieve the feeling that he is doing his best to live as a good Muslim, despite the unfavorable social conditions. He can alleviate his guilt also by assuming an Islamic identity for his own business.

There is nothing unique, of course, about such consequences of immoral economic behavior. History is replete with examples of schools, religious buildings, and works of art financed by individuals whose wealth was acquired in ways they would have been loath to publicize. For example, some of the leading universities of the United States have benefited from fortunes amassed, partly through morally questionable means, by the builders of the early American railroads. Efforts to build an Islamic economy are partly driven, then, by the very same motives that helped construct the huge endowments of certain American universities.

The second factor that has fueled economic Islamization is that an Islamic subeconomy helps its participants cope with prevailing adversities by fostering interpersonal trust. Insofar as individuals do business within networks of people who know and trust each other, they reduce their costs of negotiating, drafting, monitoring, and enforcing agreements; relative to people who must constantly guard against being cheated, they incur lower transaction costs.[32] Yet, newcomers to a growing and increasingly impersonal metropolis like Cairo or Istanbul do not have access, at least not immediately, to the most lucrative of the existing networks, if only because they lack the requisite education, connections, and social etiquette. They have access only to networks built on ties of kinship and regional origin—networks whose members tend to be poor, inexperienced, and politically powerless. The Islamic subeconomy enables these newcomers to establish business relationships with a diverse pool of ambitious, hardworking, but culturally handicapped people who, like themselves, are excluded from the economic mainstream. Their shared commitment to Islam, even if partly feigned, keeps many of their activities within social circles in which information about dishonest behavior spreads quickly, thus providing a basis for mutual trust. Their costs of doing business are lower, therefore, than they might have been, and their opportunities for economic advancement correspondingly greater.

To sum up, the prevailing standards of interpersonal trust provide a constituency for Islamic economic institutions through two channels, one psychological and the other economic. Creating a need for guilt relief, they also make the economically insecure seek a vehicle for forming networks based on trust. These observations imply that until the conditions for greater trust in business relations get restored and traders regain efficient means for dispute resolution the services of the Islamic subeconomy will remain in demand.[33]

THE SIGNIFICANCE OF ISLAMIC ECONOMICS

We come, finally, to the challenge of evaluating the impact of economic activities undertaken in the name of Islam. From a narrowly economic standpoint, the Islamic subeconomy is not a source of inefficiency. On the contrary, it is providing palpable benefits that secular economic agencies and institutions are failing to provide. Although its constituent enterprises have hardly revolutionized economic relations, they are delivering meaningful services to groups with special needs, including individuals wishing to borrow or lend in accordance with religious values, or in need of guilt relief, or simply seeking to establish economic networks.

If Islamic economic activities are also a source of social harm, a basic reason lies in their political effects, including their possible consequences for future economic policies. Islamic enterprises provide financial support to Islamist political parties and organizations that seek to restrict social, economic, and cultural interactions between Muslims and non-Muslims. They enhance the perceived strength of Islamism, thus discouraging resistance from Islamists and inviting religious activists to press new demands. Finally, they support the claims and promises of Islamism, including those that fall outside the realm of economics. All such effects are alarming, of course, only insofar as one considers Islamism a threat.

The significance of the concrete steps taken to give economies an Islamic character lies only partly, then, in their economic content. Much of their importance lies in their symbolism, implications for the distribution of political power, and cultural meaning. Remember in this connection that Mawdudi's aim was not to foster a radical shift in economic thought or to unleash a revolution in economic practices. His aim was to reassert Islam's importance as a source of guidance and inspiration, and to reaffirm its relevance to modern life. From the standpoint of these objectives, the ongoing economic activities represent a remarkable accomplishment.

They defy the common separation between economics and religion. They invoke Islamic authority in a domain that modern civilization has secularized. Finally, by promoting the distinctness of Islamic economic behavior, they help counter foreign social influences.

Like the practical economic steps that are identified as Islamic, the doctrine of Islamic economics has helped to advance Mawdudi's objectives. But its influence has stemmed less from its substance than from the cultural statement that it delivers. Islamic economics does not offer a comprehensive framework for a modern economy; for all its grand claims, it presents a package of loosely connected policies rather than a blueprint for complete reform. Its proponents support many of their positions through selective quotations from scripture, leaving it open to the charge that an Islamic justification may be found for a wide variety of mutually inconsistent policies.[34] Yet another problem is that it fails to provide a well-defined and operational method of analysis. Islamic economics is mostly prescriptive; where efforts are made to give it analytical power, it loses much of its Islamic character. As a case in point, studies that explore the operation of an interest-free economy tend to rely on a standard general equilibrium model featuring no Islamic motif except a restriction on interest.[35] Most strikingly, the agents that populate these models are replicas of homo economicus, the bête noire of every general treatise on Islamic economics. The analytical weaknesses of Islamic economics also show up in its comparisons of alternative systems. The Islamic economists contrast the actual practices of systems they want to discredit with the ideal operation of their favored alternative.

Even though the practical and intellectual developments discussed here have all contributed to Mawdudi's objectives, they have not flowed from an integrated agenda. The forces responsible for the Islamic subeconomy include needs that played no role in the growth of Islamic economics. These needs might have been met through policies and institutions without religious significance. If religion did enter the picture, this is largely because in countries where Islamic economic structures have become conspicuous Islam provides a readily available, widely meaningful, and historically salient source of moral justification. Insofar as this observation is correct, Islamic economics must matter to participants in the Islamic subeconomy less because of its economics than because of its Islamic character.

There are observers, however, for whom the significance of Islamic economics has everything to do with its substance. Murat Çizakça, a Turkish economic historian, believes that a major factor in the Islamic world's economic backwardness has been the inadequacy of credit opportunities for entrepreneurs. The development of the Islamic world will thus require, he argues, the establishment of vast numbers of venture capital firms—firms that will provide funds to promising companies in return for some of their shares.[36] He maintains, moreover, that the stated principles of Islamic banking are precisely those of venture capitalism. Like venture financiers, Islamic banks are supposed to participate in the risks of the firms they finance. As one might expect, Çizakça is highly critical of the current practices of Islamic banks. Instead of trying to differentiate themselves from conventional banks through symbolism, he says, Islamic banks should be in the vanguard of genuine venture capitalism. Çizakça makes clear that his argument is grounded in economic data and logic rather than in religion. Significantly, some of his supporters have invited the Islamic banks to stop characterizing their operations as "Islamic" and to get on with the business of genuine financial innovation.

Coming a half century after Mawdudi launched Islamic economics, Çizakça's agenda amounts to the secularization of Islamic banking. Recent years have also witnessed calls to reform the established obligatory zakat systems and to reformulate the economic ethics of Islam in the light of contemporary economic realities, needs, and knowledge. And influential Islamic economists have acknowledged that efforts to extract a new economic paradigm from religious scripture are liable to end in failure, as are efforts to develop economic institutions unique to Islamic civilization. Muhammad Nejatullah Siddiqi, a prolific and widely read Islamic economist, has written: "The craving for a de novo discipline of Islamic economics is ill-conceived. No such thing is possible. The key to Islamic economics lies in positioning the Islamic vision in place of the Anglo-Saxon economic vision. But the Islamic economic vision has to be universal and contemporary, not chauvinistic and medieval."[37]

It remains to be seen whether the most significant legacy of Islamic economics will be the impetus that it gives to overcoming Muslim suspicions of ideas and institutions associated with the West; or its contribution to the political agenda of Islamism; or the comfort it gives to individuals trying to fit into the modern urban economy; or, again paradoxically, its revitalization of the goal, taken for granted by leading Muslim thinkers during much of the twentieth century, of keeping economic ideas, practices, policies, and institutions outside the realm of religion.

CHAPTER THREE

Islamism and Economics: Policy Prescriptions for a Free Society

ONE OF THE MOST VISIBLE TRIUMPHS of the ongoing global movement known as Islamic fundamentalism, Islamic revivalism, or Islamism[1] has been the spread of Islamic banks. Throughout the Islamic world the successes of Islamic banking have alarmed many supporters of secularization, modernization, and economic development. One outspoken worrier was Uğur Mumcu, a widely read Turkish columnist who was assassinated in January 1993, probably on orders from the Islamic Republic of Iran.[2] Mumcu saw the advent of Islamic banking as part of a sinister ploy to advance Islamism, isolate Muslims from global civilization, and force Muslim nations into a despotic political union established on medieval principles.

To readers familiar with the actual practices of Islamic banks, Mumcu's fears may seem hysterical. The typical Islamic bank is a commercial enterprise whose choices are sensitive to market pressures. Notwithstanding the utopian claims of Islamist ideologists, its practices differ only cosmetically from those of conventional banks. Where an ordinary bank charges interest openly and unabashedly, the Islamic bank charges a commensurate "commission." A Malaysian observer of Islamic banking puts it more bluntly: "The only difference is whether the man behind the counter is wearing a religious hat or a bow tie."[3]

The notion that Islamic banking differs minimally from its conventional counterpart is not inconsistent, however, with the assertion that the spread of Islamic banking is socially disruptive. Even if inherently beneficial to commerce and investment, it may serve a potentially harmful political and cultural mission. Going beyond Islamic banking, this essay offers reasons for concern about the spread of Islamist economic teachings and practices. It also proposes a set of responses to the challenge of Islamism. The first policy prescription is to disseminate information about flaws of the Islamist economic agenda. The second is to show that Islamist leaders tend to overstate their popular support. The final prescription, to which secularists of Mumcu's persuasion might object, is that close attention should be paid to Islamist views on social problems. Many Islamist complaints about modernity, including various socioeconomic grievances, stem from genuine policy failures.

To prescribe public policies one must have a sense of what social order one wants to build and maintain. Let me make explicit my own ideals and biases. The organizing principles of an economy should be individual liberty and limited government. I believe that our material aspirations, not to mention many of our nonmaterial needs, are best served by a free economic order—one that accords individuals broad freedoms to produce, consume, negotiate, and exchange according to their own preferences, expectations, and abilities. In a free economy the state's central economic role is to protect property rights. It may regulate commerce, communication, and innovation only to forestall demonstrated inefficiencies. Though it may provide certain forms of social insurance, it must avoid arbitrary attempts at redistribution.[4]

The Social Significance of Islamic Banking

In and of themselves, Islamic banks pose no challenge to a free economic order. As long as they are sustained by private capital, the government gives them no special privileges, and their clients are free to use conventional banks, their operations will not violate economic freedoms. Moreover, at least where these conditions are met, the very success of Islamic banking implies that it meets an apparent social need; so it should be tolerated, given full protection of the law, even welcomed.

It has been argued that in its ideal form Islamic banking encourages certain classes of depositors, such as the retired, to carry risks better borne by others. It has also been argued that Islamic banking necessitates excessive monitoring of commercial and industrial borrowers.[5] Though justified, such criticisms are beside the point. If a septuagenarian chooses to risk her savings by placing them in a variable-return account, third parties have no reason to object—provided they will not be forced to support her in the event her investment turns sour. Likewise, if a private bank chooses to tie the returns on its industrial loans to the profits from the financed projects, third parties need not be concerned—provided, again, they are not obligated to keep the bank solvent.

Every society gives its members wide latitude to make decisions that observers might characterize as wasteful or silly. As a case in point, Americans are free to purchase nutritionally worthless, even harmful, food. Granting Muslims the liberty to "misspend" resources in running their finances according to an alleged Islamic tenet is no different, in principle, from allowing Americans to "misspend" resources on unhealthy food. Even if Islamic banks are inefficient, in itself that is no reason to oppose their right to exist.

The alarmists would agree that the practice of Islamic banking presents no reason for concern;[6] many recognize that a religious hat is no more threatening than a bow tie. They would hasten to add, however, that Islamic banking is motivated by more than the provision of a neglected financial service. A common theme in the alarmist literature is that Islamic banking represents not simply a new financial instrument but also a conspicuous, lucrative, and symbolically potent instrument of Islamism. Mumcu considered Islamic banking an affront to Atatürk's vision of a secular and Westernized Turkish Republic. In the same vein, Islamist Egyptian writers view it as both a source of financial support for Islamist activities and a vehicle for creating financial ties among Islamist activists.[7]

The link between Islamic banking and Islamism is anything but imaginary. The founders and executives of Islamic banks see themselves as contributing to the reestablishment of the primacy of Islam in the lives of Muslims. Some want the entire social order restructured according to Islamic criteria, not only economic relations but also gender roles, education, the mass media, government, and much else. An appliance manufacturer might launch a new line of refrigerators or enlarge his workforce without intending to change the basic framework of the economy, to say nothing of revising the high school curriculum or reordering male-female relations. By contrast, Islamic bankers commonly view themselves as both profit seekers and agents of social renewal. They do not ask merely to be left alone, to be permitted to withdraw from the economic mainstream. They want to be noticed and to inspire. They wish to make their preferred financial practices the norm. They consider themselves in the vanguard of a struggle to cleanse the economy, indeed the whole social system, from harmful secular influences.

The vast literature that falls under the rubric of "Islamic economics"[8] confirms that, unlike ordinary firms, Islamic banks are meant to serve a broad social mission. The literature holds that the prevailing capitalist and socialist economies generate injustice, corruption, inequality, poverty, and discontent. A major source of all these problems is interest, which pushes distressed borrowers into poverty, allows lenders to make risk-free gains without exerting any effort, and weakens social ties. By offering an alternative to interest, Islamic banking will contribute, so claims Islamic economics, to making the economy fairer, more egalitarian, and less harmful to the social fabric. But the objective is not simply to make Islamic banking more accessible. It is to make all banking Islamic. Certain campaigns against conventional banking have succeeded in making "interest-laden" banking illegal. In Pakistan all banks were ordered in 1979 to purge interest from their operations within five years, and in 1992 the Sharia court removed various critical exemptions.[9] Interest prohibitions have gone into effect also in Iran and the Sudan.[10]

The religious justification for prohibiting interest has been that the Qur'an bans all its forms, irrespective of the prevailing institutional framework and the nature of the involved loan. Actually, what the Qur'an bans is riba, an ancient Arabian lending practice whereby defaulters saw their debts grow exponentially. Although the notion that all interest is equivalent to riba has never enjoyed unanimous acceptance among Islamic authorities, to say nothing of skepticism on the part of laypeople,[11] Islamic economists[12] treat the issue as settled, and they consider anyone who questions the wisdom or feasibility of prohibiting interest as misguided, corrupt, or ignorant. They feel justified, moreover, in compelling everyone, including Muslims who reject the precepts of Islamic economics, and even non-Muslims, to abide by a ban.

For many proponents of Islamic banking, its religious rationale is far more important than its economic justification. Indeed, some respond to criticisms of the methods of Islamic banking by saying that its economic merits are secondary to its contribution to the revival of Islam. For them, the overriding objectives are the reassertion of Muslim identity, the reaffirmation of Islam's relevance to the modern world, and the restoration of Islamic authority. Islamic banking defies the separation between economics and religion. It invokes religious authority in a domain that modern civilization has secularized. Moreover, by promoting the distinctness of Islamic economic behavior, it counters the absorption of Islamic civilization into Western civilization. Many leaders of Pakistan's Jamaat-i Islami support Islamic banking as a vehicle for replacing the cautious and limited Islam of Iqbal and Jinnah with one that is relatively assertive and intrusive.[13]

THE BROADER ISLAMIC SUBECONOMY

"True Muslims," wrote Sayyid Abul-Ala Mawdudi, the Pakistani thinker who founded Islamic economics in the 1940s, "merge their personalities and existences into Islam. They subordinate all their roles to the one role of being Muslims. As fathers, sons, husbands or wives, businessmen, landlords, labourers, employers, they live as Muslims."[14] Following in Mawdudi's footsteps, contemporary Islamists consider Islam a "complete way of life," a source of guidance and inspiration in every personal and social domain. This position obviously clashes with the secularist view that religion is separable from public realms such as science, law, politics, and economics.

To discredit the notion that Islam's relevance is limited to matters of personal faith, Islamists have needed to demonstrate its comprehensiveness as a way of life. Islamic economics emerged, through the writings of

Mawdudi and others, as one component of a broad philosophical attempt to meet this challenge.[15] With the literature growing rapidly, concrete applications were quick to follow. Major efforts to exhibit the practicality, distinctness, and wisdom of Islamic economics got underway in the 1960s, and the world's first Islamic bank went into operation in 1975.[16] Subsequently, Islamic banking spread to more than sixty countries, putting it at the center of the campaign to demonstrate the superiority of Islamic economics over secular economic traditions. The practical demonstrations of Islamic economics, which go much beyond banking, may be grouped in four categories.

The first consists of efforts to give an Islamic identity to existing economic activities, mainly through symbolism. Islamic banking falls into this category. From a substantive standpoint, Islamic banks do not operate very differently from their conventional counterparts. In making loans, they adhere mainly to financial criteria; like conventional banks, they pay little attention to nonfinancial considerations. Contrary to the stipulations of Islamic economics, they tend not to give priority to long-term development projects over projects aimed at quick profits. They do not limit their business to pious Muslims, or even to Muslims. And they show no appreciable bias against projects with heavy social costs, such as highly polluting factories. They differ from conventional banks primarily in appearance. Their operations are formally under the control of a religious council. Their quarters feature signs of Islamic piety: verses from the Qur'an on the walls, veiled female and bearded male tellers, prayer rooms, and breaks during times of prayer. Finally, and as already noted, they give and take interest under various religious disguises.

Cosmetically Islamic variants have emerged for other types of businesses, too. There are now Islamic retail outlets, Islamic investment companies, even Islamic conglomerates. What makes all such enterprises Islamic, observes Nazih Ayubi, is essentially that their owners have taken to "wearing white gowns, growing thick beards, and holding long rosaries."[17] Indeed, the substantive differences between Islamic and ordinary firms are minor. Self-consciously Islamic firms tend not to deal in commodities considered un-Islamic. Thus, an Islamic grocery store does not sell pork or liquor, and an Islamic boutique does not cater to the needs of discotheque patrons. Another difference involves beneficiaries of the firm's charitable contributions. Where an ordinary firm makes donations to secular causes—an art show, a scholarship program, a sports team—the Islamic firm tends to favor explicitly Islamic causes.

If employees of Islamic firms were asked what makes their operations Islamic, a common response would be that they avoid interest. In fact, most Islamic enterprises deal in interest as a matter of course, though usually under Islamic garb. In no essential respect do their business practices differ systematically from their non-Islamic counterparts. Though Islamic enterprises have not been studied adequately, casual observation suggests that they are not exceptionally honest in their dealings with clients unlikely to be repeat buyers.[18] Nor do they appear any less prone than ordinary firms to tax evasion, or especially generous toward their employees. Though Islamic economics is highly critical of the prevailing standards of honesty, trustworthiness, and fairness in contemporary economies, nothing suggests that established Islamic enterprises behave substantially differently from ordinary enterprises.[19]

Efforts that form our first category of Islamic economic activity do no great harm. In refusing to stock dancing outfits, an Islamic boutique does not keep dancers from taking their business elsewhere. Islamists also try, however, to eliminate economic choices they find objectionable, sometimes by force. Such efforts form our second category. They include attacks on establishments deemed to foster moral laxity: video stores, theaters, bookstores, dance clubs, bars, hotels that cater to "naked" tourists, and restaurants that serve food during fasting times.[20] The attacks are aimed at destroying certain economic sectors, and the consequences have hardly been insignificant. In Egypt, attacks against tourists and tourism establishments have lowered foreign exchange earnings, harming investment and growth.[21] Such attacks serve to differentiate Islamic economic values from non-Islamic ones. They also make it known that the goals of preserving and advancing Islam take precedence over such objectives as individual liberty, financial opportunity, hospitality toward visitors, and economic development.[22]

Economically harmful attempts to establish the primacy of Islam have not been limited to violent attacks against morally controversial sectors. In various countries it is now common for employees to be pressured to attend communal prayers several times a day. During Ramadan, employees have been forced to fast, often with adverse effects on productivity. Communities have been discouraged from spending resources on nonreligious social services, lest these reduce the amount available for the construction of mosques and Qur'an schools. In one case that has received scholarly attention, Islamists seeking space for a new mosque secured the removal of a Turkish community's only health center, without bothering to find it a new location.[23] Still another example of giving primacy to religious needs lies in pressures to make governments devote more resources to religious education. In Turkey between 1976 and 1984, the number of government-run religious high schools (*imam-hatip* schools) rose from 73 to 374, largely because of Islamist pressures. For a comparison, over the same period the number of secular high schools (*lises*) rose from 927 to 1190.[24]

The third category of economic instruments for advancing Islamism consists of nongovernmental Islamic social services. Such services include hospitals, clinics, legal-aid societies, schools, dormitories for college students, youth centers, summer camps, and sports facilities. Benefiting primarily the poor, they demonstrate that organizations infused with an Islamic spirit can tackle various social problems more adequately than the government. Also, by giving a religious dimension to traditionally secular services they lend credibility to the claim that Islam is a complete way of life.

In Egypt, mosque-affiliated clinics are delivering health services at rock-bottom prices, generally more efficiently than overburdened health facilities run by the government. Where a poor Egyptian might wait three months for an X-ray at a government facility, at an Islamic clinic access to the procedure typically takes much less.[25] For another example, thousands of underprivileged Turkish teenagers have attended Islamic summer camps, their expenses paid by Islamist organizations.[26] These camps put great emphasis on religious instruction. In addition to earning general goodwill, therefore, they serve as Islamist training grounds.

It is costly to run services like camps and hospitals. By contrast, the final category of economic instruments consists of services that bring Islamists net financial gains. The most important such instrument is zakat, a religious tax on wealth and income. By tradition, zakat proceeds serve partly to deliver poor relief and partly to finance "praiseworthy activities," defined to include religious education and pilgrimage. In several countries, including Pakistan, zakat has become a legal obligation, and the government now organizes both its collection and its disbursement. In most parts of the Islamic world, however, zakat is collected and disbursed in a decentralized manner by local religious organizations.[27] Whatever the pattern, substantial shares of zakat revenue are used to finance Islamist activities. Another source of income for Islamist causes is the hides of sacrificial animals. In Turkey, such hides traditionally went to the Turkish Aviation Society. Now, a large share, in some localities the lion's share, goes to Islamist collection agencies, which have taken to portraying it as sinful to make donations to a secular authority. One estimate puts the Islamist income from a recent year's collection at around U.S. $90 million.[28]

No one knows the total income of Islamist organizations. What is known is that Islamists derive revenue from many channels, including not only zakat and hides but also donations from Islamic businesses, individuals sympathetic to Islamic causes, and unsympathetic individuals hedging their bets. There is also reason to believe that many Islamist organizations receive funds from foreign governments. The governments of Saudi Arabia, Libya, and Iran, among other countries, deliver much help to Islamist organizations throughout the world.[29] Some of the diffuse income supports Islamic services. Much of the rest is used to support an array of political activities. In predominantly Muslim countries that have meaningful elections, the candidates of Islamist parties regularly receive financial support from Islamist organizations whose primary purposes are nonpolitical.

All told, the economic activities of the Islamists hardly amount to a radical reordering of economic relations. They serve either to raise resources for Islamist advancement or to demonstrate that Islamists are capable of solving entrenched social problems. True, Islamists talk of radical change. Yet the ongoing economic activities associated with Islamism generally do not represent major departures from the economic status quo.

It is essential here to remember that Islamic economics did not originate from a need to reorder economic relations. Rather, it arose out of an impulse to demonstrate the distinctness, continuing social relevance, and priority of Islam. From this perspective, Islamists have been remarkably successful in pursuing their economic objectives. They would have been less successful, perhaps, had they advanced a detailed, coherent, and comprehensive plan for truly revolutionary economic restructuring. This is because a complete and fully explicit plan would have identified many potential losers. As matters stand, the vagueness of Islamic economics allows Islamists to appeal to a broad audience without triggering widespread anxieties about the economic consequences of an Islamist takeover. It also gives Islamists the flexibility to adjust the content of Islamic economics to changing needs and opportunities.

THE DOMINO EFFECT

Successful Islamization in one domain lends credibility to Islamization attempts in other domains. So a significant consequence of the economic activities undertaken in the name of Islam is the support they give to the broader Islamist agenda. The economic accomplishments of Islamism encourage activists to press new demands. They also discourage resistance from opponents and embolden Islamist movements elsewhere. It follows that the economic advances of Islamism may lead, through a domino effect, to further victories in both economic and noneconomic domains.

When Islamists writers insist, then, on the inseparability of economics, family structure, dress, and education, they do not mean only that in the minds of individual believers these domains are interlinked. They mean also that every move toward Islamization facilitates further moves. The spread of Islamic commerce discourages women from dressing immodestly in public settings. Conversely, as veiling becomes more common, Islamic economics is taken more seriously, and its opponents become less vocal.

In pursuing power, any political movement will rely on two complementary strategies. The first is to make people understand and accept its objectives, the second to pressure individuals of all persuasions, including skeptics and potential opponents, into supporting the objectives. Each of these strategies is apparent in the economic activities of Islamists. A philosophical contribution to Islamic economics serves primarily to persuade. By contrast, a profitable Islamic bank and a well managed clinic serve both to persuade and to build political pressure. On the one hand, they show that Islam can make positive contributions to economic justice and efficiency. On the other, they boost the perceived power of Islamism, thus compounding pressures to support Islamist positions.

Bolstering a movement's perceived strength is not riskless: it can induce a major reaction. The military response to the imminent victory of the Islamic Salvation Front in Algeria's legislative election of 1991–92 illustrates the point.[30] Yet under the right set of contingencies, a pro-Islamist turn in public opinion will make fear change sides: people who were reluctant to appear too sympathetic to Islamism will become reluctant to appear too unsympathetic. Thus, a shift in public opinion may weaken the anti-Islamist resistance, make it equivocate, and eventually crush it. Islamist leaders can never be certain about their hidden support or about their opponents' susceptibility to social pressure. Like all political players, they face uncertainty regarding the appropriate timing for action. Nevertheless, they all recognize that the likelihood of breaking the resistance to their agendas is likely to grow with increases in Islamism's perceived strength.[31]

In some places, Islamism in general and Islamic economics in particular already derive critical support from fears of being stigmatized as un- or anti-Islamic. Though many leaders of Pakistan's People's Party have serious misgivings about Islamic economics, few have gone on record with their reservations. In fact, they generally make a point of claiming that their own economic programs are consistent with, if not derived from, the economic teachings of Islam. Zulfikar Ali Bhutto, who once questioned the feasibility of organizing a modern society according to Islamic principles, began asserting in the mid-1970s that the inspiration for his socialist ideas had come from Islam.[32] A decade later, his daughter Benazir Bhutto refrained from denouncing the ban on interest, even as the Jamaat-i Islami was conspiring to topple her government. Such episodes are at once a manifestation of, and a contributor to, social pressures to appear supportive of Islamism. All fundamentalist objectives, not simply those associated with attire, gain legitimacy and immunity to criticism when a political leader appears in an election poster with her head fully covered and reading the Qur'an.[33] So, too, they all benefit when Pakistani statesmen, bureaucrats, intellectuals, and professionals exhibit reticence to take issue with the claims and practices of Islamic economics.

To sum up thus far, Mumcu's point that Islamic economics is part of a broad mission is unassailable. Islamic economics serves to differentiate the Islamic social order from prevailing social orders, to signal the strength of Islamism, and to make potential opponents practice self-censorship. As such, schemes such as zakat and Islamic banking are both objectives in their own right and instruments of the wider Islamist cause. Opponents of the Islamist agenda are justified, then, in treating Islamic economics as more than a quaint doctrine.

If this point is granted, the obvious next question is, "How should non-Islamist policy makers respond to the economic activities undertaken in the name of Islam?" I will offer three suggestions in due course, but only after making two additional points. I will note that Islamism has been grappling, not always unsuccessfully, with some deep social problems. And I will then suggest that Islamism—like other fundamentalisms—carries the potential of harming the global economy.

Islamism as Economic Instrument

Given that the rise of Islamic economics was driven largely by noneconomic factors, it is unsurprising that it has solved no major economic problem. A half century after the publication of Mawdudi's seminal writings, Islamic economics has not made Muslim economies more equal, more productive, or more innovative. Nevertheless, for reasons essentially unrelated to the principles of Islamic economics, Islamism has helped alleviate certain discontents of rapid urbanization. In particular, it has enabled metropolises like Cairo, Istanbul, and Karachi to cope with historically unprecedented demographic changes.

Because of rampant government corruption and widespread dishonesty in business relations, many businessmen of the Islamic world find it difficult to succeed without bribing government officials or deceiving their suppliers and clients. Their inevitable moral compromises give rise to guilt, a condition for which Islamism offers an array of cures. By holding savings in an Islamic account and making a point of shopping at Islamic stores, a businessman can achieve the feeling that he is doing his best to live as a good Muslim. Likewise, by donating money to a mosque and time to a Qur'an school, he can satisfy himself that, despite the adverse conditions, he is doing his share to improve the moral climate. He can alleviate his guilt also by assuming an Islamic identity for *his own* business.

It would be simplistic, then, to portray the businessmen who contribute to Islamic causes and participate in the Islamic subeconomy as mere tools of Islamist leaders, although there are undoubtedly Muslim, non-Muslim, and agnostic businessmen who take such actions under real or imagined social pressures. Many of the businessmen who have fueled the growth of the Islamic subeconomy derive important personal benefits from their activities. To them, Islamism is not just a social force to be accommodated. It is also a vehicle for emotional support and a means of fitting into a hostile economic culture.

A related consequence of rampant dishonesty is that it makes it advantageous to join a subeconomy that fosters trustworthiness. Relative to businessmen who must constantly guard against being cheated, ones who can count on timely deliveries and payments incur lower costs of operation. In particular, they spend less time, energy, and money on negotiating, drafting, monitoring, and enforcing agreements.[34] New urbanites have immediate access to networks built on ties of kinship and regional origin. As a rule, however, these networks provide fewer benefits than those composed of longtime residents, because members of the former tend to be poorer, less experienced, and politically powerless. The newcomers would like to break into the most lucrative networks. They seldom can, however, if only because they lack the proper education and the requisite social etiquette. The Islamic subeconomy offers a second-best alternative. Within it, they are able to establish business ties with ambitious but culturally handicapped people who, like themselves, are excluded from the economic mainstream. Their shared commitment to Islam, even if partly feigned, provides a basis for mutual trust. Their costs of doing business are thus lower than those of the typical newcomer operating outside the Islamic subeconomy.

The networks of the Islamic subeconomy are not limited to the private sector. Throughout the Islamic world they extend into various levels of government. Islamists elected or appointed to positions of government authority are known to grant financially valuable political favors to those outside government. They make it cheaper for Islamist businessmen to learn about regulations, obtain licenses, avoid tax audits, and pass inspections.

Hence, low standards of honesty fuel Islamism through two channels: by creating a need for guilt relief and by making the economically insecure seek a vehicle for forming networks based on trust. One reason why the Islamic world displays low standards of honesty is that overregulation and misregulation provide officials, high and low, with vast opportunities for earning bribes.[35] A related reason is that the government has been ineffective at its most essential task, namely, providing the legal foundations of a complex, dynamic, and increasingly impersonal economy. In most parts of the Islamic world, the legal system fails to furnish low-cost instruments for collecting overdue debt. Traders thus have strong incentives to join private networks for protection against being cheated.[36] Explosive urbanization has compounded the incentives by stretching government services, including legal services, to the breaking point.

In populous countries like Egypt and Turkey, there was a time when the government could employ every high school graduate in need of a job. Now it cannot even hire every applicant with a university degree. In Cairo, a university graduate may have to wait a decade for a low-paying, entry-level position. At the same time, today's young job seekers have much higher aspirations than ones of earlier generations. Populist ideologies, schooling, and the mass media have all raised their expected living standards way above what is feasible. Yet, many must wait until they are around thirty to get a stable job, rent a place, and get married. In the meantime they remain sexually and emotionally frustrated, and they feel robbed of honor and dignity.

This brings us to still another way in which contemporary Islamism helps marginalized urbanites cope with frustrations. In promoting a puritanical lifestyle, it gives the deprived a justification for accepting a bad situation they are powerless to change. In effect, it offers both sexes the means for adjusting their aspirations to their possibilities—much like the fox who decided the grapes he could not reach had to be sour.[37] Islamists communicate to their adherents that to get married and have children one need not wait for financial security. One can live as a "good Muslim," they say, even without fancy clothes, a private home, and modern amenities. They add that the affluent lifestyles many impoverished people seek to emulate are in any case immoral and un-Islamic. In some Egyptian Islamist circles, a prospective bride demands nothing from her future husband but a deep commitment to Islam. Moreover, before she accepts and her family agrees to the marriage, the groom must prove, usually through an oral quiz, that he has sufficient religious knowledge.[38]

Against this background, the Islamist obsession with veiling may be seen as another effort to alleviate the frustrations of marginalized urban youths. The veil reduces women's need to compete socially by keeping up with changing fashions. It also makes a statement against the materialism of modern civilization. Yet another of its functions is to protect the dignity of men socialized into measuring their manhood by how well they protect their women. City life offers great opportunities for the mixing of the sexes, and overcrowding in poor urban communities drastically limits family privacy. Under the circumstances, the veil attenuates the vulnerability of culturally conservative men, young and old.[39]

By no means do all veiled women belong to economically deprived segments of the urban population. Some come from upwardly mobile families that live in posh neighborhoods and have the financial means to keep up with fashions. For such women, the motivation for veiling lies primarily in its political and religious symbolism. This observation is supported by the emergence of an Islamic fashion industry, which even stages fashion shows of the latest styles in Islamic dress.[40] Relative to poor Islamist women, prosperous ones tend to wear more expensive and more stylish veils. They thus affirm their religious identity and express opposition to modern sex relations *without* rejecting the materialism of modern civilization.

start

THREATS TO THE GLOBAL ECONOMY

The encouragement of veiling is a shared characteristic of Islamist movements everywhere. Likewise, the promotion of Islamic banking is a standard element of every Islamist economic agenda. Notwithstanding such commonalities, the economic orientations of Islamists exhibit potentially significant variations. Most critically, Islamists, including Islamic economists, have always been divided on the merits of the market. The religious opposition that toppled the Iranian monarchy harbored several rival economic agendas. Schools led by Morteza Motahhari and Navab-Safavi put great faith in the market system and saw the private accumulation of capital as essential for healthy economic development. A rival school led by Ali Shariati rejected private ownership and insisted on endowing the government with vast redistributive powers.[41] In Pakistan, Mawdudi and many of his followers have maintained that Islam is sympathetic to private property and the market mechanism. But in the 1970s prominent Pakistani leaders interpreted Islam as mandating planned economic development and massive redistribution.[42]

Contemporary Islamism is capable of supporting both pro- and anti-market ideologies, because this is as true of Islam itself as it is of other major religions.[43] In the fundamental sources of Islam one can find justifications for respecting market outcomes along with ones for restricting them. One also finds precepts favoring interventions on behalf of the poor along with ones that preach tolerance of inequality. Such variations provide immense flexibility to anyone who wants to have Islam serve an economic agenda or to use ostensibly Islamic economic policies for noneconomic ends. They make it possible to ground any number of arguments, strategies, and policies in venerable traditions or timeless commandments. They enable public figures whose rhetoric may make them appear backward-looking to select among various economic positions without rejecting the authority of religion. As a case in point, they allowed the Ayatollah Khomeini and his associates to adapt to various exigencies without ever stepping outside Islamic discourse. Iran's theocracy continues to accommodate new needs, yield to social pressures, and make pragmatic adaptations—all while continuing to claim allegiance to a timeless, unchanging, and well-defined economic agenda.[44]

Modern Islamist movements possess, then, the ideological capacity and flexibility to sustain a liberal economic agenda. Even if they promote illiberal policies while in opposition, they may be able to assume a liberal orientation once in power. In any case, to pursue effectively liberal policies they need not make deliberate or explicit ideological adaptations. By giving low priority to economic issues, they may end up promoting private investment, self-management, private ownership, and free trade by default. Such unintended liberalism is all the more likely where illiberal economic goals are overshadowed by objectives concerning family, sexuality, manners, and education. Though a prominent theme in Khomeini's pre-revolutionary rhetoric was the elimination of poverty and exploitation, once he rose to Iran's helm he subordinated his stated economic objectives to the general goal of restoring the centrality of Islam in public life—even to such particular objectives as eliminating the consumption of alcohol, veiling women, banning Western music, and severing Iran from its pre-Islamic heritage. After the revolution, he dismissed demands for concrete economic reforms on the ground that economic well-being is worthy of the donkey.[45]

None of this means that the Islamists' market-constraining enactments and prescriptions, whether involving interest or planning or redistribution, should be viewed as gimmicks without long-run significance. Although there is no necessary connection between Islamism and economic illiberalism, Islamism is capable of supporting restrictions on economic liberties. Islamist leaders who, for whatever reason, desire to restrict international trade or regulate the composition of private investment will have little difficulty justifying their actions in religious terms. Also, leaders who whip up antimarket feelings as a tactical move to gain power will not necessarily be able to control the forces they unleash.

Illiberal economic policies can harm the countries implementing them. Protectionism causes the misallocation of local resources, and it insulates inefficient firms from external competition.[46] Measures to direct an economy's evolution can produce excessive bureaucratic growth, thus reorienting individual enterprise from wealth-creating economic activities to wealth-distributing political ones.[47] The colossal failures of the centrally planned economies and the persistent disappointments of countries that have pursued inward-oriented and highly interventionist development strategies bear testimony to these adverse consequences.[48] The burdens of illiberal policies do not fall entirely, of course, on the countries pursuing them. Trade restrictions generate misallocations in countries forced to produce goods obtainable more cheaply from abroad. Likewise, excessive bureaucratic meddling in one country imposes costs on anyone who consumes its products, directly or indirectly.

When a new regime starts pursuing an antimarket agenda, the consequent costs need not catch notice immediately. The new regime's apologists will be endeavoring to make its failures look like successes. Also, hardships and inefficiencies may initially appear transitional. Even when the costs gain wide recognition, however, it will not be easy to switch gears. For one thing, certain leaders may lose authority if they repudiate the policies they have championed. For another, the government bureaucracy and protected segments of the private sector will have developed a vested interest in the status quo. As a case in point, many Iranian leaders now recognize that the statist and nationalistic measures taken after the revolution of 1978–79 have imposed great burdens on the Iranian people. Accordingly, they have begun to change course: nationalized industries are now being reprivatized, and measures have been taken to encourage foreign trade, foreign investment, and joint ventures with foreign firms. Nonetheless, the Iranian economy remains more regulated and more inward-oriented than it would have been in the absence of illiberal postrevolutionary policies.[49] Even though leaders sympathetic to a radical reorientation could easily concoct an Islamic rationale for broad liberalization, they find it politically infeasible to undo all the policies they now consider unwise. The principle at work here is "path dependency": current possibilities are shaped by history. Of two societies, one market-oriented and the other antimarket, the former can retain liberal policies more easily than the latter can adopt them.

Government policies influence economic performance, but they are not the sole determinant. Education, culture, expressive freedoms, and the mass media all play important roles. Islamism seeks to reshape each of these factors, mostly for reasons other than the creation and distribution of wealth. The relevant political efforts thus carry economic implications. A culture that insists on the inerrancy of traditional sources of wisdom, treats religious teachings as unambiguous, and considers certain issues beyond controversy, may leave the societies it touches unprepared to face the challenges of a dynamic global economy. It is likely to encourage risk aversion as opposed to risk taking, cautious imitation as opposed to daring innovation, and the production of established commodities as opposed to new, and thus highly profitable, ones. In a world where some societies are inquisitive and expressively free, therefore, an Islamist-controlled society may find itself economically disadvantaged. Significantly, the Middle East's failure to match the West's economic modernization process coincided with the spread of a mindset that equates innovation with heresy and success with stability.[50] Technological creativity has always been a major source of relative economic success, and creative societies are generally tolerant of political dissent, distrustful of conventional wisdom, and open to social change.[51]

If a society starts pursuing economically unwise policies, should outsiders raise objections? As long as they respect the society's right to make bad choices, they should not hold back. Just as an individual has a right to eat foods high in cholesterol, so a society has every right to restrict its economic growth for other objectives, be it environmental preservation, political stability, or spiritual harmony. By the same token, anyone bothered by a society's economic choices, including an outsider, is entitled to offer alternatives. There is no reason, from a liberal point of view, to prevent a society from choosing to make its economy unproductive. Nor is there a reason, however, for people disturbed by its inefficiencies to keep their misgivings hidden.

When one part of the world falls substantially behind another, there can be troubling consequences for global political stability. The economically backward societies will accumulate resentments against the global economic system, against advanced societies, and even against similarly disadvantaged others. Such resentments can become a source of international friction. Whatever their source, international conflicts threaten global trade flows and transfers of capital. They also impart uncertainty to property rights, as when an ethnic group held responsible for another's economic frustrations faces the possibility of expropriation. If, then, a society run by Islamists—or, for that matter, by anyone else—performs poorly in an economic sense, other societies, too, may suffer.

Islamist movements need not sow social tensions only after achieving power, as a by-product of their economic failures. Because they thrive on drawing boundaries between Muslims and others, they may deliberately antagonize outsiders in the hope of benefiting from the consequent social and political polarization. Agitated outsiders may then get organized in self-defense, thus fueling protracted intercommunal struggles. Such a process is already under way in Egypt, where Islamic militancy has prompted Copts to organize in self-defense. Intercommunal struggles can throw property rights into jeopardy, discourage local investment, and cause capital flight, thus impairing economic growth. In the long run, of course, they may end up promoting development, particularly if they destroy political coalitions that have helped preserve inefficiencies.[52] In Egypt, today's mounting intercommunal tensions may eventually bolster economic freedoms by weakening some key elements of social control, including the state and the ideology of economic nationalism.

There is no easy answer, then, to the question of what Islamism implies for the future of the global economic order. Like other fundamentalisms, it is capable of doing economic harm, yet it can also serve as a hidden agent of economic advancement. Remember, too, that some of what passes as Islamic economics, like the establishment of Islamic enterprises, serves to alleviate potentially explosive social problems. How, then, should policy makers committed to a liberal social order respond to the economic activities of Islamists and to their calls for economic reform? What, if anything, should governments, funding agencies, research establishments, schools, and the media be doing to meet the Islamist challenge to prevailing economic ideals, structures, practices, and relationships?

The remainder of this chapter offers a case for three classes of responses. In the first place, one must expose the flaws and limitations of Islamic economics. Second, one needs to show that the economic prescriptions of Islamists have considerably less appeal than their leaders tend to claim. Finally, it is essential to devise creative solutions to the festering socio-economic problems that have fueled the rise of Islamism. The last of these policies requires efforts at understanding the grievances, activities, and ideals of Islamists.

A First Response to Islamic Economics:
Expose Its Flaws and Limitations

The first response would involve disseminating information on the actual and potential effects of Islamic economics. There is a need for writings at all levels, including works that resonate with groups from which Islamist movements draw their rank and file. For all their inconsistencies and illusions, Islamist tracts have an emotional appeal that is often lacking in secular economic writings. They connect, therefore, with large numbers. The constituents of Islamic economics must be given exposure to the counterarguments. The lion's share would have to be shouldered by non-Islamists within countries where Islamists are making credible bids for power or have already achieved control. Outsiders can help out, but in the absence of local participation their efforts are likely to be perceived as evidence of cultural bias or foreign interference.

Because modern scholarship is essentially an outgrowth of European civilization, to criticize a non-Western movement is to risk being branded a tool of Western cultural arrogance. It would be wise, therefore, to integrate evaluations of Islamic economics into discourses on the merits of competing economic approaches. If criticisms of Islamic banking come to be confused with animosity toward Islam, matters resolvable through research and debate can turn into objects of cultural confrontation, possibly causing Islamist positions to harden. Another way to allay suspicions of cultural bias is to subject economically unsound policies issued in the name of non-Muslim faiths to exactly the same treatment as those advanced in the name of Islam. The American doctrine known as "Christian economics" has a protectionist, antimarket streak.[53] If only to maintain the credibility of criticisms directed at Islamic economics, this movement should be treated no differently from the antimarket strands within Islamism. To be sure, one can strive for impartiality without managing to avoid the charge of bias. Fundamentalisms have a stake in perpetuating, if not heightening, the perception of deep divisions between themselves and some immoral, ignorant, foreign "other." Also, it is a common rhetorical tactic to deflect criticism by attributing dark motives to its bearers. This tactic is used effectively also by diverse secular leaders.

With respect to the specifics of what needs to be disseminated, efforts are needed to enhance general knowledge on the drawbacks of nationalist and protectionist policies adopted in the name of Islam, like those of Islamic Iran. Greater awareness must be fostered of the ruses that Islamic banks employ to circumvent the prohibition of interest and of the ineffectiveness of established zakat systems. It should become better and more widely understood that the distributional consequences of Islamist-favored institutions are not necessarily equalizing. There should be greater familiarity with the unimpressive economic records of countries that have implemented Islamist-led economic reforms, like Iran and Pakistan. Finally, people who appreciate that Islamic economics is a reaction to a serious social crisis, should also realize that, for all its lofty rhetoric, it fails to offer a comprehensive solution.

Much talk about Islamic economic behavior has been shallow rhetoric, for no one, from Mawdudi onward, has come close to defining it in practical terms. The Qur'an has not been of much help in this regard. Of its thousands of verses, only about one-third of 1 percent provide economic directives. And these verses offer enormous choice and flexibility to anyone who wants to use them to build an economic system. Accordingly, the juristic schools of Islam have differed on numerous economic matters. Likewise, the great Muslim thinkers to whom contemporary Islamist writers commonly turn for authority and inspiration often held conflicting positions.[54] The key implication that requires dissemination is that a wide variety of economic agendas admit Islamic rationales. They include economically harmful ones. Economic restrictions imposed for the sake of cultural differentiation or confrontation—an enforced ban on interest, limitations on financial dealings with non-Muslims—may weaken a country economically, keep it on the periphery of the emerging global economy, and make it vulnerable to foreign domination.

In suggesting that one publicize the economically unsound elements of Islamist agendas, I am not proposing special treatment of religion in general or of Islam in particular. On the contrary, I am insisting that economic challenges in religious garb be treated exactly like those in secular garb.

To exempt Islamic economics from review or criticism would be to grant it a special privilege. When a labor union or trade association demands an anticompetitive regulation, ordinarily there are many challenges. Commentators point to the regulation's disadvantages and suggest alternative solutions to the problem that it would ostensibly solve. For a weightier example, when the young Soviet Union put its economy under central control and started to preach planning as a superior alternative to the market mechanism, its antimarket campaign met with swift intellectual opposition. Ludwig von Mises, Friedrich Hayek, and other scholars argued that central planning would prove unworkable. They showed that no government agency, however powerful, can disseminate information and coordinate individual actions as efficiently as markets operating under the rule of law. Although the antiplanning literature was initially dismissed as "reactionary," it managed to erode confidence in the Soviet economic system, thus helping to set the stage for the fall of communism.

My first policy suggestion, then, is to subject Islamist economic proposals to the same critical examination that we bring to bear on any ordinary economic challenge. It is worth mentioning that secular intellectual communities have paid scant attention to the economic content of Islamist agendas. Part of the reason lies in the fragmentation of the social sciences. Most economists consider religion outside their professional domain, while few area specialists and students of religion have had training in economics. Another reason is that the simpleminded prescriptions of Islamic economics allow observers to dismiss all of its discourse as nonsense, even as its influence grows. Still another reason, at least in countries where Islamists have resorted to violence, is that thinkers with misgivings about the Islamist agenda are afraid to say so publicly. The assassinations of critics like Uğur Mumcu and the Egyptian thinker Faraj Foda have made many Muslim intellectuals reticent to speak honestly and openly about the goals of Islamism.[55]

SECOND RESPONSE: ESTABLISH THE LIMITS OF THE ISLAMIST APPEAL

A second measure to mitigate the economic damage of Islamism would be to counter the Islamists' efforts to portray themselves as spokespersons for quiescent majorities. When Islamists claim to represent the authentic voice of a society long silenced by secular pressures, they are often exaggerating.

Where Islamic banks operate alongside conventional banks, their share of Muslim deposits has remained under 20 percent; in some predominantly Muslim countries, the figure is as low as 1 percent.[56] Also, the customers of Islamic financial establishments have shown a remarkable readiness to withdraw their deposits at the first threat of insolvency.[57] By no means is it clear, therefore, that the goal of abolishing interest enjoys widespread acceptance. Nor is it clear that those comfortable with the goal consider themselves bound by the Islamist injunction against interest. An Islamic economist might reply that "genuinely Islamic" banks would be more popular than the existing "nominally Islamic" banks paying and charging interest in disguised form. Perhaps so, yet if none of today's hundreds of Islamic banks is "genuinely Islamic," it behooves us to ask why. For one thing, fewer Muslims consider interest immoral than those who extend public support to the anti-interest campaign. For another, Muslims bothered by interest generally subordinate their qualms to objectives like financial security and simplicity.

It bears reemphasis that many participants in the Islamic subeconomy are skillfully using Islamic symbolism as an instrument of economic self-advancement. Not every Egyptian who keeps money in an Islamic bank or operates an Islamic grocery store is a committed Islamist. Many Muslims who pass as Islamists know next to nothing about Islamic history, philosophy, and institutions; they have little interest in developing a distinctly Islamic social system; and they have made lifestyle adaptations under Western influences. Furthermore, Muslims who have devoted considerable time to studying Islam are not all under the spell of its angry, authoritarian, and inflexible side. Some are impressed instead by its gentle, tolerant, and pragmatic side; and they are ready to allow the coexistence of multiple interpretations of Islam, even to respect the rights of unbelievers.[58]

İsmet Özel, Turkey's leading Islamist poet, readily acknowledges that few Turks are genuinely committed to the cause of creating an Islamic social order. He claims that only 6 percent of Turkey's Muslims are true believers, though he considers this small share socially and politically pivotal.[59] Other leading Islamist writers take issue with the prevailing Islamist interpretation of Islam's economic mission. Suggesting that the established Islamic banks have little to do with Islam per se, they argue that some forms of interest are morally unassailable and that an effective interest ban would hamper Muslim firms in the global marketplace.[60] The proponents of prohibiting interest are out of touch with reality, they say. An Islamist regime could never achieve widespread compliance with a ban, except by force.

Claims regarding the genuine popularity of Islamist prescriptions can be tested through elections conducted by secret ballot or surveys that give respondents anonymity. This is because social pressures that regulate openly conveyed preferences are absent from settings where people's choices remain unknown to others. To my knowledge, there have been no systematic surveys to determine the true popularity of Islamic economics. But certain predominantly Muslim countries have held secret-ballot elections that gave voters the option of supporting an Islamist party. In many of these elections Islamists received far less support than the tenor of public discourse might have led one to expect. In Bangladesh, Islamists control several university campuses, largely because students with misgivings about Islamist causes are afraid to vocalize their views. Yet the Jamaat-i Islami of Bangladesh has never made a strong showing in national elections. In the 1991 election its support stood at 6 percent.[61] Pakistan furnishes a similar contrast. In national elections the Jamaat-i Islami of Pakistan never performs well. Its candidates routinely lose to rivals labelled un- or anti-Islamic. Benazir Bhutto, whom the Jamaat-i Islami has denounced from the day she entered politics, enjoys far more electoral support than most Islamist politicians.[62] In Turkey, one might observe, the leading Islamist party, the Welfare Party, came on top in the general elections of 1995. True, but it won with only one-fifth of the vote; four-fifths went to parties more or less committed to secular principles.

Social pressures do not necessarily benefit Islamists. On the eve of the Algerian elections of June 1990, the Islamic Salvation Front was expected to lose decisively. It went on to win handily, suggesting that fear of government reprisals had caused many of its sympathizers to conceal their inclinations.[63] The point, then, is not that the publicly expressed preferences of Muslims always overstate their genuine sympathies toward Islamist causes. Rather, it is that one should never accept at face value the claim that Islamists form a cowed majority.

Certain segments of the secular intellectual community are predisposed to rejecting particular Islamist claims. For instance, most economists will readily reject the assertion that people brought up as Muslims consider interest unjust. This is because economists are generally trained to believe that basic economic impulses and understandings exhibit no systematic differences across societies. Other segments of the intellectual community tend to be sympathetic to assertions of cross-national variation in values, goals, and attitudes. For instance, anthropologists and many area specialists are trained to notice, probe, and highlight differences, as opposed to similarities. Whatever their own values, many are prepared, therefore, to accept that Muslims are readier than non-Muslims to forgo the safety of fixed interest in favor of variable returns. Moreover, even if they find such a claim implausible, their professional norms may keep them from raising objections, lest they be accused of cultural bias. It so happens that interest has always played an integral role in Muslim economies.[64] And Islamic banking is a modern creation; nothing like it existed prior to the 1970s. Scholars who teach that Islam mandates a distinct form of banking are unwitting accomplices, therefore, to an effort at myth making. In trying to respect an ostensible cultural difference, they are enhancing the credibility of Islamists posing as defenders of an endangered local practice.

A related boost to the credibility of Islamists stems from the fact that the West has lost its once-booming cultural confidence. One manifestation of this loss is the ongoing uprising in the United States against the long-standing liberal curriculum in the humanities and the social sciences, now held responsible for deficiencies in the performance of certain groups.[65] Another is the intense self-criticism occasioned by the quincentennial of Columbus's landing in America, which stood in sharp contrast to the self-congratulatory atmosphere of a century earlier. Whatever their intrinsic merits, campaigns to denigrate Western culture as inherently racist, sexist, oppressive, and inegalitarian diminish the West's confidence in its own cultural particularities. Moreover, the resulting self-doubt makes it harder for secularist Muslims to defend Westernization, and it allows Islamists invoke Western malaise as evidence that Westernization is dangerous.

One should not seek to constrain Western self-criticism just because it yields side benefits to Islamism or, for that matter, to other fundamentalisms. Nor should one compel Islamists to refrain from cultivating the best possible image for themselves, any more than one should make Coca-Cola refrain from manipulative advertising. However, one should avoid falling for, and basing policies on, inflated claims of Islamist support. This is not a trivial point. In certain countries incumbent non-Islamist regimes are making concession after concession to the Islamists, often on the ground that Islamist demands command major support. To give one example, the Egyptian government is giving increasing coverage to religious programs on the state-controlled television network. It is also seeking the approval of religious authorities in a growing number of policy domains. Such concessions are probably short-sighted. They serve to bolster the image of Islamist strength, make non-Islamists afraid to articulate their own beliefs, and embolden the Islamist opposition even further.

THIRD RESPONSE: LISTEN CAREFULLY

The responses proposed thus far are confrontational. One is intended to discredit the arguments on which Islamists base their challenges to prevailing socioeconomic structures. The other calls into question the popularity of these challenges. By contrast, the final suggested response is conciliatory. It is to listen carefully to Islamist complaints about modernity, recognizing that some are motivated by tangible flaws of the social status quo. Secular regimes have every right to oppose misguided challenges to their policies. By the same token, they have an obligation to hear criticism. The fact that Islamists are making some outrageous demands hardly means that their complaints are equally unjustified and their suggestions uniformly worthless.

When Islamists complain about increasingly corrupt government, they are not pointing to a nonexistent problem. Government corruption is as old as government itself, yet its allocational and distributional consequences have gained importance with the state's expanding control over economic and social life. Nor are Islamists unjustified in accusing incumbent regimes of wasting human resources. Many countries feature enormous unemployment and underemployment, partly because of excessive centralization and bureaucratic inefficiency. One need not be a militant antisecularist to see that basically secular regimes in Egypt, Turkey, Algeria, and Pakistan—to name just a few of the countries with vociferous Islamist movements—have not been entirely successful at answering the frustrations of their swelling populations. Secular elites would respond that they, too, recognize the problems of corruption and unemployment, adding that they have proposed various reforms. Yet, the measures that many of them champion would probably compound the prevailing problems. For example, Mumcu tended to support widespread economic regulation. He never quite appreciated that Turkey's huge public sector creates enormous opportunities for favoritism, influence peddling, and graft, or that various bureaucratic controls inhibit job growth. His approach to fixing the Turkish economy—tighter government controls, better planning—amounted to a more vigorous application of policies responsible for past economic disappointments.

While criticizing incumbent governments, Islamists have also been tackling certain social problems with considerable creativity. These efforts are not necessarily part of a grand plot to achieve power. Some Islamist services have emerged partly, if not mainly, to plug gaps left by poorly functioning economies. As noted earlier, Islamic clinics, dormitories, clubs, camps, and schools serve various underprivileged and disaffected groups. That these services contribute to the wider Islamist cause does not diminish the benefits they bring to individuals who are not committed Islamists. Secular policy makers would do well, therefore, to explore how these services operate and why so many people are turning for help to Islamists.

Islamists do not necessarily offer viable solutions to problems such as unemployment and official corruption. In restricting economic freedoms, certain Islamist agendas would probably exacerbate existing problems. This is no reason, however, to dismiss all the grievances that underlie such agendas. On the contrary, the dangerous aspects of the agendas compound the urgency of finding ways to alleviate the discontent that accounts for their popularity. Unless secular authorities reduce government excesses, limit the state's economic authority, and create an economic environment conducive to free exchange under the rule of law, illiberal fundamentalist agendas will enjoy appeal. A century ago, when Engels denounced work conditions in British factories, his criticisms prompted non-Marxists to institute reforms. This was doubtless a factor in the subsequent containment of communism. In any case, some Islamists are on the right track with respect to solving critical economic problems. Those who wish to restrict the economic reach of government and implement regulatory reforms are not just identifying serious sources of inefficiency. They are also helping to build a consensus for a shift in direction.

Adam Smith is widely remembered for the *Wealth of Nations* (1776/1937), his treatise on the connection between market freedoms and economic prosperity. Less well known is his first major treatise, the *Theory of Moral Sentiments* (1759/1976), which explores, among other matters, how social and moral norms help ensure the social stability that allows human civilization to flourish. The lesser appeal of Smith's earlier treatise epitomizes the scant attention in secular discourse to the psychological, social, and economic functions of norms. Where Islamists, like other fundamentalists, take norms very seriously, many secular intellectuals and policy makers tend either to dismiss them as unimportant or to treat them as sources of inefficiency. The study of economic development is revealing. International differences in economic growth rates are commonly attributed to differences in resource endowments, trade policies, and social stability. Economists in the mainstream generally pay little attention to cultural variables like work habits, demand for education, attitudes toward innovation, and family structure.

Islamic economics promotes the view, we saw earlier, that behavioral norms contribute critically to economic success. They are right about the importance of norms,[66] even if they tend to overrate the social virtues of altruism and underrate those of selfishness. This is not to say that social definitions of right and wrong should stay fixed. Nor is it to deny the importance of laws, rules, and regulations. My point is that in vast reaches of human activity norms remain a cheap and effective way to discipline and coordinate individual actions.

If one requirement of a free economic order is that individuals enjoy broad economic freedoms, another is that they accept responsibility for their own circumstances. Certain Islamist inclinations go against this requirement: for instance, the tendency to blame foreigners for domestic economic ills—a tendency evident in Mawdudi's writings on the corrupting influence of Western culture. But not all Islamists are on the look for scapegoats. In South Asia the Tablighi Jamaat encourages self-improvement and self-reliance; its members are expected to decline gifts from others and to become more generous and more honest.[67]

The observed support for Islamism should never be taken at face value, I have argued, for some of it might be feigned. Islamist leaders would not necessarily object to this warning. They would quickly call, however, for equal caution with regard to the apparent support for secularist agendas and the observed opposition to public displays of religion. A prominent theme in the Turkish Islamist literature is that, since the Atatürk reforms of the 1920s, Turkish Muslims have had to keep their religious feelings private, at least in spheres officially divorced from religion. Here are a few revealing titles from Islamist presses: *The Postponed Islamic Life*, *Speaking in Difficult Times*, and *The Minister Who Recognized "Allah" after His Death*.[68]

The last title refers to Hasan Âli Yücel, minister of education from 1938 to 1946, a Westernizer known as a tough foe of traditional Islam. The book alleges that, contrary to his outward appearances, Yücel was deeply religious. After his retirement, it claims, he regretted having supported the suppression of Islam, as evidenced by a long religious poem he penned. Yücel did not publish the poem during his lifetime, though he instructed his heirs to publish it as soon as he died. The episode testifies, the book concludes, to Yücel's fear of being denounced as a closet obscurantist. The veracity of the account is not a matter to be settled here. What matters is the book's central message, which is that Turks have tended to be less supportive of the secularist agenda in private than they have appeared in public. An implication of the message is that efforts to eject religion from domains such as politics and economics owe their apparent support to social pressures against overt dissenters.

That certain Islamists are prepared to intimidate, censor, and silence their opponents does not refute that they, too, have had their expressive freedoms curtailed. When Islamists promote public displays of religiosity and cultivate religious symbols, this is partly, then, in reaction to past pressures that have made them lead insincere lives. The pressures could have come from official controls, established religious organizations, or simply the weight of public opinion. Whatever the cluster of sources, the pressures imply that the ongoing spread of Islamism stems from more than a rise in individual religiosity. A complementary factor is that religion is everywhere becoming more vocal, more open, and more demanding than it was, say, in the 1960s, when secularization was pushing religion progressively into the private realm.[69]

The notion that Islamists feel expressively constrained is not one with which intellectuals of a secularist persuasion have much familiarity. Conscious as they are of the Islamist threat to their own artistic, literary, sexual, intellectual, and political freedoms, generally they overlook that Islamists feel expressively limited and threatened. The source of this ignorance is that secular intellectuals rarely bother to talk to Islamists, listen to their grievances, or read their writings. Were they to make an effort to understand Islamist concerns, they would encounter unmet spiritual needs. They would find that secular policies and pressures, like government controls on Islamic expression or the sanctions of secular public opinion, have left a huge void in some individuals. Such a realization would pave the way, perhaps, for fruitful communication between Islamists and their adversaries.

CONCLUSION

The central objective of this essay was to propose how policy makers committed to a free economic order should respond to the rise of Islamic economics and the Islamic subeconomy. Insofar as efforts to bring Islam into economic discourse and to confer a religious identity on formerly secular economic practices are pushing long-submerged perspectives to the surface, they advance individual liberties. The spirit of the free order calls for openness about thoughts, wants, and anxieties, including religious impulses. It offers the freedom to give one's actions whatever meaning one chooses, possibly some religious meaning. In itself, therefore, it is not a problem that certain social services are being defined as Islamic. Nor is it problematic that there now exist Islamic banks, Islamic grocery stores, and Islamic fashion shows. If Islamic economic enterprises give comfort to Muslims who consider Islam a well-defined way of life, they should be regarded as positive developments. The legitimacy of a social order is enhanced, not diminished, when a person who ascribes religious significance to a loan's form can shun interest openly, proudly, and without apology.

Yet, certain Islamist economic goals conflict with economic freedoms. Economic protectionism, which some Islamists favor, would curtail individual rights to free exchange. Likewise, forcing all Muslims to shun interest would interfere with basic economic liberties. Such moves should be opposed vigorously, regardless of their source and irrespective of how they are justified. They should be rejected because they trample on essential freedoms and also because they can be socially costly. Forcing all Muslims to shun interest would relegate Muslims to the fringes of the international economy.

The promotion and enforcement of free economic order requires, therefore, drawing a distinction between the liberty to live by Islamist economic rules and the liberty to impose such rules on others. The latter liberty clashes with the liberties of others, so it may be rejected. Thus, one may grant the freedom to live by the rules of Islamic economics without recognizing a right to impose these rules on entire societies.

Islamists might never agree to make abiding by its tenets a matter of personal choice. But there is room for optimism. The fact that they are making a primary issue out of allowing people to speak their minds, be themselves, and follow the calls of their conscience has an important implication. It means that Islamists may be, or may eventually become, amenable to granting reciprocal rights of self-expression to others. Perhaps, then, the focus of discourse on Islamic economics should shift to matters of openness and reciprocal tolerance. A common ground could eventually emerge from an understanding that to force Islamic economic prescriptions on everyone is morally and practically equivalent to pressuring Islamists to hide their own religious identities and views.

Relative to Christianity, Islam has a good historical record with regard to religious tolerance. Historically, therefore, Muslims have felt less pressed than Christians to institute formal protections against religious tyranny. Contemporary conditions in many parts of the Islamic world are ripening, however, for a broad attempt at protecting freedom of thought and expression. With huge numbers of secularists and Islamists feeling expressively oppressed by one another, a stalemate between the two groups may fuel a mutual willingness to agree to a reciprocal exchange of basic liberties.[70] The liberties might include economic freedoms, including both the right to shun interest and the right to deal in it fearlessly.

Stop

CHAPTER FOUR

The Genesis of Islamic Economics:
A Chapter in the Politics of Muslim Identity

THE TWENTIETH CENTURY HAS WITNESSED the emergence of an economic doctrine that calls itself "Islamic economics." Of all economists of the Muslim faith, only a small minority, known as "Islamic economists," identify with some variant of this new doctrine. Yet it is socially significant, if only because it advances the sprawling and headline-grabbing movement known as "political Islam," "Islamic fundamentalism," or simply, "Islamism."

The declared purpose of Islamic economics is to identify and establish an economic order that conforms to Islamic scripture and traditions.[1] Its core positions took shape in the 1940s, and three decades later efforts to implement them were under way in dozens of countries.[2] In Pakistan, Malaysia, and elsewhere, governments are now running centralized Islamic redistribution systems known as zakat. More than sixty countries have Islamic banks that claim to offer an interest-free alternative to conventional banking. Invoking religious principles, several countries, among them Pakistan and Iran, have gone so far as to outlaw every form of interest; they are forcing all banks, including foreign subsidiaries, to adopt, at least formally, ostensibly Islamic methods of deposit taking and loan making. Attempts are also under way to disseminate religious norms for price setting, bargaining, and wage determination. For every such initiative, others are on the drawing board.

From these developments one might infer that Islamic economics arose to advance an economic agenda. In fact, it emerged in late-colonial India as an instrument of identity creation and protection; at least initially, the *economics* of "Islamic economics" was merely incidental to its *Islamic* character. The purpose of the present essay is to substantiate this claim.

Almost no research exists on the origins of Islamic economics. Part of the reason, no doubt, lies in the rhetoric of the doctrine: Islamic economics claims to be uncovering and propagating the fixed, transparent, and eternal teachings of Islam, which makes questions about its origins seem tantamount to investigating the origins of Islam itself. In this view, Islamic economics has existed since the dawn of Islam, and the role of the modern Islamic economist is simply to rediscover forgotten teachings. Whatever the exact connection between the substance of Islamic economics and the precepts of Islam, the alleged antiquity of the doctrine is a myth. Certain economic ideas and practices now characterized as inherently Islamic are new creations; others, while not new, acquired religious significance only recently. Moreover, even the concept of Islamic economics is a product of the twentieth century. So it is hardly obvious why the doctrine exists, to say nothing of why it has generated Islamic norms, banks, and redistribution systems.

Compounding the puzzle is the Islamic world's generally low level of economic development, at least relative to Europe and North America. Given the prevailing pattern, it is not self-evident why Muslims, however devout, would look to Islam for solutions to economic problems. True, the heritage of Islam offers principles, policies, and practices of relevance to modern economic conditions; and in the religion's early centuries Muslim-ruled lands made remarkable economic progress. But if these scarcely disputed facts justify and explain Islamic economics, why did the doctrine not emerge earlier? If the answer is that the Islamic world's persistent state of underdevelopment has led to a search for alternative economic programs, there is the point that the Islamic world passed its economic prime many centuries ago. The need for economic reforms has been present for much longer than Islamic economics has been in existence.

JUSTIFYING CULTURAL SEPARATISM

Islamic economics emerged toward the end of India's colonial period as part of a broad campaign to preserve the religious identity and traditional culture of the country's sizable Muslim minority, more than a fifth of the total population. In the 1930s, against a background of mounting agitation for Indian independence, increasing numbers of Muslims came to fear that a Hindu-dominated India would subject them to hostility and discrimination.[3] Their worries were compounded by a rise in the indebtedness of Muslim farmers, mostly to Hindu moneylenders who were prepared to expropriate the lands of defaulters.[4] Although the British had erected obstacles to expropriation, it was uncertain that a Hindu-led government would uphold the protections.[5] Responding to such anxieties, certain Muslim leaders began arguing that the Muslims of India formed a distinct nation entitled to a state of their own. Before long, the idea of Pakistan was born, and within a decade and a half the new state became a reality.

There were Muslim notables who resisted the idea of a separate state. They argued that Muslims needed not political independence but cultural autonomy and, further, that the two goals were incompatible. Foremost among these leaders was Sayyid Abul-Ala Mawdudi (1903–79), the founder of Jamaat-i Islami (Party of Islam), first in India and then in Pakistan. Mawdudi objected to a national homeland for India's Muslims on the ground that they were a "brotherhood" entrusted with "a comprehensive system of life to offer the world." Were they to practice Islam faithfully, the matter of a national homeland would become "absolutely immaterial."[6] He did not deny the existence of threats to Indian Islam. But his favored solution was cultural reassertion rather than political separation. Specifically, he wanted his community to turn inward and revive the traditions that once brought it power, glory, and prosperity. As part of the required rediscovery, he promoted the idea of Islamic economics. We do not know who introduced the concept into Indo-Islamic discourse. Clearly, however, it gained currency through Mawdudi's sermons, speeches, and publications. In addition to "Islamic economics," Mawdudi coined or popularized many other terms that quickly became key elements of Islamist discourse, including "Islamic ideology," "Islamic politics," "Islamic constitution," and "Islamic way of life."[7]

In his voluminous writings,[8] Mawdudi argued that if India's Muslims were to survive as a community, they would have to treat Islam a "way of life," not merely as a system of faith and worship.[9] A minority of Muslims were "true Muslims," as they were "completely immersed in Islam." Religion fully controlled "their heads and hearts, their bellies and private parts." But the majority barely practiced Islam. "They believe in Allah," he observed, "offer their prayers to Him, solemnly tell their beads in praise of Him, [and] partially abstain from what is forbidden." Beyond certain limited realms, however, they lead lives that have "no smack of religion whatsoever." Their "likes and dislikes, daily transactions, business activities, [and] social relations" have nothing to do with Islam, being based solely on "personal considerations and self-interest."[10] The latter group of "partial Muslims" had never accomplished anything of value, claimed Mawdudi. On the contrary, by relegating Islam mostly to the private domains of daily life, they had weakened their community and fueled the ascent of "infidels."[11] And their limited adherence to Islamic norms, he felt, posed a greater danger to Indian Islam than the looming transfer of political power to the Hindus. In any case, he went on, a Muslim community could lose its religious identity even within a polity characterized as Islamic. The creation of Pakistan, he feared, would instill in its citizens the illusion of communal safety, thus accelerating the diminution of Islam's relevance to daily life.

Such reasoning convinced Mawdudi and his companions that the Muslim nationalists were proposing the wrong solution to the wrong problem. Whereas the nationalists wanted territorial partition to achieve political independence, what was needed was cultural reassertion to ensure religious survival. To reinvigorate their culture, Muslims needed to make a point of keeping their religiosity continuously in public view.[12] In every domain of activity, they had to be conscious of how their behaviors differ from those of non-Muslims, making themselves easily distinguishable as Muslims. Economic activity is carried out partly, if not mostly, outside the home. In principle, therefore, it could serve the cause of heightening Islam's visibility. For example, if Muslim traders were to follow Islamic contracting procedures, and if Muslim consumers were to make choices in ways distinctly Islamic, Islam would gain salience, enabling new generations to grow up in an environment where Islam appears highly relevant to everyday decisions. A factor making it especially important for Muslims to keep their economic behaviors "Islamic" was, Mawdudi felt, the growing significance of economics. "New complications have been introduced in the production, distribution, and acquisition of the necessities of life," he observed. "As a result of this, there is such a plethora of discussion and scientific research about economic problems that . . . the other problems of mankind seem to have paled into insignificance."[13]

Bringing economics within the purview of religion was central, then, to Mawdudi's broader goal of defining a self-contained Islamic order. Whatever one thinks of his agenda, he was onto something real: with technological progress, economics was indeed becoming increasingly important to daily life everywhere. In a technologically primitive and static world, where family background determines one's career, where one plants and sells crops in the ways of one's grandparents, where one has little to spend on nonsubsistence goods, and where markets offer little variety, economics may be vital to physical survival but economic decision making does not absorb much attention. By contrast, in a technologically advanced world, where career choices have to be made, where women pursue and interrupt careers outside the home, where investment choices require monitoring, and where markets offer abundant choice, economic decision making absorbs considerable time. It follows that if economic choice is considered a secular activity, economic advances will make Muslim existence look increasingly secular. But if it is considered a religious activity, then economic development need not reduce Islam's perceived role in the lives of Muslims.

WESTERNIZATION AND MUSLIM DISUNITY

Why did the Muslim nationalists overlook the dangers that Mawdudi identified? His own explanation was that many had attended colleges, like Aligarh University, founded expressly to equip Muslims with Western knowledge. Brainwashed to think like Westerners, the nationalists were trying to refashion Islam in the image of irreligious Western materialism.

In relation to the matter of a homeland, for example, they were making a fetish out of issues not even raised in the Qur'an, such as federalism, parliamentary democracy, and limitations on the franchise.[14] Yet, the ideology of "Muslim nationalism" was a contradiction in terms. How, asked Mawdudi, could nationalism be compatible with a universal religion that transcends local identities? He went so far as to indicate that the envisioned state would not be worth serving. Pakistan would be "pagan" and its leaders "Pharaohs and Nimrods," he once claimed.[15] But once Pakistan came into being, he simply accepted the new reality and expanded his mission to include making the state itself Islamic.[16] Distinguishing between a "Muslim state," whose citizenry happens to be largely Muslim, and an "Islamic state," which follows Islamic principles, he began fighting against what he considered Western influences on Pakistan's social, economic, and political systems.

Over time, Mawdudi's anti-Western rhetoric would become less strident and his positions more nuanced. Around the time of India's partition, however, his central concern was the impact of the West—the civilization, once called Western Christendom, that comprises Western Europe and North America, plus their cultural offshoots elsewhere. In addition to altering how Muslims think, the West was changing relationships among Muslims. Growing numbers of Muslims, he observed, were admiring Western literature, adopting Western customs, playing Western sports, and dressing like Westerners. Becoming socialized to consider Western culture superior to their own, they were judging Islam by Western criteria, rather than judging the West by Islamic criteria. They were looking down on their brethren, making the Muslim community appear to have two segments, one modern and progressive, the other traditional and backward. To make matters even worse, they enjoyed an advantage in obtaining civil service jobs for which English literacy had become a prerequisite.

But if the Muslim community was splitting, the culprits, as Mawdudi saw it, were not only his fellow Muslims who saw Westernization as an instrument of personal advancement. The West itself was using its recent material advances to make Muslim achievements seem unimpressive. "Your honor, which no one dared to touch," he told a congregation, "is now being trampled upon."[17] There existed, in fact, Western statesmen and intellectuals who were open about their low opinion of non-Western cultures; and some of them had singled out Islam as particularly uncivilized and irrational. For example, the Islamicist Duncan Black Macdonald had said: "The essential difference in the oriental mind is not credulity as to unseen things, but inability to construct a system as to seen things. . . . The Oriental feels no need to explain everything; he simply ignores the incompatible; and he does so conscientiously, for he sees only one thing at a time."[18] True to this view, Macdonald believed that to make peace with the twentieth century, Muslims would have to abandon Islam. He approved of efforts to limit Islam's social role. The Young Turks of the Ottoman Empire were on the right track, he felt, as they were "prepared to assimilate the civilization of Christendom, prepared to make the attempt, at least, to bring the Muslim peoples within the circle of modern life." They were ready, he perceived, to modernize Islam. Where Islam stood in the way of their program, they knew that it was Islam that had to yield.[19]

Such statements are now generally considered crude and simpleminded. In the days before India's partition, however, they were commonplace, as Edward Said has shown in his polemic against "Orientalism."[20] For Mawdudi and his followers, they constituted evidence that Westernizing Muslims had put themselves in the service of a new crusade against Islam. Khurshid Ahmad, a member of Mawdudi's inner circle and later a prominent contributor to Islamic economics, cites Lord Macaulay, the British statesman, as saying: "We must do our best to form a class who may be interpreters between us and the millions whom we govern—a class of persons, Indian in blood and colour, but English in taste, in opinion, in morals, and in intellect."[21] The clear implication, it seemed, was that Islam had to be defended.

THE LOGIC OF CULTURAL SEPARATISM

Mawdudi had been raised in a family suspicious of modern knowledge, and he had not received a formal Western education.[22] These factors probably contributed to his apprehensions about the West, making him overlook the West's diversity and equate Western cultural expansionism with the West itself. But whatever his motivations and perceptions, he was right that contacts with the West were making increasing numbers of India's Muslims reject their own heritage. At his arrival on the political stage, his fellow Muslims were overwhelmingly illiterate; according to the 1931 census of India, only 6.4 percent of those aged five or above could read, and the educated minority tended to have attended traditional schools that emphasized religion and avoided modern science.[23] The community was mostly destitute, and it boasted disproportionately few of India's major entrepreneurs.[24] Dissatisfied with these conditions, ambitious Muslims, like growing numbers of India's non-Muslims, and like millions of poor people in other parts of the world, were discovering that the key to prosperity lay in adopting new technologies and developing new habits of mind.

Mawdudi was right, too, that India's Muslims were behind other major groups in making the requisite adaptations. Whereas 1.2 percent of all Indians aged five or above were literate in English in 1931, only 0.9 percent of the Muslims were. And, as of two decades earlier, 1.5 percent of all Indians were in professions requiring more than an elementary education, but just 1.3 percent of the Muslims. The latter comparison is especially striking because the advanced professions were predominantly urban, giving entry advantages to Muslims, who were disproportionately urbanized.[25] Two historical factors contributed to these patterns. Indian Islam drew its adherents primarily from the lower end of the caste system. And Muslims were statistically overrepresented among the artisans whose skills depreciated with industrialization.

Finally, Mawdudi was also justified in believing that Westernization was weakening the control that religion exerted on personal worldviews and interpersonal relationships. His writings anticipated Thomas Luckmann's "religious privatization" thesis,[26] which proposed that as Western religion got pushed from public to private domains it became less of a restraint on individual religiosity and lifestyles.[27] Indeed, in Europe and North America the adherents of the typical religious denominations were exercising ever greater discretion over how they would practice their religion. If being an Episcopalian once meant that one attended Episcopal services every Sunday, it was now possible to attend occasionally, or not at all. Moreover, such diversity within denominations was becoming as acceptable as diversity across denominations had become in earlier centuries; and, as a consequence, religion was losing its importance as a determinant of marriage, residential choice, and employment.[28] Based on the West's ongoing evolution, then, it was reasonable for Mawdudi to expect the Westernization of India's Muslim community to weaken official Islam's control over the minds and behaviors of individual Muslims. It was reasonable, too, for him to expect the practice of Indian Islam to become increasingly diversified, although his rhetoric exaggerated the likely effects.

His favored response—to reverse Islamic privatization through displays of Muslim religiosity in a wider array of public settings—rested on a universal principle of group solidarity. In every society movements eager to preserve or rebuild group solidarity emphasize visible markers of group identity. Such markers limit contacts across group boundaries and encourage those within.[29] An extreme form of their use involves the stigmatizing behavioral codes of religious sects popularly known as cults. Many sects require their members to behave in ways that nonmembers find strange and repulsive. The requirement binds the members to each other, as no one else accepts them.[30]

In late-colonial India, Mawdudi was not the first to promote Islamic norms to cultivate Muslim solidarity. The Muslim nationalists had encouraged Muslims to distinguish themselves by wearing the fur hat that came to be known as the "Jinnah cap"—partly in response to Hindu identification with the "homespun" headgear known as the "Gandhi cap."[31] Nor was a campaign to enforce Islamic behaviors a break with Islamic history. Traditionally, Islam had insisted more on orthopraxy (behavioral correctness) than on orthodoxy (doctrinal correctness). As a case in point, the regular recitation of sacred texts was generally considered more important than comprehension of their meaning;[32] even in non-Arab lands, the call to prayer and the prayers themselves were almost always in Arabic, a language few understood.[33] Significantly, no major Islamic language has a word meaning orthodox, and the designation for Islam's largest major branch is "Sunni," which means orthoprax. A good Muslim is usually not someone whose beliefs conform to an accepted doctrine, as Protestant Christianity defines a good Christian. It is someone whose commitment to Islam is evident through observable behaviors. The Islamic counterpart to the Christian concept of heresy is *bid'a*, which means deviation and has traditionally been interpreted to mean behavioral nonconformism.[34]

The originality of Mawdudi's program lay, then, not in his insistence on Islamic orthopraxy but, rather, in his efforts to update the content of this orthopraxy to meet a new challenge. He did not try simply to restore or reinvigorate decaying customs. Nor did he limit the scope of his agenda to domains of activity already under Islamic regulation. Sensing that Europe's Enlightenment and Industrial Revolution were having irreversible and universal effects, he sought to redefine Islamic orthopraxy in a way that would allow, even encourage, certain adaptations without a loss of communal identity. Economic change was central to modernization. So, unless Muslims were taught how to make their economic adjustments in ways recognizably Islamic, identity loss would be inescapable. One of the pressing challenges facing the Islamic world, Mawdudi thus reasoned, was to specify, by developing Islamic economics, the economic components of a *new* Islamic orthopraxy. Although Mawdudi presented the agenda as a return to Islam, it was, in an important sense, a manifestation of Westernization. The idea of a distinct discipline of economics originated in Europe; no such category of knowledge existed in the intellectual heritage of Islam. Commentaries now classified as Muslim economic thought were not, except recently under Western influence, considered a separate branch of intellectual discourse.

PREVIOUS CAMPAIGNS OF RENEWAL

The novelty of the concept of "Islamic economics" is evident in the intellectual evolution of Mohammad Iqbal (1876–1938), the Indian poet-philosopher who, a generation before Mawdudi, became a dominant voice for Islamic reassertion. In 1902, before becoming an Islamist, Iqbal published a book called *Ilm-ul Iqtesad* (Science of Economics). Given the subsequent evolution of his thought, the most striking aspect of this work is its irreligious character. A few years later, by the time Iqbal had embraced Islamism, he no longer considered economics a key instrument of change. Not that he had lost sight of the Islamic world's economic backwardness. In 1909 he observed that India's Muslims had "undergone dreadful deterioration. If one sees the pale, faded faces on Muhammadan boys in schools and colleges, one will find the painful verification of my statement." Yet, his proposed solution to this crisis of underdevelopment lacked an economic dimension. He wanted his fellow Muslims to stop "out-Hinduing the Hindu" and to reinvigorate the traditions that had brought their ancestors glory and prosperity.[35]

One might infer from Iqbal's prescription that on economic matters, too, the solution lay in the rediscovery of old Islamic principles. However, the concept of a specifically Islamic form of economics is absent from Iqbal's work. Significantly, the major bibliographies of Islamic economics list none of his writings.[36] Iqbal's disinterest in developing an Islamic form of economics is shared by other figures who, in one way or another, made significant contributions to Islamic thought in the decades before Mawdudi came on stage. The speeches and writings of such activists as Muhammad Abduh, Jamal ad-Din al-Afghani, and Sayyid Ahmad Khan reveal no interest in the Islamization of economics.[37]

Nor did the development of Islamic economics ever become an objective of pan-Islamism—the diffuse international movement that, from the late nineteenth century onward, sought to unite the world's Muslims under one flag. The pan-Islamists were alarmed by the military advances of Europeans, and especially by threats to Muslim holy places. They thus promoted the ideal of supranational Muslim solidarity to resist the Europeans more effectively.[38] A few showed some interest in economic matters. For example, certain pan-Islamists worried about the economic exploitation that accompanied loss of political independence, and a few favored an economic war against non-Muslim rulers, including the withholding of taxes.[39] But the notion of identifying or rediscovering distinctly Islamic economic practices was absent from their campaigns—to say nothing of cultivating an economic doctrine grounded in Islamic teachings.

Although Muslim activists of the late nineteenth and early twentieth centuries exluded the development of Islamic economics from their agendas, collectively they paved the way for Mawdudi's initiatives. By calling for a return to Islam, however much they differed in what they meant, they prepared the masses for Mawdudi's broad Islamization campaign. Mawdudi's argument that Islam is a comprehensive way of life was hardly new. What makes him stand out is that he took this view seriously and sought to identify its concrete implications. At the time that Mawdudi set to work, vast numbers of Muslims, in India and elsewhere, were acutely aware of the Islamic world's political powerlessness and economic backwardness in relation to the West. They had developed various responses, including ones diametrically opposed to Islamization. One response, *secularist modernism*, was to accept the advantages of Western civilization, privatize Islam in the image of unobtrusive Protestant Christianity, and attempt to join the West. This response became the official policy of modern Turkey under its first two presidents, Atatürk and İnönü. Indeed, the post-Ottoman Turkish regime sought to import Western civilization in toto, and part of its strategy was to drive Islam to the periphery of social life, shifting the primary loyalty of Turks from religion to nation. A second response, less radical in appearance, was *Muslim modernism*, exemplified by the movement for Pakistan. It pursued Westernization without recognizing any conflict between this objective and the promotion of an Islamic identity. One of its hallmarks was to identify Islamic precedents for reforms formulated to meet secular goals. Unlike secularist modernism, which essentially rejects the sacredness of Islamic scripture, Muslim modernism pays lip service to the comprehensiveness of Islamic wisdom, pretending that Islam is its ultimate source of authority. The difference is one of stylistic and tactical choice, however, not a matter of substance. For reasons unrelated to religion, either type of movement may decide to promote, say, restrictions on imports. The first will justify its policy through secular theories of economic development. The second will do the same, but offer also a more or less vague religious rationale.

Both secularist and Muslim modernism entailed Westernization, differing only in how openly they rejected Islamic authority. By contrast, two other responses were resolutely against Westernization, and each treated Islam as the primary source of wisdom. Its extreme variant, *conservative Islamism*, simply rejected Western civilization and embraced familiar cultural forms without pursuing change. By Mawdudi's time, it was more popular among the masses, including low-level religious functionaries, than among religious leaders of his own stature. Mawdudi's own response, which may be called *reformist Islamism*, was to seek a religious revival that promotes modernization without Westernization. He differed from conservative Islamists in perceiving an urgency to meet the Western challenge creatively. And he differed from all modernists in insisting that the reforms have an Islamic character. He refused to pursue reforms with an eye toward satisfying world opinion.[40]

Sources of Variation

Mawdudi claimed to speak for all Muslims, except the Western-educated minority he considered "partial Muslims." In truth, he never enjoyed the support of a majority of India's Muslims, to say nothing of widespread support from Muslims outside India. As we have seen, Muslims responded to the Western challenge in various ways. One reason lies in differences in upbringing, education, and crosscultural exposure. A Westernizing society would put people with traditional backgrounds at a disadvantage. Although they might make certain adaptations, they would find it difficult to achieve the privileges available to people with Western educations and contacts. A related factor is that certain individuals had a vested interest in preserving traditional patterns of authority; preachers, for example, had reason to believe that in a Westernized India or Pakistan their powers would shift largely to modern professionals. Like local textile producers anxious about external competition, local religious functionaries felt threatened by competition from foreign sources of cultural authority.

Still another source of variation lay in the capacity to cope with cultural clashes. People differ in their ability to synthesize elements from different cultures, as they do in the ability to prevent conflicts through compartmentalization. Consider the Muslim requirement to fast from dawn to dusk during Ramadan. Especially when Ramadan falls in summer, fasting workers may experience a fall in productivity. Those with high professional standards may feel morally torn, therefore, between fulfilling a sacred obligation and the duty to be productive. Such individuals will tend to be relatively receptive to responses that entail choosing one culture over the other.[41]

Mawdudi was aware of the inner conflicts that Muslims commonly experienced; he understood that many Muslims felt torn between East and West, old and new, tradition and adaptation. If the West's influence were controlled, he reasoned, such tensions would subside. The task would require providing distinctly Islamic alternatives to behaviors Muslims had come to define as Western. If work enjoyed religious meaning, and work and worship were perceived as parts of a continuum, the modern Muslim would have a unified personality, rather than a bifurcated one. Mawdudi's agenda shared a key characteristic with that of secularist modernism: the aim of discarding certain cultural influences to prevent cognitive and moral dualism. Moreover, its instrument for fostering Islamization, an updated Islamic orthopraxy, was equivalent to the secularist campaign to weaken Islamic culture by encouraging the adoption of Western appearances and lifestyles.

Turkey's headgear law of 1925, which forced Turkish men to discard the fez in favor of Western headgear, aimed at cultural reconstruction. The law may seem comic or trivial, and it tramples on what is arguably a basic liberty. Nonetheless, it was of great significance at the time. "Dress, and especially headgear," it has been observed, "was the visible and outward token by which a Muslim indicated his allegiance to the community of Islam and his rejection of others. . . . The fez proclaimed at once his refusal to conform to the West and his readiness to abase his unimpeded brow before God."[42] The Turk adopting a Western appearance would be identifying publicly with the West. He would also be concealing a major symbol of his Islamic heritage. Other Turkish reforms of the 1920s, including the abandonment of the Arabic script for the Latin, were also intended to solidify Turkey's visible identification with the West. In neighboring Iran, likewise, the lifestyle reforms that Reza Shah Pahlavi undertook in the 1920s and 1930s were aimed at giving immediate visibility to Iran's Westernization.[43] Mawdudi's agenda, like these Westernization campaigns, was based on the insight that the coexistence of Western and Islamic cultural influences fueled personal tensions and social instability. It differed, of course, in its choice of which cultural influence was to be eliminated.

Both secularists and reform-minded Islamists were conscious of past reforms that generated mental dualism, like the educational reforms of the mid-nineteenth century. Rulers of the era, including those of Egypt and the Ottoman Empire, sought to equip Muslims with the advantages of Western knowledge without altering the traditional educational system. Specifically, they set up Western secondary schools without reforming the primary curriculum. The result of this juxtaposition was a bifurcation of the knowledge and values of educated Muslims. One side of them considered Islam as central to every question; the other ignored Islam altogether. One side accepted traditional Islamic values, with an emphasis on community, authority, and stability; the other glorified values of the European Enlightenment, including freedom, innovation, and progress. Mental dualism could be avoided through a unified system of education, itself situated within a unified culture.[44] But there was more than one possible form of unification. Atatürk's Turkey and Reza Shah's Iran had chosen one strategy; two decades later, Mawdudi was pursuing an alternative.

THE IMAGINED UMMA

Mawdudi also shared with the secular modernists a commitment to focusing historical and emotional attachments on one particular civilization. Atatürk and Reza Shah, seeking to enhance identification with the West rather than Islam, led efforts to recover, embellish, teach, and celebrate the pre-Islamic histories of their nations, with particular emphasis on the West's Middle Eastern cultural roots. Each hoped to foster a new self-awareness that would distance their peoples from the broader Islamic world.[45] For his part, Mawdudi appealed to the old notion of the universal Muslim umma, or community, which is expected to operate according to traditional principles of Islamic solidarity. Essentially undifferentiated except by gender, the umma is supposed to transcend tribal, national, regional, and local ties. Having its own laws, values, and convictions, it is to be the individual Muslim's principal source of identity and the focus of his loyalty.

To strengthen consciousness of the umma, Mawdudi drew attention to similarities and historical bonds among the world's Muslim peoples. He also discounted their cultural, linguistic, historical, and political differences, making it seem that such distinctions would lose significance, even dissolve, if only Muslims were willing to restore the vitality of their umma.[46] In his historical writings, examples of Muslim diversity and discord appear as aberrations. What is similar in the cultures of different regions is Islamic and thus authentic and important; what is different is foreign, accidental, and superficial. Likewise, harmony among Muslims is natural, disharmony a sign that they are spurning the dictates of Islam.[47]

Mawdudi's umma was not a real community identifiable through ongoing and observable interactions of members who know one another personally. It was an "imagined community,"[48] because its typical member could know, and be known to, very few of its millions of other members. Indeed, the concept was sharply at variance with prevailing social realities.[49] Economic relations among Muslim nations were minimal; they all traded primarily with Europe. Also, significantly, many Muslims were exhibiting strong commitments to ethnically, linguistically, and regionally defined communities far smaller than the Islamic umma. As a case in point, just decades before the establishment of Jamaat-i Islami, Indians fighting to save the caliphate in Istanbul got frustrated first by Arabs who fought Turkish rule in the hope of creating a new Arab Empire and then by Turkish leaders who abolished the caliphate and committed Turkey to secularism. Equally revealing, during Mawdudi's own career, there was never any unity even among the minority of India's Muslims who wanted the Islamic umma reinvigorated. There existed various interpretations of Islam as well as serious disagreements over tactics and strategy.[50] Nor were the differences among regionally separated Muslims typically minor compared to those among Muslims and non-Muslims living together. India's Muslims, like the Hindus among whom they lived, upheld hereditary divisions of caste. In their embrace of innate inequality, they stood closer to Hindus than to Muslim Arabs, who, like Christian Arabs, accepted the principle that people are born equal.[51]

In addition to minimizing the political, cultural, and historical obstacles to strengthening the Islamic umma, Mawdudi ignored technological impediments. Specifically, he made no allowance for falling transportation and communication costs. Such technology-driven trends would produce two conflicting effects. On the one hand, they would allow better contacts among geographically distant Muslims, thus facilitating the unity and homogeneity of the umma. On the other, they would stimulate Muslim exposure to non-Muslim influences, making the umma's desired isolation progressively harder to achieve. Insofar as the latter effect dominated, Muslim and non-Muslim lifestyles would continue to converge, and individual Muslims would find it ever easier to develop cross-civilizational loyalties. But to address such possibilities would have complicated Mawdudi's message and perhaps weakened its appeal. However well he may have understood the forces producing a global village, his political mission required him to treat them as controllable.

To recapitulate, Islamic economics emerged in India at a time when its Muslims were intensely preoccupied with defining themselves. Were they Indians entitled to equal citizenship rights in a secular state? Should they respond to Europe's formidable material advances by absorbing its knowledge without limit? The Jamaat-i Islami's position was that Muslims should endeavor to strengthen their communal identity by pursuing lifestyles that would distinguish them from non-Muslims. To avoid ambiguity as to what behavior was properly Islamic, Mawdudi and his colleagues ventured to update the norms of Islamic orthopraxy. Among the fruits of their efforts was Islamic economics. They tried also to promote solidarity within the global community of Muslims. Muslims were to interact mostly with one another, minimizing relations with outsiders.

THE MYTH OF ISLAM'S "GOLDEN AGE"

The matter of group identity is hardly unique to Islam. Every society harbors individuals with confused identities as well as movements seeking to define and tighten group boundaries. Cohesive groups provide their members familiarity, trust, easy communication, and emotional comfort. These benefits create a natural constituency for activists promoting identity-related platforms. If the Jamaat-i Islami and the Muslim League became significant political players in pre-partition India, this was partly because, in their different ways, each spoke to concerns involving group identity. Yet, individual political commitments always reflect motives richer than identity construction. Mawdudi's early works sought to establish that Islamic solidarity and uniformity would yield Muslims benefits beyond security of identity, including material benefits.

To convince an audience of a social agenda's material advantages, one may appeal to theory, evidence, or both. The communist movements of the early twentieth century relied almost exclusively on theory: invoking "scientific laws" articulated by Marx and Engels, they tried to make a classless society seem both desirable and possible. As I have observed elsewhere,[52] neither Mawdudi nor his followers provided as ambitious a theory to substantiate that Muslims would live better within a segregated Islamic umma than they would within a multireligious society. Mawdudi's chief instrument of persuasion was what he considered the evidence of Islam's "Golden Age"—the thirty-nine-year period that spanned the Prophet Muhammad's leadership of the original umma and the tenure of the four "rightly guided" caliphs who succeeded him at the community's helm.[53] He presented the Golden Age as a period of efficiency, justice, cooperation, and self-sacrifice. It was a vast improvement over the preceding era of ignorance (jāhiliya), he proposed, and never have its achievements been replicated.

Mawdudi went on to argue that after the fourth caliph "governmental reins, once again, passed into impious hands . . . fine arts like dancing, music, and painting, which are strictly un-Islamic, found patronage." There have been several attempts to reconstruct Islam, he held: at various times and places, uncompromising agents of revival (mujāhids) have worked toward "cleansing Islam . . . and making it flourish more or less in its original pure form." Their successes always proved short-lived, however, because they neglected to produce a "universal ideological movement" relevant to "all walks and spheres of life." He considered his own mission a fresh attempt at Islamic renewal, one that would succeed where others had failed because it was comprehensive.[54]

Cognitive psychologists observe that in individual calculations losses loom larger than equivalent gains.[55] Their findings suggest that, all else being equal, people are more responsive to a promise of improvement when it is framed as eliminating a loss than when it is presented as providing a new gain. Accordingly, reformers commonly use historical reference points that make experienced changes look like degeneration.[56] In focusing on a period revered by Muslims, then, Mawdudi was using a tactic that has been employed to great advantage in countless settings. Whatever the accuracy of his interpretation of Islamic history, his vision of the Golden Age fostered a sense of loss. It was also easily communicated, because it was long part of Islamic discourse, and Islamists of previous generations, including India's own Iqbal, had worked to keep it alive.

Scientific evidence on Arabian living conditions during the earliest period of Islam is actually scant. Standards of living were doubtless primitive, however; most Arabians lived under harsh conditions at levels close to subsistence.[57] Not until later times, the Umayyad and Abbasid eras that Mawdudi dismisses as times of decadence, did Middle Eastern living standards reach levels that were advanced for the period. Moreover, the early Islamic community was not exactly a paragon of harmony and cooperation. Three of the first four caliphs met their ends at the hands of fellow Muslims, an indication of sharp disagreement. Moreover, by the end of the Golden Age tensions ran so deep as to produce the Sunni-Shiite split that, fourteen centuries later, remains a source of discord.[58] Yet literal accuracy about early Islamic history would have defeated Mawdudi's purpose, which was to make Muslims attribute their problems to the degeneration of Islamic society under "un-Islamic" influences. Had his sermons and essays pursued historical accuracy, he might well have been ignored.

The histories of various Muslim peoples feature extended periods of steady economic growth, scientific creativity, and artistic flourescence. One need only think about the high periods of the Abbasid Caliphate, Muslim Spain, Safavid Iran, the Ottoman Empire, and Mughal India. If these periods received scant attention in Mawdudi's writings, this was because they belied his basic thesis. To invoke the glories of these cosmopolitan states would have undermined the argument that Muslims do best when they withdraw into their own communal shells. It might also have refuted the alleged perfection of the Golden Age: if developments in these periods represented protracted changes for the better, then the Golden Age was surpassable and, hence, imperfect.

A CLASH OF CIVILIZATIONS?

The campaign to make Muslims avoid non-Muslim influences and seek inspiration solely from Islam impinges on Samuel Huntington's thesis that the dominant source of global conflict is now culture rather than ideology or economics. The centerpiece of contemporary international politics, says Huntington, has become "the interaction between the West and non-Western civilizations and among non-Western civilizations."[59] Whatever the empirical validity of his argument, it matches the thinking prevalent within Jamaat-i Islami at its founding. As far as Mawdudi and his companions were concerned, Islam and the West could not coexist, and the two were locked in combat for the identity and loyalty of Muslims.

Huntington's thesis has been criticized for underestimating the homogenizing effect of economic development and also people's receptivity to cross-cultural influences. It is true that urbanization, industrialization, and modern education are attenuating differences between non-Western and Western lifestyles. Even so, such transformations have fueled vociferous movements of cultural resistance. Precisely because they are so disruptive to traditional lifestyles, campaigns to protect local values and institutions are commonplace everywhere. The movement led by Jamaat-i Islami presumed that in the absence of efforts to counteract non-Muslim influences the distinguishing features of Islamic civilization would wither away.

Another criticism has been that civilizations are difficult to define. Indeed, their boundaries are somewhat arbitrary, and every major civilization harbors much diversity. Yet these facts do not keep cultural protectionists of various stripes from acting as if the civilizations they would preserve are well-defined entities. As a case in point, Mawdudi ignored the differences between the aspirations of individual Muslims. At the time he was writing, there were vast differences between the lifestyles of secularized Muslims in Istanbul and those of devout Punjabis, and between consumption patterns in a Bengali village and those of an Arabian palace. Nevertheless, he claimed to speak for all Muslims, irrespective of background and circumstance. This is especially significant in view of the ambiguities of defining who is a Muslim. In 1954, following disturbances that arose when Pakistan's Ahmadiyya sect declared Mirza Ghulam Ahmad a prophet, a committee was formed to investigate the question. Just as Israeli rabbis argue interminably on the definition of a Jew, religious leaders could not agree on what makes a Muslim.[60]

The notion of civilizational conflict is sometimes dismissed as the product of a "Eurocentric" thought process. There exist, of course, many Westerners who subscribe to some variant of the clash-of-civilizations thesis.[61] In no way, however, does this negate the Jamaat-i Islami's homegrown conviction that Islam is party to a war of civilizations. Nor does it negate the emergence of Islamic economics as a weapon of civilizational resistance. Unsurprisingly, the theme of clashing civilizations appears in all early contributions to Islamic economics. Outside the Indian subcontinent, the first major contribution came from Sayyid Qutb (1906–1966) of Egypt, who concentrated on matters of social justice. Under Mawdudi's influence, Qutb characterized Islam as a comprehensive and self-sufficient system. True Islam, he wrote, "does not try and has not tried to copy" other systems; nor does it "establish any connection or similarity with them."[62] Like Mawdudi, he commonly honored this goal in the breach: prominent themes of his writings, like full employment and even social justice itself, betray Western influences. However, following the pattern established by earlier Islamists, he presented these concepts as intrinsically Islamic, partly through twisted interpretations of the Qur'an.[63] Whatever the validity of his interpretations, they supported the view that Islam offers a comprehensive system in conflict with the West.

The theme of civilizational conflict is prominent also in the works of Muhammad Baqir al-Sadr (1931–1980), an Iraqi cleric who produced highly regarded expositions of Islamic economics and played a leading role in the religious opposition to Iraq's Baath-led secular regime. His major work, *Iqtisaduna: Our Economics*,[64] extends Mawdudi's contrast between the Islamic economic system and its main rivals, capitalism and socialism.[65] Al-Sadr was especially eager to prove Islam's superiority to socialism, because at the time Arab socialism was gaining appeal: he devoted eight times as much space to refuting socialism than he did to discrediting capitalism.[66]

The Iranian Revolution of 1978–79 has been characterized as a "cultural earthquake."[67] Indeed, its leaders stressed that its primary aim was to restore Islam's role in providing group identity, social cohesion, and moral guidance. Khomeini repeatedly spoke out against poverty and exploitation, and he supported certain economic reforms. But he subordinated economic objectives to the general goal of restoring the centrality of Islam in private and public life. Communism and the West were both at war with Islam, he believed, and they had already brainwashed many Muslims. Iran's challenge was much broader, therefore, than the matter of choosing an economic direction.[68]

These examples, to which more could be added, establish that in various countries Islamists themselves have long defined their struggle in terms of a civilizational clash precipitated by Western aggression. Huntington's central point was not news to *them*; it merely confirmed what they had maintained for decades, although they portrayed as self-defense what Huntington considers Islamist hostility. The cases also illustrate that the economic initiatives of Islamists have been perceived as components of a broad counteroffensive against Westernization. By no means do all Muslims share Huntington's perception; to varying degrees many hope or believe that present tensions will subside. By the same token, Islamists are not alone in considering themselves engaged in a civilizational war. Diverse secularists agree that a bitter war is under way among two incompatible civilizations. A columnist for *Al-Ahram*, Egypt's generally anti-Islamist semi-official daily, wrote in 1993 that his country's politics involved a "struggle between two contrasting cultural models . . . one Western in outlook, the other Islamic."[69]

Clearly, many Muslims, including Islamists and secularists, have considered Islam and the West to be at war over the hearts and minds of Muslims. Have they had a valid point? Insofar as the answer is yes, has economics indeed been among the battlegrounds? If the term "clash of civilizations" refers to a conflict that substantial numbers of participants define in civilizational terms, the evidence does indeed point to a long-standing civilizational struggle. Moreover, economics has become one of the battlegrounds, for there are Muslims who consider Western economic thought, policies, and institutions a threat to their cultural identity, along with others uncomfortable with efforts to give economics an Islamic cast.

These observations do not presuppose that every Westerner or every Muslim is party to a civilizational clash. One can speak of a military conflict between two countries when only a minority of each country's citizens is actively engaged in battle, the rest pursuing their daily routines without interruption. Likewise, one can speak of a clash of civilizations even if the noncombatants outnumber the committed combatants.

"Clash of civilizations" may mean, alternatively, that the members of a designated group are having trouble synthesizing, or selecting among, the civilizations with which they are in contact. Contemporary Muslims have not been particularly resistant to technologies or products with Western origins. The diffusion of foreign-generated machinery, appliances, and pharmaceuticals is never instantaneous; however, at least in recent times, major innovations have spread to Muslim countries quickly by historical standards.[70] Nor is there reason to believe that Islamists are opposed to modern science and technology, or that they refrain from adopting new technologies.[71] The Ayatollah Khomeini disseminated his Friday sermons through audio cassettes; and when he returned from exile to assume Iran's helm, he did so on a jumbo jet. Hence, looking merely at production and consumption patterns, one finds no clear evidence of an incompatibility between Islam and the West, or between Islam and modernization.

Yet, evidence of cross-civilizational diffusion in production and consumption does not imply that relevant decision makers perceive their choices as costless. Even if their choices are voluntary, they might feel distressed over what they have to give up; to experience guilt and resentment is part of being human. For example, a person who drives to work in a French-built car, lunches at McDonalds, and watches televised sports may end his day feeling anxious that his lifestyle resembles that of a Parisian. A common theme in Islamist discourse, we saw earlier, is that pious Muslims feel distressed over the choices they make in becoming modern. Mawdudi's writings developed this theme from the beginning, as have other social commentators from all over the Islamic world. In a book banned in Iran under the Pahlavis, the Iranian social critic Jalal Al-e Ahmad coined the word "Westoxification" to describe what he perceived as widespread social alienation resulting from contacts with the West.[72] In the same vein, many of Turkey's new Islamists argue that Western civilization has created a consumer culture breeding perpetual disappointment and unsatiation. Believers also suffer, they say, from an inability to keep true to their values in the face of innumerable temptations to get richer and step up consumption. Failing to lead what they consider a properly Islamic life, they become distressed.[73] The same theme had been articulated decades earlier by the early opponents of Turkish Westernization. In his memoirs, the Islamist poet Necip Fazıl Kısakürek explains that he became disillusioned by Westernization upon recognizing that it made him feel culturally displaced. He rediscovered Islam, he recalls, in searching for what Rimbaud, the French poet, calls *la vrai vie absente*—the missing genuine life.[74]

The notion of a clash of civilizations is consistent, then, with a rapid diffusion of new technologies and goods. In fact, such diffusion may be among its basic causes.

IDENTITY CONFUSION AND ITS REPERCUSSIONS

Implicit in the foregoing argument has been that individuals derive a measure of inner satisfaction from a secure and unambiguous identity. Since our focus is on economic thought and behavior, it is worth recognizing that many influential schools of modern economics downplay, if not ignore, matters of identity. Indeed, much of economics treats the benefits of identity as nil and its social role as negligible, thus avoiding the need to address how people cope with identity-related concerns. In reality, we have seen, the need for a well-defined identity competes with needs that every school of economics recognizes, like food, shelter, and financial security. Moreover, just as a person whose house suffers damage will undertake repairs, people whose identity has lost focus or become depreciated will try to redefine themselves and establish a clearer sense of who they are. The repair task may involve, we have seen, efforts to reformulate economics itself.

That identity concerns account for the emergence of Islamic economics does not mean, of course, that these explain every facet of its subsequent evolution. Once the doctrine had been outlined, various actors found it a convenient vehicle for advancing political and economic aims unrelated to identity. A second watershed in the evolution of Islamic economics occurred with the Arab oil boom of the 1970s. Led by Saudi Arabia, the boom's major Arab beneficiaries felt obliged to step up their support for pan-Arab and pan-Islamic causes, and Islamic economics was among the causes that received vast assistance. Accordingly, the first Islamic commercial banks started operation in 1975, as did the Islamic Development Bank, established to transfer petrodollars to predominantly Muslim developing countries through interest-free instruments. The period of the oil boom saw also the enhancement of the institutional infrastructure of Islamic economics. New institutes of Islamic economics came into being, and departments of Islamic economics were started in various parts of the Islamic world. Also, journals of Islamic economics began publication, and well-funded international conferences of Islamic economics became a regular occurrence.

Once Islamic economics acquired the trappings of an academic discipline, it gained new complexities. Researchers steeped in Islamic economics went looking for new problems to address, and various applications of Islamic economic principles, including Islamic redistribution and Islamic banking, stimulated new debates. To this day, however, Islamic economics has remained precoccupied with defining the modern Muslim identity. One cannot make sense, therefore, of contemporary Islamic thought on economics, or of economic practices identified with Islamism, without paying attention to the genesis of Islamic economics a half century ago. The major stimulus to the emergence of Islamic economics was the perception of Mawdudi and his Indian companions that the Indo-Muslim community was losing its identity.

CHAPTER FIVE

The Notion of Economic Justice in Contemporary Islamic Thought

IN THE MASSIVE CONTEMPORARY LITERATURE that has come to be known as "Islamic economics,"[1] a frequent claim is that an Islamic economic system would serve economic justice better than existing capitalist and socialist systems. An Islamic system, it is said, would be free, on one hand, of the exploitation and severe inequalities that characterize capitalism and, on the other, of the class struggles and intolerable restrictions that are the hallmarks of socialism.[2]

The challenge at hand is to describe and evaluate the notion of economic justice that appears in this body of literature. I begin by defining the main principles of justice to which the Islamic economists subscribe. Then I present a synopsis of the injunctions they put forward as means of ensuring that society adheres to these principles. By and large, I go on to argue, these injunctions rest on a faulty model of human civilization, and they leave far more room for interpretation than Islamic economists acknowledge. In many contexts, moreover, the injunctions bring the principles of justice into conflict, both with one another and with other Islamic principles. On the basis of these observations, I suggest, finally, that an Islamic society will inevitably contain seeds of disharmony. Although Islamic economists downplay the possibility of discord, they pay considerable attention to mechanisms for minimizing its scope and magnitude. Prominent among these are educational measures designed to engender a consensus that conforms to Islamic principles.

Islamic economics did not emerge as a discipline in its own right until the mid-1960s. Earlier years saw the appearance of some books, articles, and pamphlets, most notably the still widely cited works of Sayyid Abul-Ala Mawdudi and Sayyid Qutb.[3] But these works showed neither an interest in nor an appreciation for the economic concepts and tools developed in recent centuries, primarily in Europe and North America. The Islamic economists who have appeared on the scene lately tend to be of a different mold: having been exposed to modern currents of thought, they are more willing to borrow ideas and methods from non-Islamic writings. Perhaps as a consequence, in some respects their standards of analysis are higher. Still, there are broad substantive continuities between the earlier and later writings. Like their predecessors, contemporary Islamic economists ascribe immense importance to the interest ban and Islamic forms of redistribution. More important for us here, they subscribe to the same two principles of justice. It is entirely appropriate, therefore, to treat the earlier and later writings as a single body of literature, provided one recognizes that this literature has gained sophistication.

In any case, I am restricting the analysis to the monographs, essays, conference proceedings, and journal articles published in English between 1970 and mid-1987. The bulk of these writings were issued by a handful of publishers: the Center for Research in Islamic Economics (Jeddah), the Islamic Foundation (Leicester, United Kingdom), the Institute of Policy Studies (Islamabad), Sh. Muhammad Ashraf (Lahore), and Islamic Publications (Lahore). I shall pass over the writings that are providing ideological support to attempts to restructure the Iranian economy along Islamic lines, some of which have been published, in English, by Mizan Press (Berkeley, California).[4] Including these writings in the present analysis would have required consideration of the doctrinal differences between the Sunnis and the Shiites. I venture to say, though I shall not defend this statement here, that as far as economic justice is concerned, the inconsistencies, ambiguities, and disagreements of the Sunni-dominated literature are found also in the mostly Iranian, Shiite-dominated literature.

Inconsistencies, ambiguities, and disagreements exist in all the great bodies of literature that point the way toward a just world, including the diverse writings whose roots lie in Judaism, Christianity, Marxian socialism, and Third World nationalism. But the objective here is not to perform a comparative analysis. It is to evaluate the notion of economic justice in one particular literature: contemporary Islamic economics. Only at the end shall I return to the parallels with other literatures, and then simply to put the argument into perspective.

PRINCIPLES

For a society to achieve economic justice, say the Islamic economists, it must conform to two general principles: equality and fairness.

The principle of equality forbids gross inequalities in the distribution of goods: whereas "moderate" inequality is acceptable, "extreme" inequality is ruled out. A society would not be considered properly Islamic if it allowed some of its members to live in luxury while others eked out an impoverished existence.[5]

The principle of fairness is that people's economic gains are to be "earned" and their losses "deserved." It requires the economic system to treat similar economic contributions similarly, and different contributions differently. "There is to be no discrimination," says a leading Islamic economist, "due to race or color or position. The only criterion of a man's worth is character, ability, and service to humanity."[6] In the same vein, another states that "no economic entity [should be] deprived of its due share in the national product."[7]

The first of these principles is concerned with the outcome of the economic process, the second with the process itself. The principle of equality bars the distribution of wealth generated by this process from being grossly unequal. The principle of fairness, by contrast, requires the economic transactions, which determine the distribution, to be fair.

Injunctions

The literature offers numerous injunctions as means for bringing economic relations into conformity with the principles of equality and fairness. These take the form of prohibitions, restrictions, obligations, and responsibilities. There is no need here to provide an exhaustive survey of these injunctions, in all their details and ramifications.[8] The following synopsis will simply identify the injustices they are intended to prevent, demonstrate how they vary in terms of specificity, and provide a basis for evaluating the logic on which they rest.

A much heralded obligation is the redistribution scheme known as zakat. It entails taxing certain wealth holders and certain income earners at rates varying between 2.5 and 20 percent, and using the proceeds to aid disadvantaged members of society, including the poor, the handicapped, the unemployed, dependents of prisoners, orphans, and travelers in difficulty. The coverage of zakat is controversial. Some writers consider it to be limited to those categories of wealth and income for which rates were specified in the early years of Islam. Others consider it to include categories unknown until recently, such as factories and motorized vehicles, although the reformist writers do not agree among themselves as to the limits of the coverage and the applicable rates. But regardless of how they perceive zakat, all Islamic economists see it as a powerful instrument for bringing an economy in line with the principle of equality.[9]

Another injunction regarded as having an important equalizing effect is the Islamic law of inheritance, which spreads a deceased person's wealth among all his immediate relatives. One contributor to the literature describes the law's essence as follows: "[A] person may not dispose of more than one-third of his property by testamentary directions. . . . The rest of the inheritance must be divided among the prescribed heirs in specified shares."[10] The shares are determined according to the exact number and relationships of the survivors, so the distribution of estates assumes an endless variety of configurations. In accordance with the principle of fairness, full siblings of the same sex have identical entitlements, which rules out primogeniture. The law promotes equality by interrupting the growth of family estates.

In addition to such formal obligations, there are informal injunctions intended to equalize the distribution of goods. Most important, the individual is to make charitable donations to the needy. In this connection, a Pakistani Islamic economist writes that "capacity for contribution to social welfare . . . is to be measured by the amount one is able to spare after enjoying the standard of living which is commonly enjoyed by men of one's rank and station in life."[11] As a consumer, meanwhile, the individual is encouraged to enjoy the earth's bounties, but without drifting into extravagance, even if he can afford to do so after having met his formal obligations. The following warning by a widely quoted Islamic economist is typical: "After a certain limit, consumption of cloth may turn into extravagance. As extravagance is prohibited, the individual must stop at this point."[12] Extravagance violates the principle of equality because, by definition, it entails consumption well beyond the average level for society.

An injunction that appears in numerous guises is the obligation to behave altruistically, in other words, to demonstrate an unselfish concern for the welfare of others. It requires the individual both to refrain from actions unduly harmful to others and to take positive steps in the public interest.[13] In the terminology of modern economics, the individual is to bring into his calculus the negative and positive externalities of his actions. This injunction, which is intended to serve both principles of justice simultaneously, comes into play primarily in discussions concerned with personal consumption, resource allocation, and industrial relations.[14] To give one example, an industrialist deciding whether to build a particular factory must take into account not only his expected personal profits but, in addition, the air pollution the factory would generate and the new employment opportunities it would provide. Many writers stress that the relevant externalities are not limited by geographical, national, racial, familial, or occupational boundaries.[15]

The pursuit of monetary gain is legitimate, provided it does not involve unfairness. An industrialist must pay "fair" wages to his employees and charge "just" prices to his customers.[16] Moreover, he is to make every effort to share with his customers what he knows about the goods he is selling, including their possible defects.[17] To this end, he must avoid equivocal speech and refrain from concluding a deal until the buyer knows all there is to know. The main objective of this insistence on openness is to protect the consumer from exploitation and give him a fair deal. The injunction also promotes, some writers claim, the principle of equality.

Of all the injunctions cited, the most celebrated is the prohibition of interest. The rationale for the prohibition differs depending on whether the loan involved is a consumption loan or a business loan, although in both cases the principle of fairness is central. If interest is charged on a consumption loan, the lender makes money without exerting any effort and without giving the borrower something in return. If it is charged on a business loan, the lender's return is fixed, while that of the borrower is variable. (A bank deposit is treated as a special kind of business loan, where the depositor is the lender and the bank, the borrower.)

How are the implied injustices to be avoided? In the case of a consumption loan, the lender is to earn no return at all: when the loan comes due, he is to get back only what he has lent. In the case of a business loan, the lender and the borrower are to share, according to a predetermined formula, the profits or losses from the investment financed by the loan. Mindful of the possibility that an interest-paying borrower could end up with a significantly higher return than the lender, as when an industrialist earns a 30 percent return on an investment financed through a loan obtained at 5 percent, the Islamic economists contend that an interest ban would also help to equalize the distribution of wealth.[18]

The prohibition of insurance as a profit-oriented business rests on similar reasoning. Most Islamic economists have no objection to insurance per se, just as they are not opposed in principle to lending and borrowing. They recognize that by spreading unanticipated losses among its members a well-designed insurance scheme can serve the principle of equality. Nevertheless, they feel that profit from insurance constitutes unearned gain, "the callous exploitation of the misery of . . . helpless common folk."[19] To prevent exploitation, they say, the state must be empowered to take over most areas of the insurance business and to regulate the rest.[20]

Transactions involving speculation rooted in avoidable ignorance are considered objectionable, again on the ground that they may result in unearned gain for one party and undeserved loss for the other. Thus, the sale of a pregnant camel is prohibited because her value depends on the sex of the offspring, which, until known, may generate speculation. Likewise, an orange tree in blossom may not be sold because neither the quantity nor the quality of its yield can be predicted exactly. It is also considered illegal to trade a piece of cloth that has not been examined carefully by both parties, lest they misperceive the cloth's properties.[21]

Throughout the literature one encounters prohibitions of the activities of middlemen, a catchall category that includes such diverse groups as commodity speculators, real estate agents, and stockbrokers. Invariably, the opposition is based on the belief that such activities result in unearned gain. Commodity speculation, undertaken in the expectation of profiting from fluctuations of supply and demand, is the most frequent target of attack.[22] There is a consensus that speculation over basic commodities is highly unjust. Certain writers argue that speculation does not violate the principle of fairness when it involves luxuries, although they fail to specify criteria for distinguishing between the two categories of commodities.[23]

Modes of agricultural cultivation are also a concern of the Islamic economists. Sharecropping, a practice whereby a laborer cultivates a landowner's plot in return for a fixed share of the output, is the favored mode of most writers, who consider it to be analogous to profit and loss sharing in industry and trade. They maintain that sharecropping entails praiseworthy cooperation by owners of complementary factors, land and labor, and that the landowner's returns are no less justified than those of the depositors of an interest-free bank.[24] Other writers oppose sharecropping on the ground that a landowner who does not participate personally in cultivation is not entitled to a return.[25] Still others take an intermediate position. Among them is the author of a trilogy on Islamic economics, who writes: "If there is a spirit of goodness and benevolence behind [a sharecropping] contract and either [party] expects only to receive his due . . . then it is the best form of cooperation, partnership and friendship. But if this spirit is lacking and the weakness of the cultivator becomes the instrument of [the] landlord's oppression and exploitation . . . then this form of cultivation is not permitted. . . ."[26] He adds that sharecropping should not be allowed where it would turn the landowner into an idler or a parasite.[27]

Predictably, perhaps, the practice of renting land, which involves a fixed payment from the laborer to the landowner, comes under harsh indictment. Like interest, it places the contract risk entirely on one party: the laborer's return depends on the size of his harvest, while the landowner's return is fixed. In addition, the practice enables the landowner to lead a comfortable life of leisure while the laborer struggles for his subsistence. Still, some authors are prepared to exclude a class of cases from the prohibition. A landowner can justly rent his land, they say, if he is pursuing socially beneficial activities and, in particular, if he is defending Islam.[28]

Various Islamic economists consider certain other market structures and forms of economic organization to be unjust. There is widespread agreement that, in allowing exceptionally high returns, unregulated private monopoly gives rise to grievous injustices. "Islam views with extreme disfavor," says a Nigerian proponent of Islamization, "the monopoly of resources by a few self-seeking millionaires."[29] Some writers consider the publicly held corporation of modern economies at odds with Islam's principle of fairness. The facility of liquidating the corporation's shares encourages, they say, its shareholders to desert it at the slightest sign of trouble, compounding the remaining shareholders' expected losses. However, the majority consider the modern corporation praiseworthy, on the ground that it involves risk sharing.[30]

ILLUSIONS

By and large, the Islamic economists treat the Islamic injunctions as unambiguous guidelines for attaining economic justice. The following remark is typical: "If the Islamic teachings on the earning of wealth are followed, the norm of justice to employees and consumers is applied, provisions for redistribution of income and wealth are implemented, and the Islamic law of inheritance is enforced, there cannot be any gross inequalities of income and wealth in Muslim society."[31] There is a strong consensus, moreover, that the set of injunctions is not dynamic but static: eternally applicable, without revision, to all societies.

One thus gets the impression that in an Islamic economy the attainment of *substantive* justice would be a *procedural* matter.[32] Regardless of economic and social conditions, the two substantive principles of justice would be met by having members of society follow the specified injunctions. This position harbors two distinct claims. First, that just behavior entails conformity to the stated Islamic injunctions. Second, that these injunctions are just, in the sense of promoting the principles of equality and fairness better than other sets of injunctions. Here I wish to evaluate the second claim—to question whether the promoted injunctions can reasonably be expected to secure the two principles of justice.

The purpose of zakat, we have seen, is to promote equality by redistributing wealth from the haves to the have-nots. It is by no means self-evident, however, that zakat would achieve this purpose. Since it entails taxing only some categories of income and wealth, and then at various rates, its distributional impact would depend on the composition of society's output. Its narrow version places the burden of taxation entirely on categories of income and wealth known in the early years of Islam, notably agriculture, mining, and precious metals. With industrialization and the explosion of the service sector, these sources of income and wealth have dwindled in importance, even in the least developed countries. Also, most of today's poor households are concentrated in agriculture, and most rich households outside agriculture.[33] It is possible, therefore, for zakat to reinforce existing inequalities. This conjecture is supported by a study of one of the narrow zakat schemes in existence.[34] What about the broader schemes that have been proposed? They may well play an equalizing role, although this remains to be demonstrated. The impact of any particular scheme will depend on characteristics of the economy to which it is applied. A scheme that serves as a strong equalizer in a heavily agricultural and industrial contemporary economy could lose its potency as services for which rates have not been specified gain in importance.

Regarding the injunction to take into account negative and positive externalities of one's actions, it is appropriate to ask how individuals are to compute and predict these. In most contexts, this is an enormously difficult task, if only because human abilities to acquire, store, retrieve, and process information are severely limited. Thus, individuals willing to abide by this injunction would not necessarily succeed in doing so. Nevertheless, the Islamic economists are confident that in an Islamic system the individual would incur no major problems in distinguishing between collectively harmful and beneficial actions.[35] One basis for their confidence is a conviction that the Qur'an and the Sunna provide considerable guidance. Another, criticized further on, is the belief that in many important contexts there will emerge a consensus coinciding with the public interest.

Overly optimistic assessments of human nature and capabilities also pervade discussions concerning other injunctions. On the subject of helping the needy, the Islamic economists have a tendency to write as if it were perfectly obvious who is "needy." Likewise, when exhorting employers to pay fair wages and sellers to charge just prices, they write as though everyone will attach identical meanings to "fair" and "just." They simply evade the treacherous task of making these concepts operational. Yet if ten members of an Islamic society, all well versed in Islamic economics, were asked to quantify the need of a certain person out of work—or the fair price of ripe tomatoes, or the just wage of a novice bricklayer—they might well produce ten different answers. True, on some issues agreement would be easy. No one trying to follow the injunction to help the needy would favor letting an unemployed person starve. But there is no reason to expect automatic agreement on the nature or magnitude of assistance.

As we have seen, the Islamic economists would give the state an active role in preventing injustices associated with insurance. Further on we will see that they accord to the state many other roles in preventing injustice. They take it for granted, in this connection, that officials in charge of identifying and correcting injustices will be both able and willing to carry out their duties in full. Such optimism is unwarranted, because no state official has unbounded cognitive abilities and because the powers at the disposal of an official constitute assets that can be used for self-enrichment.[36] Throughout the history of Islam, in fact, there have been state officials, many of them pious, who have abused their powers by putting public resources to personal use, conferring privileges on relatives and friends, subsidizing prosperous groups at the expense of the poor, and in other ways.[37] Of course, not all Islamic economists disagree with this interpretation of the past.[38] My reason for touching on the historical record is to highlight the lack of a convincing explanation as to how abuses observed in the past can be avoided in the future.

The prohibition of interest, deceptively straightforward in an abstract setting, poses a practical problem that is rarely even acknowledged. Under inflation, is the borrower of a consumption loan obligated to compensate the lender for changes in purchasing power? Certain writers who address the issue refrain from taking a position. And those committed to a particular view are divided, with some saying that fairness requires the indexation of loans, others that it bars indexation.[39] For the proponents of indexation, an unresolved issue is whether the relevant price level is to be based on the lender's consumption basket or on that of the borrower.

Profit and loss sharing, the favored alternative to interest in the case of a business loan, presents another problem that has received little attention. Suppose an old person takes his savings to the only Islamic bank in his neighborhood. The bank proposes a profit and loss sharing contract whereby it would receive 99 percent of any profits and, correspondingly, incur 99 percent of any losses. Is this deal fair from an Islamic standpoint? If the answer is "no" or "not necessarily," what are the lines of demarcation? One writer holds that shares are to be determined by custom—as if a practice becomes fair by virtue of being customary.[40] Another writer, using a mathematical model, says that shares are to be determined through the interaction of the supply and demand for contracts—as if, once again, an equilibrium allocation could never be lopsided.[41] Only one writer, as far as I am aware, recognizes that the literature effectively evades the issue.[42]

The point of all these criticisms is not that one ought to impose even tighter restrictions on economic transactions or that one ought to regulate every aspect of the economy; rather, it is to expose as an illusion the belief that the Islamic injunctions would guarantee economic justice.

DISAGREEMENTS AND INCONSISTENCIES

This belief is all the more surprising when one considers that the Islamic economists themselves disagree as to what the Islamic injunctions are. We have already encountered differences on indexation, the scope of zakat, sharecropping, and publicly held corporations. Another fundamental controversy concerns the limits of public ownership. Quoting verses of scripture and passages from Islamic classics, some writers maintain that the principle of equality requires public ownership of trade facilities, industrial raw materials, and even land.[43] Quoting different verses and passages, others hold that public ownership is not necessary in these areas, except when social welfare would improve.[44] Thus, Islamic justifications exist both for both sharply curtailing private property rights and for according them wide protection.

There is a similar controversy over the method of financing public projects. "A progressive taxation system," says one prominent Islamic economist, "seems to be perfectly in harmony with the goals of Islam."[45] Another disagrees: "Progressive taxation assumes illegitimacy of the income of the rich. The rising slabs represent taxation with vendetta. Only a proportional tax at a fixed rate (on the pattern of zakat) is to be levied on the accumulated wealth of the capable taxpayers without any distinction."[46] Yet another Islamic economist sees merit in both positions: "Proportional taxation becomes Islamic if income and wealth are already distributed according to Islamic economic egalitarian criteria. . . . However, in the existence of maldistribution of income and wealth . . . a progressive system of taxation should be invoked."[47]

Underlying this particular controversy is the fact that the principle of equality is subject to diverse interpretations. Indeed, writers tolerant of "moderate" inequality often disagree over the limits of moderation.[48] Of course, such disagreement is anything but new to Islam: even the early caliphs saw the limits differently.[49]

On the disbursement of zakat funds, writers disagree as to whether funds collected in one year can be spent in another. Some hold that rollovers are inconsistent with the spirit of zakat.[50] Others disagree, saying that cyclical fluctuations in economic activity require larger disbursements in some years than in others.[51]

Such disagreements disconfirm that in an Islamic economy the attainment of substantive justice would be a procedural matter. On many central issues the Islamic economists subscribe to contradictory injunctions, which means that, even though they share the same substantive objectives, they disagree as to the procedures needed to reach them. A person trying to weigh the merits of an Islamic economy might wonder: "whose Islamic economy is *the* Islamic economy?"

If we ignore actual and potential disagreements among Islamic economists, we notice that the injunctions defended by any given writer are not always consistent with one another. Take the prohibition of interest on business loans and bank deposits, usually defended on the ground that fairness requires the borrower and the lender to share risk. This interpretation of the principle of fairness would also seem to require employees to earn variable, as opposed to fixed, wages. Yet, many of the most vehement opponents of interest favor fixed wages, and some say explicitly that variable wages are unjust.[52] If wages were variable, the argument goes, a fall in a firm's revenues might lower its employees' wages to the point that they would have trouble obtaining even subsistence goods. This situation would violate the principle of equality.

Leaving aside the question of why zakat funds or other reservoirs of altruism could not be brought into play, let us pursue the implications of coupling fixed wages with the absence of interest. It means, for instance, that a grocery worker is shielded from market risk as an employee, but not, if he puts his earnings in an income-producing bank account, as a saver. Correspondingly, the owner of the grocery store bears the entire risk of his operation, while his neighbor the banker shares his own risk with the grocer's employee. A given grocer, banker, or employee need not find this arrangement undesirable or unreasonable. He may or may not, depending on a host of factors. My point is simply that the Islamic economists do not apply the principle of fairness consistently.

A subtler inconsistency involves the injunction against speculation caused by avoidable ignorance. Through examples, the Islamic economists try to show that the injunction would effectively block all transactions where the buyer and the seller might have avoidable differences over relevant characteristics of the traded commodities. But these examples do not make a case. Consider, first, the prohibition against selling a pregnant camel, and the associated suggestion that one may sell her after she has given birth and the sex of her offspring has been revealed. Does all avoidable ignorance end with the termination of pregnancy? The mother could have a brain tumor, detectable through modern veterinary technology, which would make her expected life span very short. In practice, therefore, she could change hands with both buyer and seller expecting her to live ten more years, instead of the six months she actually has left. The buyer would then suffer what the Islamic economists call an undeserved loss, and the seller would reap an unearned gain.

For another example, take the ban on selling an orange tree in blossom, which carries with it the permission to sell the tree after it has borne fruit. Islamic treatises suggest that avoidable ignorance vanishes once the oranges have ripened. In fact, the juiciness, sweetness, and vitamin C content of ripe oranges—to mention three of the characteristics that make them desirable—become known with greater precision when they are cut open, eaten, and analyzed. Traders of ripe oranges can thus reduce their ignorance through scientific sampling and testing.

The inconsistency, then, is to insist on the elimination of some types of ignorance without demanding even the reduction of others that traders are capable, in the present state of technology, of reducing substantially. This inconsistency is the inevitable result of attempting to eliminate all avoidable ignorance. Since one can always reduce ignorance through more tests, the approach will lead to arbitrary decisions, unless one bans trade altogether. In modern economies, ignorance on the part of traders is reduced through mechanisms such as commodity standards, product brands, and warranties.[53] A measure of ignorance is deliberately tolerated, apparently because traders consider the cost of elimination prohibitive. But the trade-offs in question rarely appear in the Islamic economists' repertoire.

The prescriptions that permeate the contemporary literature, such as those involving pregnant camels and orange trees in blossom, are by no means new. They figure prominently in classical jurisprudence, as solutions to recurrent commercial problems that threatened social stability. If in the absence of certain information a transaction tended to breed resentment, Islam's jurists tied the transaction's legality to that information's availability. They thus hoped to minimize the incidence of disputes.[54]

The jurists did not always agree among themselves as to which informational imperfections were problematic enough to call for regulation. Nor, when in agreement on this count, did they always agree on the nature of regulation. In a recently published study, Nabil A. Saleh records, in encyclopedic fashion, differences among the various schools of law.[55] He documents, for instance, that whereas the Shafii, Hanbali, and Ibadi jurists categorically prohibited the sale of unripe fruits, the Malikis and some of the Hanafis allowed "the sale of fruits . . . which ripen in succession during one harvest, if such sale accompanies the sale of what has already ripened."[56] Apparently, there were also differences over the definition of ripeness. For the Malikis, Shafiis, Hanbalis, and Ibadis, fruits ripened and became ready for sale when they turned sweet. For the Hanafis, by contrast, they ripened upon passing the flowering stage and attaining their final appearance.[57] Surprisingly, Saleh does not consider such inconsistencies an obstacle to defining the Islamic economic order. Even though he ignores the question of choosing among conflicting positions, he suggests that his study will actually facilitate Islamization.[58]

Priorities

Certain inconsistencies in the contemporary literature arise partly because justice is not the sole objective of the Islamic economic system. Among other objectives are efficiency, growth, employment, and industrialization. A few authors appeal to such goals in justifying their reluctance to ban all transactions involving avoidable ignorance.[59]

Apparent inconsistencies involving modes of cultivation are also traceable to other goals. As we saw earlier, the Islamic economists would prohibit the renting of agricultural land except in cases where the owner is engaged in socially beneficial activities, notably the defense of Islam. A landowner defending Islam is presumably away from home for extended periods of time. Therefore, unlike his sedentary counterparts, he might not be able to monitor his property cheaply. Allowing him to extract a fixed rent, as opposed to a variable share, eliminates the need for monitoring. As such, the fixed rent contract can be interpreted as a compromise that allows the abridgment of justice for the sake of cost minimization.

Other inconsistencies can be attributed to clashes between principles of justice themselves. Take the contradiction between the prohibition of interest and the requirement that wages be fixed. Each of these cases features a clash between fairness and equality. In the former case, the clash is resolved in favor of fairness; in the latter, in favor of equality. The resolutions differ because of an implicit assumption that workers are much poorer than investors. From this assumption, which does not always correspond to reality, it follows that workers would suffer more severely from a decline in wages than investors would from a drop in their returns. Hence, the principle of equality prevails in the case of wages, but not in the case of investment returns.

Certain disagreements among Islamic economists can be ascribed, likewise, to clashes between the two principles of justice. The dispute concerning progressive versus proportional taxation, like potential disputes over such notions as need, fair wage, and just price, can be linked to variations in weights accorded to fairness and equality.

A few Islamic economists recognize that the principles of fairness and equality may conflict with each other or with a goal such as efficiency. One writer remarks: "Islam emphasizes the priority of justice over efficiency. . . . This is not to say that efficiency is not a relevant consideration, but only that it is not decisive."[60] Illustrating the implications of this ordering, he notes that it calls for a ceiling on commercial profits, although he does not discuss how the ceiling is to be determined.[61] On the subject of resource allocation, another writer provides a long list of relevant criteria, from consumer preferences to project profitability to Islamic ideology. It may prove impossible, he says, to satisfy all at once, in which case they must be weighted according to importance. He does not specify how the weighting is to be done.[62] Yet another writer detects a conflict over inflation. After noting that erosion of the purchasing power of money does injustice to providers of interest-free consumption loans, he states:

This implies that any activity . . . which significantly erodes the real value of money should be considered to be a national issue of paramount importance and treated with a sense of concern. Nevertheless, there are other goals which are of equal, or greater, importance. If there is an unavoidable conflict between the realisation of these goals, and a compromise becomes inevitable, then the goal of stable real value of money may be somewhat relaxed provided that the damage done by such relaxing is more than offset by the realisation of other indispensable national goals and provided that such relaxing is undertaken only as long as absolutely necessary and does not become a permanent feature of the policies of the Islamic state.[63]

Which other goals are "indispensable," and what determines when they "more than offset" the ravages of inflation? On these crucial points, we are offered little guidance.

Most writers do not even bring up the issue of priorities. They appeal to one principle on wages, another on interest; then, on modes of cultivation, they switch principles in mid-discussion, without, however, offering a rule to govern such switches. Philosophers characterize this style of argumentation as "intuitionist," since it involves using intuition to strike a balance among different principles.[64] In intuitionist arguments, compromises are struck among principles as a matter of course; however, because priorities remain implicit, they offer limited assistance in novel contexts.

Interestingly, a leading Islamic economist admits that in resolving conflicts among Islamic goals "the appeal to intuition cannot be avoided altogether."[65] But he immediately reverses himself, dismissing the arbitrariness that intuitionism imparts to one's judgments. Islam's holy laws specify, he says, how various considerations are to be weighted. He goes on to argue that "the so-called controversy between equity and efficiency is not real in Islam."[66]

No intellectual enterprise as ambitious as Islamic economics can be entirely free of inconsistencies or avoid intuitionist argumentation. Our cognitive limitations as human beings preclude us from producing a fully coherent blueprint of the socioeconomic system we favor. They force us to segment our blueprint and to bring to issues and problems disparate constellations of impulses, aspirations, assumptions, and logical processes. They prevent us, moreover, from articulating the complete rationale behind every feature of the blueprint.[67]

Still, while total coherence may well be a mirage, blatant inconsistencies can be avoided through careful and systematic reflection. Yet, as we have seen, even the few Islamic economists who notice certain inconsistencies attempt to deal with these in the most superficial manner. They eschew the painstaking task of bringing order over doctrine—a task to which generations of judges and social thinkers, including Muslims, have devoted their careers.[68] The task involves more than bringing coherence to abandoned injunctions of past centuries, as when an attempt is made to explain why fourteen centuries ago the caliph Umar I declared that dates are subject to zakat, but not pomegranates.[69] It involves bringing coherence to current practices as well. Consider, for example, the employment preferences that Saudi Arabia and the Gulf Emirates give to non-Muslims from the Far East.[70] Given that many well-qualified Muslims are out of work and that workers from the Far East are less likely to cause political trouble, is this policy justifiable according to Islamic standards? As far as I can ascertain, the literature provides little help in resolving issues of this sort.

The Islamic economists may object on the ground that Islamic thought is equipped with a methodology for resolving inconsistencies and handling novel issues. A major component of this methodology, many Islamic economists say, is analogical reasoning (*qiyās*), whose purpose is to apply established priorities to new contexts.[71] It is true that medieval Islamic treatises feature extensive legal commentaries on analogical reasoning, as well as scores of applications.[72] However, these do not amount to an operational system for the coordinated determination of priorities. Nor is this surprising. For reasons just explained, establishing similarities between a novel case and familiar cases involves, even in the best of circumstances, a measure of arbitrariness. Also, perceptions and values are inevitably colored by personal experiences and local conditions.[73] Islamic jurists often produced a series of judgments on a single case.

Even if I am wrong and classical jurisprudence does provide an operational system for the determination of priorities, one would not know this from contemporary Islamic economics. Nowhere in this literature does one find a set of general rules to govern analogical reasoning. Instead, one finds an abundance of unsynthesized, disparate examples of analogical reasoning by medieval Islamic writers. When contemporary Islamic economists resort to analogical reasoning themselves, they do so in what seems to be an arbitrary manner.

CONSENSUS

The Islamic economists claim, as mentioned at the outset, that an Islamic economy would be free of the economic injustices allegedly rampant in capitalist and socialist economies. In various contexts, however, it is unclear what Islamic justice requires; nor is it obvious what compromises are to be struck on account of other considerations.

These ambiguities have a far-reaching practical implication: even in a society composed entirely of pious Muslims eager to build the economic system championed by Islamic economics, no one would possess definitive criteria for judging whether particular economic actions, policies, or institutions were just. Two members, equally well-meaning and learned, could easily differ on whether a certain market institution conforms to Islam's twin principles of justice. Because of their differences, moreover, they might suspect each other of subscribing to un-Islamic principles, which would disturb the envisioned social harmony.

Yet, most Islamic economists minimize, and some dismiss altogether, the possibility of discord. In the belief that the institutions of an Islamic society would be geared toward the reconciliation of individual differences, they maintain that people would eventually attain a consensus (*ijmāʿ*).[74] Some writers seem quite confident that this consensus would be in line with Islamic principles. One claims that "when new situations have been met by analogy or otherwise," the consensus of the community will prevent it from "drifting into heresy."[75] He builds his case partly on a saying commonly attributed to Prophet Muhammad: "My people shall never agree on error."

There are two distinct circularities in this position. First, the ability to determine the acceptability of a consensus presupposes a consensus on what is properly Islamic. However, the Islamic economists do not even agree among themselves on implications of the Islamic principles. Second, the authenticity of the Prophet's saying is itself based on the consensus of the Islamic community. There is no guarantee that this consensus will endure, for scholarship has cast doubt on whether the saying belongs to the Prophet.[76]

In any case, the Islamic economists are not really prepared to leave the economy's design to the community's consensus. They would not lend their approval to a consensus they consider at odds with Islamic principles—one, for example, that consents to the legalization of interest. Revealing a refusal to take the Prophet's saying literally, they also offer concrete measures to ensure the acceptability of the community's consensus. Coercion, some say flatly, is not one of these: people are not to be forced to support opinions or interpretations with which they disagree. The emphasis is to be on teaching the Islamic interpretation of history, inculcating Islamic principles of justice, and fostering a sense of brotherly cooperation. Through these educational measures, the argument goes, beliefs, opinions, and preferences will become harmonized, equipping society for the establishment of a consensus compatible with Islamic stipulations.[77]

This argument, too, is problematic, for it rests on a pair of premises shown to be doubtful. The first is that there is a unique Islamic economic system, characterized by a well-defined ensemble of institutions, practices, and behaviors. The second is that there exists a class of knowledgeable leaders—presumably the Islamic economists themselves—who can teach what the system entails. Both premises conflict with the fact that the Islamic economists are seriously divided over many basic features of the economy. How can teachers who disagree among themselves forge a consensus in the wider community?

A measure of consensus is essential, of course, to the smooth functioning of any society. If people are to live and work together in harmony they must agree on what is good or right, at least where this affects basic social issues.[78] The Islamic economists are justified, therefore, in according consensus a primary role in establishing their preferred social order. Where they err is in thinking that more Islamic research and teaching will lead to a particular consensus—to communal acceptance of a God-given set of injunctions, which unambiguously defines the just economy. They over-look that perceptions of justice are shaped in significant measure by per-sonal experiences, over which no Islamic establishment can possibly exer-cise full control. Which consensus, if any, comes into being will thus depend on people's experiences. Moreover, since each generation has a distinct set of experiences, over time one particular consensus might give way to another, or disappear altogether.[79]

There is nothing novel about the Islamic economists' conviction that inconsistencies and disagreements will disappear through the formation of consensus. Since the eighth century, Islamic scholars have accorded consensus an indispensable role in the creation and maintenance of social stability.[80] Yet a veritable consensus never emerged—not even on the definition of consensus itself. Whereas al-Shafii, the founder of Sunni Is-lamic jurisprudence, defined consensus in terms of the entire community of believers, other jurists were apt to perceive it in terms of the leading scholars.[81] Nor did educational efforts to create consensus put an end to sharp divisions over major social and economic issues.

The medieval jurists of Islam might be excused for underestimating the strength of the forces that could make Muslims differ in their inter-pretations. After all, the religion was still in its infancy at the time they wrote, and their methods for achieving consensus had just begun to be tested. Today's Islamic economists have much less justification for trust-ing that consensus will emerge and endure. Over the past fourteen centu-ries Islamic education has not prevented groups from pursuing, in the name of Islam, diametrically opposite causes. Under the banner of Islamic fairness, some have campaigned vigorously for raising certain prices that others, also touting the fairness principle, were clamoring to lower. For another illustration, wealth accumulation has been defended on the grounds of fairness and efficiency, just as it has been attacked as inimical to equality. It is obvious, too, that interpretations of Islam have a propen-sity to change over time. Until relatively recently, for instance, slavery was tolerated, indeed regulated by the Islamic establishment.[82] Today, many Muslims consider slavery unjust. Revealingly, the Islamic economists ig-nore the subject, except in listing the freeing of slaves among the uses of zakat funds.[83]

Concluding Remarks

Notwithstanding their ambitious claims, the Islamic economists have not established that the injustices they find in existing social orders would be absent from an Islamic order. They have shown neither that the distribu-tion of wealth would be relatively more equal in an Islamic order nor that an Islamic order would be fairer, even by their own standards of fairness. Their proposed injunctions are riddled with inconsistencies, and their conviction that Islam's consensus mechanism would eliminate these collides with their own divisions over many crucial matters.

As I mentioned at the outset, certain flaws of Islamic economic thought afflict other ideologies as well. Just consider the diverse schools of social thought that developed around that electrifying cry of the French Revolution, "Liberty, Equality, Fraternity!" Each can be faulted for failing to specify how these three goals are to be attained and for harboring inconsistencies. In fact, whenever and wherever an attempt has been made to bring about these goals, major conflicts have erupted over what they require. Witness how the limits of liberty have never ceased to be controversial. It has become apparent, too, that goals sometimes pull in opposite directions. Thus, economic liberties have been found to generate inequality, and many egalitarian measures have been coercive.

These patterns point to the existence of a universal process preventing social doctrines from becoming totally clear and consistent. I argued earlier that this process is linked to limitations of the human mind. The Islamic economists see the matter differently. While agreeing that other doctrines are deeply flawed, they believe that Islamic thought, being divinely inspired, is exempt from the perils of human weakness. They thus ignore that, like the doctrines they indict, Islamic economics rests on human reasoning and interpretation.

Of course, systems of thought are never alike in every way. They differ in the severity of their ambiguities, inconsistencies, and illusions. They also differ substantively. A key difference between Islamic economics and other popular doctrines lies in the emphasis placed on liberty. In many doctrines liberty is a supreme goal, on par with fairness and equality. In Islamic thought, by contrast, liberty is barely an issue. It enters writings only through unsupported assertions that in an Islamic order transgressions of individual liberty would be minimal. The positions taken by Islamic economists make clear, however, that in the event of conflict between an Islamic requirement and individual liberty, it is liberty that must yield.

CHAPTER SIX

Islam and Underdevelopment:
An Old Puzzle Revisited

ON OCTOBER 29, 1923, the day Turkey was proclaimed a republic, the new regime's founder, who would eventually assume the name Atatürk, spoke to a reporter on culture and religion. The Turkish nation should remain religious, he said, explaining that religion is not necessarily inimical to progress. He added, however, that his fellow Turks were being held back by a "confused and artificial religion riddled with superstitions."[1] Under his leadership, Turkey would abolish the Islamic caliphate and declare secularism one of its guiding principles.

Atatürk was not alone in viewing Islam, or at least popular Islam, as irrational and retrogressive. Many educated Muslims of his day shared his perception, as did most Westerners. To many, it seemed self-evident that Islam was inimical to economic development. Muslims were overwhelmingly illiterate, whereas in the West mass education was already more than an ideal. Few Muslims appreciated, and even fewer were seeking to capitalize on, the discoveries and innovations that, in the West, were transfiguring production processes, ushering in new commodities, and elevating living standards. Muslim trade with the outside world, even some of the trade within it, was largely under the control of Europeans, whose local representatives came chiefly from religious minorities. Muslims had established few banks, and their treasuries were depleted. The contrast between Europe's ongoing advances and the Islamic world's backwardness was stark enough to make Islam seem antithetical to economic modernization.

Three-quarters of a century later, certain heavily Muslim countries are on the World Bank's roster of high-income countries, with others in the middle-income category. Still, the world's poorest countries contain disproportionately many with predominantly Muslim populations. From a scientific standpoint, then, it is natural to question whether there exists a causal relationship between Islam and economic development. To be sure, statistical correlation does not imply causation. Establishing causation requires identifying one or more mechanisms to account for the correlation.

The purpose of this essay is to classify and critique some of the proposed mechanisms and to distinguish them from the crude arguments that enjoyed currency at the time that Turkey became secular in a bid to limit

122 • Chapter Six

Islam's social power. At the end, I shall lay some groundwork for an integrative theory. It should be recognized that the relevant literature is remarkably limited in view of Islam's importance in global affairs. Significantly, the English-language development textbooks currently in vogue tend not to explore linkages between religion and economic development, to say nothing of addressing the economic role of Islam in particular.[2]

One reason for the paucity of scientific interest in investigating the connections between Islam and development lies in the uncommonness of interdisciplinary contacts between economics and religion. Economists, even ones connected to the Islamic world, generally know little about the scientific study of religion; having learned to ignore hard-to-quantify cultural variables, most operate as if these have no economic effects, positive or negative. For their part, scholars trained in the languages, history, or politics of the Islamic world tend to lack sophistication in economics. Another reason for the paucity of relevant analyses is "cultural relativism"—the inclination, which gained momentum through anthropological studies of the 1930s, to treat cultures as incomparable. In requiring every culture to be studied on its own terms, cultural relativism has discouraged comparative studies on the economic effects of cultural variables. Still another reason for the scarcity of inquiries into the economic impact of Islam lies in efforts to avoid emboldening groups perceived as hostile to Muslims.[3]

Certain findings and arguments in this essay can doubtless be abused. But this is not a sufficient reason to avoid an honest analysis or to suppress troubling data. The principal victims of self-censorship could be the very peoples one is trying to protect. In any case, whatever the extent of current anti-Muslim prejudice, it is unlikely to disappear by ignoring potentially discomforting possibilities. On the contrary, a dispassionate analysis that dispels myths might serve as an antidote to religious prejudice.

STATISTICS AND TRENDS THAT DEMAND EXPLANATION

Some evidence suggesting a possible link appears in the regressions of Table 6.1, which include the 132 countries covered by the *World Development Report* for 1995. In each regression, the dependent variable is the logarithm of per capita income, drawn from the *Report*.[4] The only independent variable of the first regression is the share of Muslims within total population,[5] as provided by the *Britannica Book of the Year, 1995*.[6] This regression indicates a statistically significant negative relationship between the two variables, but its fit is poor.

A considerably better fit is obtained from the second regression, which includes additional independent variables. Membership in OPEC, the oil cartel, turns out to be a significant contributor to income, and location

TABLE 6.1
The Relationship between Islam and Per Capita Income

	(1)	(2)
Constant	3.33	3.55
Share Muslim	−0.41***	−2.07****
	(−2.57)	(−2.87)
Squared Share Muslim		1.76**
		(2.29)
OPEC member		0.42*
		(2.20)
Subsaharan Africa		−0.67*****
		(−5.77)
R^2	0.04	0.34

Note: 132 countries were included in the regressions. Asterisks *, **, ***, ****, and ***** denote significance at the 0.03, 0.02, 0.01, 0.005, and 0.0000 levels, respectively. The t-values are shown in parentheses beneath the regression. R^2 is the multiple correlation coefficient adjusted for degrees of freedom. In each of the regressions the dependent variable is the logarithm of per capita income, and in the second the last two independent variables are dummies.

in sub-Saharan Africa, the world's poorest region, a highly significant depressor. The Muslim share of the population remains a very significant negative determinant of income. The positive coefficient for the square of the Muslim share of population is statistically significant, indicating that a U-shaped function fits the data better than a linear one. The curvature reflects the fact that the African, South Asian, and East Asian countries with large Muslim minorities tend to be poorer than countries with Muslim majorities, located mostly in the Middle East.[7]

A complementary indication is given by the Muslim share of global income. If in every country Muslims earned, on average, exactly the average per capita income, the data of the previous exercise would show the Muslim share of global income to be 5.98 percent. As Figure 6.1 reveals, this figure is strikingly less than the Muslim share of the global population, which is 19.22 percent. The assumption that Muslims and non-Muslims have the same average income in every country is obviously unrealistic. In most of the countries where Muslims live in substantial numbers, they are generally poorer than non-Muslims. So the reported contrast probably understates the actual discrepancy.

One could refine these statistical exercises by collecting additional data, considering further variables, taking account of differences in the purchasing powers of currencies, and constructing a more sophisticated mea-

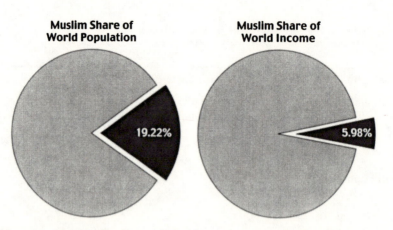

Figure 6.1. The Muslim Share of World Income Is Much Lower Than That of World Population.

sure of development. But such refinements are unlikely to alter the general pattern. In any case, our objective here is to critique the causal mechanisms proposed to account for the incontrovertible fact that Muslims tend to be relatively poor.

Few will deny that the level of economic development—whether measured by per capita income or by variables like trade, literacy, science, scholarship, and technology—has long been lower in the Islamic world than in West.[8] In the mid-nineteenth century, the contrast was captured in a famous couplet by the Turkish intellectual Ziya Paşa:

> I passed through the lands of the infidels, I saw cities and mansions;
> I wandered in the realm of Islam, I saw nothing but ruins.[9]

There is variation, however, in perceptions concerning the beginnings of the West's economic superiority. A fashionable view, grounded in the fact that several Muslim states continued to challenge Europe militarily right up to the eighteenth century, is that the West did not achieve economic dominance until the seventeenth century, if not later.[10] Whatever the exact date when the West overtook the Islamic world—regardless of how development is defined, it cannot be determined precisely—the catching up actually began much before. The Islamic world was clearly more advanced than the West around the tenth century. If it had fallen behind by the seventeenth, the reason is that centuries earlier Europe began undergoing fundamental social transformations destined to produce huge economic payoffs.[11] As Europe was laying the preconditions of the impending Industrial Revolution, Islamic civilization underwent its own transformations, of course. Moreover, the decline of the Islamic world's relative economic position was interrupted, if not temporarily reversed, by reflowerings of economic activity in Spain and Anatolia, among other places. Still, the overall trend favored the West for the better part of a millennium.

If the Islamic world was at one time economically more advanced, one reason is that it stood at the forefront of scientific and technological innovation. By the thirteenth century, Islamic learning and creativity were past their peak. A telling indication lies in the temporal distribution of the great scientists included in an "encyclopedia of Muslim scientific pioneers" issued, significantly, by an Islamist publisher.[12] Of the scientists it lists, 64 percent produced their pathbreaking works before 1250, and 36 percent did so between 1250 and 1750; not one lived after 1750.[13] Although the ranks of the world's leading scientists now include Muslims, the Muslim contribution to scholarship and innovation remains small in relation to the Muslim share of the world population. In a book replete with relevant data, Pervez Hoodbhoy reports that on a per capita basis Arab scientific output is a mere 1 percent of Israeli scientific output.[14] Although only 20 percent of all Muslims are Arabs, the comparison is roughly indicative of the Islamic world's current participation in scientific progress.

M. A. Cook and Roger Owen, among others, have observed that in absolute terms the Islamic world continued to grow even as it declined relatively.[15] Their observation raises the distinction between *extensive* and *intensive* growth. Extensive growth takes place when population growth raises total income with no increase in income per capita; it has occurred since the dawn of history. By contrast, intensive growth involves increases in income per capita; much rarer, it is ordinarily driven by the technological, organizational, institutional, perceptual, and moral changes associated with economic development.[16] In terms of this distinction, what is at issue here is not extensive growth in the Islamic world. Rather, it is the relatively poor record of intensive growth during a long period that began in the Middle Ages.

THREE THESES

The explanations advanced by scholars who have reflected on the above patterns fall into three categories.

The Economic Irrelevance Thesis

In the first category, which comprises what may be called the *economic irrelevance thesis*, are arguments to the effect that the economic fortunes of Muslims have had nothing to do with Islam per se. The most forceful exponent of the thesis is Maxime Rodinson.[17] Although the fundamental sources of Islam contain numerous economic precepts, proposes Rodinson, none has constrained economic behavior in any significant way. In practice, he maintains, Muslims have always been able to pick and choose among them; in addition, they have found it easy to reinterpret particular precepts in the face of changing conditions. Rodinson does not deny that Islamic civilization experienced a protracted economic descent. But there is no evidence, he claims, that the descent was driven by beliefs or values rooted in Islam; it was caused by changes in material conditions—changes to which the worldviews and moralities of Muslims merely adapted. If at various times Muslims have appeared to resign themselves to poverty, the reason is not, in this view, that Islam counsels laziness. Rather, it is that resignation has been a rational response to the futility of resisting political obstacles to economic advancement.

The insurmountable obstacles were created, according to Rodinson, by European imperialism. This claim begs the question of why Islamic civilization succumbed to colonialism. Rodinson does not provide an answer. Instead, he infers that, because Islam posed no obstacle to capitalist development, one cannot prove that in the absence of European imperialism the Islamic world would not have developed in the manner of Europe. As K. S. Jomo points out, neither can one prove the opposite.[18] In any case, the Islamic world's relative economic decline began well before the onset of European imperialism. So its essential causes were probably primarily internal.

A qualified variant of the economic irrelevance thesis belongs to Eric Jones.[19] Every society, observes Jones, faces numerous obstacles to economic growth, all rooted in individual inclinations to better themselves at the expense of society. Ordinarily, these obstacles frustrate possibilities for intensive growth, which is why growth in per capita income has everywhere been minuscule through most of history. From this perspective, it is easy to understand why the Islamic world developed slowly after roughly the tenth century; the challenge is to explain the rapid development of Europe rather than the slower development elsewhere. Moreover, there is no reason to look for special factors that depressed the Islamic world's economic performance; if anything, one must explore the factors that overcame Europe's own obstacles to growth. Jones adds that Islamic injunctions seemingly inimical to growth—the ban on interest, restrictions on speculation—have routinely been circumvented. At the same time, he recognizes that efforts at evasion impose social costs. They produce, he says, "a certain brake on the economy, conceivably even a lower average probability of independent growth than in, say, Christendom."[20] He insists, however, that this "brake" hardly precludes self-generated growth. His argument boils down to the view that the connection between

Islam and economic development is, while not imaginary, quite weak; if material circumstances are ripe for development, the beliefs and values of Muslims will not stand in the way.

The Economic Advantage Thesis

When I return to the arguments of Jones and Rodinson, it will become clear that, for all their shortcomings, they provide insights that any broad synthesis must accommodate. For now, let us turn to the second category of explanations, which form the *economic advantage thesis*. From a strictly logical standpoint, this thesis, which holds that Islam supports economic development, does not conflict with the Islamic world's undeniable economic descent. Islam's effects on growth could have been consistently positive, yet eventually overwhelmed by other factors. One variant of such an argument is a standard feature of Islamic economics—the school of thought that, since the 1940s, has been trying to restructure economics on the basis of Islamic teachings.[21] Observing that many verses of the Qur'an encourage effort and enrichment,[22] Islamic economics proposes that the economic prescriptions of Islam—its financial regulations, contracting guidelines, distributional instruments, and behavioral norms—provide an ideal framework for economic development. For proof, it says, one need look only at the impressive economic record of the first Islamic society in seventh-century Arabia.

What is known about the economic evolution of early Islamic civilization is actually quite limited. There is no doubt, however, that during the first few centuries of Islam regions under Muslim rule, including the Middle East, North Africa, and Spain, flourished economically. Nor is there doubt that the commercial and financial regulations introduced under the rubric of Islamic law fueled the observed economic growth[23] or that they influenced the economic evolution of Western Europe.[24] Yet there is no inherent conflict between the economic successes of early Islamic civilization and the proposition that Islam itself discourages economic development. For one thing, the early successes could have occurred in spite of the religion's growth-inhibiting features; the primary source of development might have been, for example, the mixing of cultures brought about by conquests, conversions, and political reorganization. For another, even if Islam promoted growth for a while, it obviously failed to ensure quick adaptations to later opportunities. Islam may have been less conducive to economic growth under certain conditions than under others.

If Islam contributed to the economic ascent of Islamic civilization, it might have influenced the subsequent descent. Conversely, if factors other than Islam account for the long descent, nonreligious factors probably played a role in the prior ascent. The challenge for the social sciences is to identify social mechanisms that account for both the ascent and the descent. The promoters of the economic advantage thesis typically attribute the ascent to institutional and moral changes brought by Islam, but the descent to forces that made Muslims become, after a brief "Golden Age," progressively readier to pursue un-Islamic economic activities. In this account, which resembles Sumerian and Hebraic stories of man's fall from Eden, the accomplishments of Islamic civilization after the mid-seventh century—even the high Abbasid caliphate and the expanding Ottoman Empire—appear as degeneration. The account leaves unaddressed why Islamic civilization fell victim to corrupting influences. And in treating the ideal economy as static, it overlooks that civilizations decline when they fail to adapt to changing circumstances.

A variant of the economic advantage thesis deals with the reality of the Islamic world's poor economic record by downplaying the West's economic achievements. In the view of Ahmad Haffar, for example, the West's economic expansion offers little worth emulating; having spawned psychological and social problems, it should not even be called development. The key to development worthy of the name lies, Haffar maintains, in a return to the pristine simplicity of the "Golden Age."[25]

The Economic Disadvantage Thesis

The undeniable imperfections of modernity do not negate, of course, the many improvements that have accompanied economic growth, like the near disappearance of famines and the huge extension of life spans. Thinkers whose views form our last broad category of explanations, the *economic disadvantage thesis*, take such improvements for granted. In contrast to Haffar, their focus is on why the Islamic world experienced a relative decline; why the decline lasted so long; why Muslims were slow to industrialize; and why the Islamic world remains, in spite of its oil wealth, relatively poor. Only some of the explanations provide clearly articulated causal mechanisms; as the next four sections will show, the simplest involves little more than an enumeration of symptoms. The more sophisticated explanations describe a social equilibrium or a dynamic process. None offers, however, a complete account of the underlying forces.

I start with the least satisfactory variant: the *permanent* economic disadvantage thesis.

ISLAM ITSELF AS PERMANENT BARRIER TO DEVELOPMENT

Before the mid-twentieth century, a frequently and openly expressed view in Western scholarship was that Islam stood for unchangeability. Under the rubric of "Orientalism," many studies treated Islam as defining and promoting a social system lacking a capacity for adaptation. Lord Cromer, effectively the British governor of Egypt from 1883 to 1907, put the claim succinctly: "Islam cannot be reformed: that is to say, reformed Islam is Islam no longer; it is something else." He went on: "Little assistance in the work of reform can, therefore, be expected from the steady orthodox Moslems, who cling with unswerving fidelity to their ancient faith, and whose dislike to European civilization often increases as that civilisation advances." Accordingly, he saw Christian Egyptians as "if not the only possible, at all events the principal agent for administering the country, except in so far as it is administered by Europeans."[26] A complementary view was advanced by the French scholar Ernest Renan, who held that early Islam and its Arab propagators were hostile to science and philosophy. Knowledge advanced under Arab domination, he claimed, only when Persian and Hellenic influences were powerful. All religions had discouraged free inquiry, but Islam, because it extended the rule of dogma to the temporal realm, had always stood in a class by itself.[27]

Many other such opinions can be cited; Edward Said reviews some of the most categorical.[28] Curiously, they share with the economic advantage thesis that undergirds modern Islamic economics the view that Islam defines a timeless and closed socioeconomic system, differing only in their treatment of the presumed fixity as a handicap rather than a blessing. For many of today's Islamic economists, it is a mistake for Muslims to emulate the transformations of the West; for Orientalists of Cromer and Renan's persuasion, the problem has been that Muslims cannot Westernize as long as they remain Muslims. Underlying these contrary positions is the common presupposition that the corpus of Islamic law never changes. In fact, and as the exponents of the economic irrelevance thesis emphasize, it is always changing through extensions, contractions, and reconstructions. Although the Qur'an itself is never called into question within acceptable Islamic discourse, it does indeed get reinterpreted. As a case in point, its verses generally read as prohibiting all forms of interest have at certain times and places been reinterpreted as excluding the nonexploitative forms.

Nevertheless, Cromer and Renan viewed Islam as a promoter of fatalism and a deterrent to experimentation. It is true, of course, that the literal meaning of Islam is submission and also that the Qur'an harbors verses reasonably interpreted as counseling fatalism.[29] Also true, perhaps, is that individuals trained to attribute phenomena to the works of an interventionist deity are less likely to question the status quo. But no major religion is free of fatalistic elements. Besides, if the main obstacle to growth has been what Islam teaches, one needs to identify the social mechanism responsible for the persistence of that teaching; neither Renan nor Cromer took that step. A related problem is their failure to accommodate variations in Muslim attitudes toward socioeconomic change. In any case, they did not seriously investigate whether commitment to Islam is associated with conservatism or lower productivity. On the basis of the economic backwardness they saw, they simply took it for granted.[30] In the process, they generalized the nadir of Islam's economic performance into an indictment of Islamic civilization as a whole.

The tendency to treat Islam as a source of growth-inhibiting attitudes without specifying how they get produced and reproduced did not end with Cromer and Renan's generation of commentators. The same gaps appear also in the works of modernization theorists whose heyday was the quarter-century following World War II. An influential member of the school, Daniel Lerner, wrote in his best-known work, *The Passing of Traditional Society*, that "the top policy problem, for three generations of Middle Eastern leaders, has been whether one must choose between 'Mecca or mechanization' or whether one can make them compatible." He himself believed that Muslims faced a veritable choice—one that would ultimately get resolved in favor of "mechanization," with "Mecca" losing much of its relevance.[31] Lerner did not explain why "Mecca" had been, and remained, an obstacle to modernization. He simply observed that Islam, in its prevailing form, was inimical to the structural changes essential to the Islamic world's progress.

The leading development economists of the postwar years shared the modernization theorists' view that the Islamic world's economic development would require, at the very least, the reinterpretation of Islam. For example, Arthur Lewis, in his textbook on economic growth, argued that "some religious codes are more compatible with economic growth than others. If a religion lays stress upon material values, upon work, upon thrift and productive investment, upon honesty in commercial relations, upon experimentation and risk bearing, and upon equality of opportunity, it will be helpful to growth, whereas in so far as it is hostile to these things, it tends to inhibit growth."[32] He did not provide an exhaustive classification of religions according to their support for development. But his examples make clear that he considered Islam a deterrent to growth. While he cites several religious minorities as having contributed to development, he mentions the "Moslems in India" as an example of an economically lethargic minority. Lewis follows this example with commentary on how some minorities adopt precepts "hostile to economic development," but he explains neither how such precepts arise nor why they persist. The same pattern is found in the works of Irma Adelman and Cynthia Taft Morris.[33] In identifying various social determinants of economic performance, they use a scale that ranks religions according to the degree to which they encourage people to control their own fate. With A⁺ the highest rating and D the lowest, Islam receives a B for cultivating "moderately fatalistic attitudes toward man's capacity to alter his destiny." The authors take such attitudes as given, however, without explaining either their origins or their diffusion.

The modernization and development theorists of the early post-World War II decades, like their Orientalist predecessors, formed their views about Islam through intellectual trends that treated religion as an intoxicant to be overcome by human progress.[34] Many of them held low opinions also of the major Eastern religions;[35] and they generally supported efforts to move vast domains, including economics, outside the realm of religion. If they considered Islam less supportive of development than, say, Christianity, a basic reason was that secularization had gone further in predominantly Christian countries than in predominantly Muslim ones. And they could make essentially unsupported claims about the consequences of Islam because their readers were unlikely to pose questions.

Not that the modernization perspective was monopolized by thinkers largely ignorant of Islam. It was accepted also by certain prominent students of Islamic civilization, who helped cultivate the view that the Islamic world's economic development depended on its secularization. A case in point is Niyazi Berkes, whose works on Turkish history link every social advance to a retreat of Islam.[36] Ottoman citizens, Berkes observes, learned of Western scientific advances through schools run, if not also established, by foreigners. The religion-based curricula of traditional schools remained essentially static until they were closed in the course of Atatürk's reforms of the 1920s. Almost all the leaders who initiated the modernization campaigns of the Ottoman Empire and its successor states, Berkes goes on, had enjoyed sustained exposure to Western philosophies. Equally revealing, the novel ideas generated by the European Enlightenment reached the empire's non-Muslim peoples before they did the Muslims.

There is much additional evidence, recorded by Berkes and others,[37] that religious authorities held jurisdiction in a vast array of legal, social, and educational matters. Although in principle Islam rejects priestly mediation between God and believer, in practice the religious establishment has always exercised substantial control and influence over how Muslims, including Muslim rulers, interpret Islam. Berkes is also on the mark in observing that clerics commonly took conservative positions and that successive reformers had to overcome clerical opposition.

Yet, some of Berkes's own accounts belie the notion of an unyielding religious barrier to progress. The fact that the first printing press to serve Muslims was established as late as 1727—almost three centuries after the Gutenberg press—is commonly attributed to resistance from clerics and scribes. Berkes shows that such resistance was actually minimal, although printing, when it arrived, was restricted to books without Islamic significance.[38] The long delay resulted mainly, he finds elsewhere, from a confluence of several nonreligious factors, including low demand for books, limited availability of paper, and lack of essential technical infrastructure.[39] He observes, likewise, that clerics raised no major objections to the establishment of Western-type schools in engineering and medicine. Moreover, fears of Islamic resistance to innovation often proved unfounded. To avoid offending presumed Muslim sensitivities, students at the first modern medical school of the Ottoman Empire were initially taught anatomy from wax models rather than corpses. But when corpses were finally introduced into classes, no objections followed. Equally significant, the school of medicine had little trouble recruiting Muslim students.[40] Muslims who enrolled in the school were not representative of the wider population; their ranks would not have contained individuals heavily pressured to stay away from modern medicine. Nevertheless, the episode shows that Muslims wishing to get a modern education did not always face insurmountable obstacles.

Such examples from Berkes's own publications lend some support, then, to Rodinson's thesis that Islam alone does not account for the Islamic world's failure to keep up with Europe economically. Like Rodinson's observations about the ease of circumventing Islamic precepts, they thus compound the puzzle as to why the Islamic world declined so dramatically, at least in relative terms, from the heights it reached a millennium ago. Indeed, to prove that Berkes overstates his case does not negate the incontrovertible evidence of the Islamic world's long descent; it merely raises a new set of questions. If clerical resistance was not decisive, why was the Islamic world slow to embrace modern medicine? Why did the Muslim demand for books grow too slowly to keep the printing press an economically unviable technology until the eighteenth century, when Jewish refugees from Spain began printing books for Ottoman Jews as early as 1493? One need not appeal to fatalism, scripture, or the religious establishment to sense that the answers to such questions must have a religious dimension.

The next two sections introduce arguments more sophisticated than those just critiqued. While recognizing that individual perceptions and attitudes matter to economic evolution, they seek also to explain the origins of these dispositions. Accordingly, they treat the economic effects of Islam as variable rather than fixed; they allow particular elements to support change at one time and hinder it at another. As we shall see, these new arguments hold that social circumstances raised the salience of stability-fostering religious features; and they maintain that the resulting reinterpretations of Islam helped legitimize the status quo.

Static Worldviews Associated with Islam

One argument starts from the observation that the overriding objective of Middle Eastern states was to keep their rulers in power. The measures taken to meet this objective fostered some trade and production, but they also bred ideological and institutional sclerosis.

Halil İnalcık develops this perspective in his analysis of the "Ottoman economic mind."[41] The Ottoman rulers, he explains, sought to keep their major cities prosperous, and to this end they developed commercial centers and strove to control vital trade routes. However, interested first and foremost in their own security, they put a premium on economic stability. Accordingly, they enforced price controls, regulated exports, established charitable foundations, kept the burden of taxation largely on the countryside, and, most important, restricted basic organizational changes. The system was productive enough to enable the conquest of similarly governed territories. But it proved a serious handicap once a socially transformed Europe overtook the Ottoman Empire economically and militarily. Mentally conditioned by a long history of territorial expansion to believe in the adequacy of their established social system, the Ottoman rulers could not figure out, at least not immediately, why they were falling increasingly behind.

What became a progressively critical flaw of the Ottoman economic mind was thus its focus on social stability. This focus slowed the emergence of the concept we now call economic development. Nothing in İnalcık's account identifies religion as the driving force behind ideological and institutional inertia. He observes, however, that Islam came to support the status quo through its legitimation of policies aimed at social stability. For example, the Islamic *hisba* rules, originally developed by Arabs seeking religious justification for market regulations,[42] were used by Ottomans to give religious cover to various anticompetitive measures, even to their overall economic philosophy. When Europe's evolution made the Ottoman economic system increasingly inadequate, this religious significance then made major changes look like a defeat for Islam rather than a victory for Ottoman society, thus raising the obstacles to reform. Put differently, the status quo's religious significance increased the perceived costs of change.

We will see shortly that this interpretation has its limitations. But let us move on. The economic mentality identified by İnalcık matches the dispositions that Ibn Khaldun, in his famous theory of the flowering and decay of Muslim states, attributes to the elites of states beyond their prime.[43] Ibn Khaldun observed that Muslim states were typically founded by nomadic warriors motivated by the promise of booty and glory. The warriors would subjugate, unite, and organize sedentary populations, then settle down themselves. Their descendants, raised in calm and comfort, would possess neither the predatory urges nor the dynamism that led to their state's creation. Content to preserve their gains, they would make their states vulnerable to conquest by a fresh band of ambitious nomads prepared to work for a more advanced socioeconomic order. In Ibn Khaldun's account, then, the main source of economic progress is conquest motivated by looting; without conquest, states would only decay, because they lack an internal engine for change. The religious connection comes from the legitimacy that Islam has bestowed upon conquest. Not only did conquest play an important role in the first Islamic state's expansion but the fundamental sources of Islam justify its use in promoting conversions. Insofar as the emphasis on conquest discouraged the creation of new wealth, religion would have restrained intensive economic growth.

At the time Ibn Khaldun wrote, the Islamic world was more than two centuries away from the peak of its European expansion. It is amazing, therefore, that he worried about the decline of scientific learning in Muslim countries and that he expressed admiration for philosophical advances in "the land of Rome."[44] Evidently, he sensed that an internal engine of economic development would ultimately outperform an external one based on conquest. This is not to say that his thesis fully explains the Islamic world's relative economic decline. Most critically, it leaves unexplained why the inefficiencies of Muslim states went unchallenged from within. Even if one accepts his account of why the rulers of these states became lethargic, one needs to explain why their subjects produced no challengers. What, exactly, kept Muslim societies from generating the ideas, experiments, and movements necessary to keep them economically powerful vis-à-vis their outside competitors? İnalcık's observations raise similar questions. While it is easy to see that the Ottoman rulers—like rulers elsewhere—had a vested interest in political stability, it is not self-evident why the nonruling masses put up with constraints on their economic advancement. One might observe that, even in its heyday, the Ottoman Empire was no stranger to mass uprisings. The Celali revolts of the sixteenth century provide a case in point.[45] However, these uprisings were generally disorganized movements. And their participants usually sought forced redistribution rather than fundamental social reforms to promote wealth creation.

A third perspective on the static nature of the Islamic worldview focuses on the social standing of Ottoman merchants. Sabri Ülgener observes that the Ottoman craft guilds participated in efforts to legitimize their own market sharing practices and to delegitimize the competitive practices of merchants, including speculation, arbitrage, price cutting, advertising, and product improvement.[46] There are obvious complementarities between Ülgener's observations and those of İnalcık. Stability-seeking Ottoman rulers would have preferred craftsmen to merchants because the former were stationary whereas the latter moved around. And they could expect the minimization of intraguild competition to improve political stability in the short run.

Yet, to show that certain segments of society gain from particular values does not, by itself, establish how those values spread and endured. Ülgener's account does not elucidate why the social standing of Ottoman merchants generally worsened over time; or why the merchants proved incapable of correcting their negative images; or why Islam came to be associated with a morality unfavorable to dynamic competition. These puzzles are compounded by the fact that the founder of Islam was himself a merchant remembered—some of the recollections are doubtless apocryphal—to have cautioned against interfering with market competition. Given that early Islamic thought harbors certain procompetitive traditions, it is especially puzzling that Muslim merchants, along with Muslim consumers who stood to benefit from greater competition, failed to counter the anticompetitive influences of the guilds.

In any case, the low social standing of merchants provides nowhere near a complete explanation for the Islamic world's protracted economic descent. After all, the politically powerful treated merchants with contempt even in places that ushered in the modern economy. "The business elite in England," observes Jack Goldstone on the basis of recent studies of premodern England, "virtually never penetrated into the aristocratic elite; up to 1800 wealth gained a better lifestyle, but the daughters of the aristocracy still did not deign to marry into the business classes, and the latter remained a socially separate, and lesser, group."[47] A similar observation may be made with regard to the anticompetitive regulations of the guilds. As Jones reminds us, analogous regulations existed also in Europe, where the guilds reacted just as defensively to the rise of modern industry.[48] The difference between Europe and the Islamic world was not, then, that their guilds behaved differently but that in the former the rulers were quicker to appreciate the social costs of guild privileges. Even small differences in attitudes and policies might have produced, over decades and centuries, large variations in economic performance. Likewise, over a long time span even small differences in the treatment of merchants might have produced cumulatively large effects.

A related puzzle raised by Ülgener's thesis lies in the continuing influence of the economic morality that became associated with Islam. The foremost objective of the contemporary doctrine of Islamic economics is to replace the individualistic economic morality that has spread through contacts with the West with a communalist morality akin to that of the

medieval Middle East. As we shall see, a strictly individualist morality
encourages people to pursue their own ends without having to consider
the social consequences. By contrast, a communalist morality focuses attention on communal needs. The justifications that Islamic economics offers in support of its prescriptions—charge just prices, pay fair wages,
avoid interest and speculation—always reflect a concern for balancing
individual needs against those of society.[49] The communalist economic
morality of Islam has had, of course, its counterparts in other religions,
including Christianity. But in the centuries leading up to the Industrial
Revolution, expanding segments of Christendom moved away from communalism and toward individualism.[50] As Ülgener and others observe, the
moral transformation that accompanied the rise of European capitalism
essentially bypassed the Islamic world. This observation does not, of
course, explain the divergence in economic performance. Insofar as moral
transformation supports economic development, studies that identify a
static worldview uncover a symptom of underdevelopment, but without
specifying the underlying causal mechanism. In essence, they identify stability without accounting for its source.

Ossification of Muslim Perceptions and Knowledge

İnalcık's observations concerning the Ottoman economic mind, like those
of Ülgener, raise the further question of why this mentality long remained
impervious to the mounting evidence of Ottoman decline relative to Europe. When a civilization that has enjoyed military, political, and economic dominance starts falling behind, one expects it to produce diagnoses. Indeed, in the seventeenth and eighteenth centuries increasing
numbers of Muslims wrote about the reality and causes of the Islamic
world's descent. Bernard Lewis shows that, with few exceptions, they
saw Europe's advantages as consisting basically of superior weaponry.[51]
Practically none showed awareness of the new economic values and institutions that were undergirding Europe's growing military superiority. Accordingly, the major Muslim-led governments hired Westerners to provide
guidance on military modernization, but for a long time they made little
effort to understand Western society, culture, or economic practices. Until
well into the nineteenth century, reports Lewis, "not a single work of
economic content was translated into Arabic, Persian, or Turkish."[52]

Not that Muslim observers of the Islamic world's decline ignored economic problems. Among the factors they commonly identified as contributors to economic enfeeblement were corruption, favoritism, oppression,
greed, and high taxes. Such problems had arisen, most felt, because values
and institutions supportive of past glories had eroded. The appropriate

remedy was to rediscover, reinvigorate, and reinstitute the structures that had once proven effective. In contrast to Europe, where incumbent social institutions were being challenged in the name of progress, until well into the nineteenth century the Islamic world produced no major movements pursuing radical social change.[53]

In interpreting such findings, Lewis finds no fault with the essence of Islam. "There is nothing in Islamic doctrine," he writes, "to oppose economic progress, though there is much in the social and legal practices of Muslims that needs careful reconsideration from this point of view."[54] He then lists a series of moral transformations that were essential for the Islamic world to regain economic dynamism: changes would have been helpful, for example, in views of generosity and meanness, in rankings of professional status, and in attitudes toward enterprise, experiment, and originality. The traditional values that Lewis treats as obstacles to development overlap with those advanced by Ülgener and İnalcık. Mistrust of novelty is central to İnalcık's explanation of economic decline, and the low status of merchants is key to Ülgener's explanation. But the thrust of Lewis's argument extends beyond the identification of growth-inhibiting values and practices. The Muslim observers of the decline generally made poor diagnoses of the ongoing trends, he observes, and they failed to identify the social structures driving Europe's economic advances.

For Lewis, then, the persistence of stabilizing structures was a symptom of decline, not a basic cause. It was rooted in the ossification of Muslim perceptions. Most Muslim observers appreciated at least some of the material products of Europe's transformation; in addition to weaponry, many took an interest in shipbuilding techniques and new medicines. But they could neither imagine major socioeconomic reforms nor appreciate the factors responsible for a steady stream of useful innovations abroad. What explains the perceptual rigidity? In particular, why did it take centuries for Muslims to recognize the limitations of their prevailing social structures in relation to the evolving ones of Europe? The main barrier, Lewis argues, lay in a system of education that taught people a finite set of information, rather than how to "use their own judgment, exercise their critical faculties, and decide things for themselves."[55] More so than in Europe, schools made students memorize facts and venerate classic books, so their graduates saw knowledge as something to be acquired rather than discovered and expanded. The scientific method, which relies on observation and experiment, was essentially absent—a claim supported by the earlier-mentioned time trend of path-breaking Muslim contributions to science. Also significant is the lack of curiosity about Europe, which contrasts sharply with European curiosity about the Middle East. By the end of the eighteenth century, Lewis reports, Europeans had produced ninety-five books on Arabic, Persian, or Turkish grammar, along with twenty-one dictionaries. Yet, "for an Arab, a Persian, or a Turk, not a single grammar or dictionary of any Western language existed either in manuscript or in print. It was not until well into the nineteenth century that we find any attempt to produce grammars and dictionaries of Western languages for Middle Eastern users."[56]

Did Islam contribute to shaping the educational system that limited curiosity and innovation? Lewis answers in the affirmative.[57] In early Islam scholars, jurists, and theologians more or less freely developed answers to problems that scripture and tradition left unresolved. Their innovations helped sustain an internal engine of growth, and they also contributed to the fluidity of Muslim worldviews. Somewhere between the ninth and eleventh centuries, however, freedom of innovation ended when it was declared that independent judgment was no longer permissible—when, in the traditional formulation, "the gate of *ijtihād*" was closed. This closure meant that all answers were already available and that, therefore, one needed merely to follow and obey. In treating Islamic learning as having attained perfection and the Islamic world as self-sufficient, it gave legitimacy to values, attitudes, and practices that promoted stability and discouraged inquisitiveness. It also helped support an educational system that emphasized rote learning and memorization at the expense of problem solving.[58]

Like the works of Ülgener and İnalcık, those of Lewis are rich in relevant historical observations, and they provide critical insights into the forces behind the Islamic world's economic decline. And they, too, refute Rodinson's popular thesis that this decline is attributable simply to political structures. They suggest, on the contrary, that private preferences and private knowledge, not just their politically shaped public manifestations, contributed to the observed trends. As Joel Mokyr observes, the tendency to discount the importance of desires and mentalities is common to much contemporary historical thinking on the performance of civilizations; it is hardly limited to scholarship on Islam.[59] Yet Lewis's insights, however relevant and valuable, do not sketch a model that would satisfy a social scientist. Why was it acceptable to end independent judgment? Why did the malcontents within Muslim communities—as in any society, they existed—not see it as a source of their problems? What, precisely, restrained the impulses of Muslims who stood to gain from introducing one innovation or another? Granting that the prevailing educational system must have limited inquisitiveness and innovation, it could not have extinguished new ideas or the desire for change. A full model of the obstacles to the Islamic world's quick economic recovery must explain why potential innovators, few as they may have been, were unable to overthrow a system that blocked their ambitions. It must also provide the mechanism that kept Muslims who came in contact with Western Europe from appreciating the huge transformations underway.

I shall propose some of the missing links in the essay's final section, which will attempt also to reconcile various observations discussed in earlier sections. But first I turn to an additional version of the economic disadvantage thesis, one that finds the Islamic world's relative economic decline rooted in its communalist culture.

COMMUNALISM

In discussing Ülgener's argument, we encountered the observation that Islamic civilization remained largely communalist even as Western Europe turned increasingly individualist. Ülgener is by no means the first to sense the economic implications of this cultural divergence. In the waning days of the Ottoman Empire many reformers saw the West's individualism as the key to its dynamism. A leading Turkish Westernizer lauded "Anglo-Saxon culture" for its "spirit of individual liberty and enterprise," its "sense of individual authority and responsibility," and its emphasis on "the individual's dignity and integrity."[60] For their part, the opponents of Westernization counted individualism among the Western traits to be discouraged. Even as they admired Western science, they insisted on Islam's moral, social, and political superiority. To overcome economic backwardness, they argued, Muslims needed only to regain their unity, revive their communal links, and rediscover the essence of Islam; to adopt Western individualism would be to trade a perfect religion for a human-designed, and thus inferior, moral system.

Both sides in the struggle over Westernization understood, then, that it would promote individualism at the expense of communalism. The essence of communalism is that one's rights and duties spring from one's status in the community; "good" is the common good of society, which is generally small and considered self-contained. By contrast, individualism provides broad personal freedoms concerning activities, occupations, beliefs, and responsibilities; and, in approving of self-determined thought and conduct, it seeks to create the conditions that maximize the enjoyment of such freedoms.[61] Both individualism and communalism are present in every society, and many individuals feel their pull simultaneously: people who behave as individualists in market competition often act as communalists within their own households. Yet, the relative powers of these moralities vary across time, across individuals, and across civilizations.[62] Communalism was a stronger force in medieval France than it is in modern France; and at present it is more potent in the Middle East than in Europe.

The most rigorous attempt to explain how the moralities of communalism and individualism influence economic development bears the signature of Avner Greif.[63] Greif's fundamental insight is that a society's dominant morality shapes its "cultural beliefs," which are its members' expectations with respect to actions that other members will take in specific contingencies. Individualism and communalism give rise to different cultural beliefs and, hence, different trading patterns.[64] Within a society where communalism dominates, dishonest merchants quickly develop an unfavorable reputation because of the closeness of their interpersonal relations; and they endure large costs because of heavy communal participation in efforts to punish them. To protect the value of their assets they remain honest, except when the temptation to cheat is huge. By contrast, in a society whose dominant morality is individualism merchants carry no personal responsibility for enforcing social values; hence, the stick of communal punishment is too light to ensure trust among merchants. The critical consequence is that established merchants are tempted to take advantage of one another under a wider set of contingencies. These differences have far-reaching implications concerning business relations. Under communalism, the prevalence of trust usually makes merchants hire one another as their partners or agents. Under individualism, they commonly hire nonmerchants, even people from outside their own community. In each of these cases, the underlying cultural beliefs are self-sustaining under a broad set of conditions.

From this simple logic, Greif derives several implications that shed light on the economic evolution of two groups of medieval merchants: Genoese traders from the Latin and increasingly individualist part of the Mediterranean basin, and Maghribi traders from the Muslim-dominated and steadily communalist part. The latter group, while Jewish, shared the communalist values of the Muslims among whom they lived, which makes the contrast relevant to our concerns here. Greif's argument would make one expect Genoese society to exhibit relatively greater upward mobility, to display greater division of labor, and to enjoy stronger incentives to refine contract law, improve the efficiency of the courts, and promote standardization.

All these implications are borne out by surviving records. They are consistent, moreover, with the emergence of capitalism in Europe rather than in the Islamic world. The rise of European capitalism was preceded, Franz-Xaver Kaufmann observes, by several social mastertrends: a lengthening of chains of action through a growing capability to control complex networks of production, administration, research, and mass communication; the transformation of legitimate political power from absolute dominance to the rule of law; and the metamorphosis of religion through the secularization of various domains.[65] Like many other scholars, Kaufmann traces the origins of these mastertrends to the tenth and eleventh centuries. The significance of Greif's contribution lies in its demonstration of how the mastertrends might have resulted from variations in commercial patterns, rooted themselves in an earlier divergence in cultural beliefs.

Generations of economic historians have noted that after the first few centuries of Islam commercial relations between Europe and the Middle East grew mainly at the initiative of the Europeans.[66] Although recent research has discredited the extreme view that Muslims played a consistently passive role in European-Middle Eastern trade,[67] no one seriously doubts that Europeans increasingly dominated these economic relations. Trade between these two regions was conducted mostly by European companies—a pattern that holds even today. Greif's insights offer an explanation for this pattern: merchants from individualistic cultures are relatively better prepared for cross-cultural trade, because they are less dependent on communal bonds and already accustomed to forming agency relations with people outside their own social circles. Significantly, various Muslim-ruled states—Spain, Egypt, Syria, Persia, the Seljuk sultanates, the Ottoman Empire—extended unilateral privileges to traders from European countries as early as the twelfth century. Muslim governments offered "capitulations," as the concessions came to be known, even as they conquered European-held territories and gained control over maritime trade routes. While commentators have tended to attribute the capitulations to political considerations,[68] Greif's logic would assign a more basic role to economic factors rooted in cultural differences. Yet another pattern that this logic illuminates is the contrast between regional trade patterns. Intra-European trade expanded much more rapidly than trade within the Islamic world, essentially through the support of institutions fostered by individualism. Given that trade contributes to growth, the result was a growing disparity in living standards.

The gist of Greif's argument is that communalism hampered modern economic development. It obviously calls into question the thesis that Max Weber developed in the *Protestant Ethic and the Spirit of Capitalism*.[69] Weber's view, which traces the origins of capitalism to the ideological creativity of the Protestant Reformation, was quickly challenged. For example R. H. Tawney showed that the basic institutions of capitalism were already in place by the time of Europe's great religious upheaval of the sixteenth century.[70] While Tawney's observations imply that capitalist institutions preceded and created the capitalist spirit, Greif's argument resurrects the reverse causation. It differs from Weber's classic work, however, in tracing the genesis of the capitalist spirit to a period at least half a millennium before the Reformation.

Two possible objections merit consideration. Does this argument not clash, one might wonder, with the important, even dominant, role that

142 • Chapter Six

Muslims have played in building trade relations outside Europe? In fostering extensive trade networks in sub-Saharan Africa and East Asia, Muslims have indeed helped establish the institutional foundations for long-distance trade in regions economically more primitive than the Muslim-ruled Middle East. Their contributions have included the introduction of economic regulations into places previously without written laws, and the spread of Arabic as a commercial lingua franca—a facilitator of communication, and thus exchange, among regions previously segregated by linguistic differences.[71] These observations do not conflict with the Islamic world's disadvantages relative to Western Europe. Although Muslims made major contributions to the development and dissemination of individual contract law, they left the development of corporate contract law to Europe. Likewise, after instituting rules to regulate interpersonal credit, they let Western Europe develop the institutional framework for modern banking. For reasons already outlined, this passing of the torch of institutional creativity put Muslims at a disadvantage in their relations with the West. However, it need not have hampered their relations with regions where economic institutions were even less developed than those of the Middle East. Just as a moderately experienced chess player might lose to a master and proceed to beat a novice, Muslim traders could succumb to competition from European traders without losing their dominance in other parts of the world.

The second possible objection concerns the social merits of civic ties. Is it not the case that economically advanced regions exhibit more participation in communal activities than impoverished areas? And might this discredit the notion that communalism constitutes an economic handicap? Robert Putnam's work on Italy's regional inequalities does indeed show that civic community is more developed in the prosperous north than in the relatively backward south.[72] It also demonstrates, however, that the northern civic community is characterized by overlapping social networks: individuals typically belong to many associations, within each of which their interpersonal ties tend to be weak. By contrast, civic engagement is more limited in the south, where cooperation is generally based on strong kinship ties. The difference reflects the legal system's greater effectiveness in the north than in the south, where the absence of a state able to enforce laws and contracts sustains the Mafia.

The most relevant implication is that individualism promotes growth not by breaking social ties but, rather, by weakening and diversifying them. Its economic advantages work through the proliferation of associations, the generation of overlapping memberships, and the expansion of individual choice in the matter of civic participation. The limits of communalism, as evidenced by the strength of kinship ties in southern Italy, lie in their prevention of networks of civic engagement that cut across social cleavages. Strong ties based on blood bonds sustain cooperation within small groups, whereas weak ties that link nonrelatives nourish wider cooperation and sustain greater social complexity.

Putnam's findings on Italy do not, then, refute Greif's argument. They do indicate, however, that the effects of individualism and communalism work through channels that extend well beyond cooperative arrangements among merchants. Despite this limitation, Greif's argument affords an explanation that is more complete than any other explanation discussed thus far. In particular, it defines two separate equilibria, one sustaining the dominant cultural belief of Western Europe and another preserving that of the Islamic world. Of course, it leaves unexplained the origins of the economically potent cultural differences. But all social analysis has an essentially arbitrary starting point, and to think that the seeds of today's civilizational differences can be identified precisely would be to succumb to the fallacy of absolute priority. For a more reasonable criticism, the argument leaves unexplained why, until about a century ago, the Islamic world produced no diagnoses of the growth-retarding effects of its cultural beliefs. Why did ambitious Muslims, seeing the obstacles to their economic advancement, not recognize the ideological source of their disadvantages? Why did rulers threatened by the rise of Western Europe fail to appreciate the economic disadvantages of their communalist cultures? Why, in the face of mounting competition from Europe, did Muslim merchants lack solutions to their economic losses? The essay's final section proposes certain tentative answers.

THE ROLE OF PUBLIC DISCOURSE

There is an element missing from all variants of the economic disadvantage thesis, although it is implicit in that of Bernard Lewis: the connection between, on one hand, public discourse concerning economic institutions, policies, and possibilities, and, on the other, private understandings. To specify this connection, one must identify the social mechanisms through which public discourse gets formed and maintained; and one must then explore how public discourse shapes individual perceptions, information, and knowledge. These steps would connect some of the diverse insights presented in previous sections. They would also make sense of why Muslims with everything to gain from social reforms remained, for the most part and for many centuries, essentially wedded to the social status quo.

The relevant mechanisms are developed in my book *Private Truths, Public Lies*, though within a general context rather than the particular one of Islamic civilization.[73] It shows how inefficient social structures can survive indefinitely when people privately supportive of change refrain from publicizing their dispositions. The motivation for such *preference falsification* is the desire to avoid the punishments that commonly fall on individuals who enunciate unpopular public positions. One of its by-products is the corruption of public discourse. This is because individuals choosing to misrepresent their personal wishes will also, to keep others from seeing through the falsification, conceal their perceptions and knowledge pointing to the desirability of change. It follows that unpopular structures sustained through preference falsification might, if the condition lasts long enough, achieve increasingly genuine acceptance. The transformation would occur partly through population renewal: in the absence of criticisms of the status quo, the society's new members would fail to discover why change might be beneficial. The argument applies to both the privileged and the underprivileged. If public discourse treats a social structure as optimal, even its victims may fail to see how its destruction would improve their lives.

Social pressures nourished by preference falsification do not necessarily retard economic growth. Such pressures can stimulate growth by keeping public opinion favorable to policies and institutions supportive of production, innovation, and trade. By the same token, they might harm growth if it is people with economically sound ideas, rather than ones with economically hazardous ideas, who find it prudent to keep their thoughts to themselves. The argument does not presuppose the existence of individuals either privately or publicly committed to doing social damage. People may induce others to engage in preference falsification simply to protect their own narrow interests or out of fear that free debate would weaken social solidarity. If sufficiently many people have reasons to limit debate on a social matter, the resulting social pressures will keep others from speaking honestly; and the consequent preference falsification will then induce preference falsification on the part of others. Such a bandwagon effect can result in an equilibrium under which preferences and ideas inimical to the status quo remain unexpressed. Once established, of course, an equilibrium can outlast the individuals whose self-censorship helped put it in place. Later generations may refrain from challenging the public consensus either because the prevailing social pressures make this imprudent or because the consensus itself limits their awareness of potential improvements to the social order. Either way, individuals would help retard growth inadvertently through their support of policies and institutions that happen to limit economic development.

Armed with additional concepts, let us now return to the insight that individualist societies enjoyed an advantage with respect to modern economic development. This insight raises the question of whether the members of communalist societies understood the economic limitations of their cultures. As we saw, Bernard Lewis's work on the Muslim observers of the Islamic world's stagnation shows that before the nineteenth century not even the educated demonstrated much appreciation for cultural sources of the West's unfolding strengths. Until that time, the Islamic world's communalist practices enjoyed almost total public support; although individuals routinely behaved in ways that violated certain communalist precepts, they rarely challenged the merits of communalist principles. One reason was probably that individuals favoring cultural reforms tended to conceal their wishes, lest they be accused of harboring animosity to Islam. The "closure of the gate of *ijtihād*" and the paucity of scientific research after the thirteenth century both point to an intellectual environment inhospitable to the open and honest exchange of ideas. In preserving their own reputations, individuals opting to hide their views would have impoverished public discourse. They would also have compounded the social obstacles to seeing and appreciating alternatives to the cultural status quo.

When the once-flourishing Islamic craft guilds encountered competition from superior yet cheaper European goods, their response was generally to seek the restoration of their noncompetitive, fraternal, and rather egalitarian traditions. Economic innovations thus took place initially outside the guilds, and guildsmen eager to adapt new technologies found that they could do so more easily within new economic structures.[74] One reason why exit became a common course of action on the part of change-oriented guildsmen is that those seeking to alter guild practices often suffered social sanctions. A result of these sanctions was to impoverish public discourse on the guilds' mounting problems, thus breeding ignorance about possible solutions and blocking reform-oriented collective action. These observations are in line with Ülgener's observations on the persistently low social status of merchants relative to that of craftsmen. The potential beneficiaries of steps to make the social atmosphere more hospitable to merchants were in the grip of an ideology hostile to free competition. The ideology owed its durability partly to protections against public challenges. In Europe, of course, the guilds behaved similarly. The relevant difference is that policies to protect the guilds enjoyed less public support there than they did in the Middle East.

The traditional educational system played a critical role, as the works of Berkes show, in conditioning individuals to accept the social status quo as optimal. That system could not easily be challenged, for its religious content allowed educational reform to be associated with hostility to Islam. Indeed, public discourse was highly inimical to altering the traditional curriculum; and the very rarity of dissent discouraged potential reformers from speaking up, thus reproducing the incentives against honest curricular debate. At least in relation to primary education, this equilibrium held until the twentieth century, letting foreign-established schools become the primary agents of instructional reform. What about the delays in educational innovation in contexts more or less free of social pressures against change? Although the special economic factors invoked by Berkes were doubtless relevant, these delays could also have arisen as the by-product of an impoverished intellectual atmosphere. The very factors that kept schools wedded to memorization produced graduates with poorly developed critical faculties. Such graduates would have had a low demand for books.

The foregoing interpretation amounts to saying that the relative openness of the West's public discourse created an engine of growth that the Islamic world, because of its expressive constraints, failed to develop. This failure was noted also, as we saw, by İnalcık and Ibn Khaldun. What the present perspective adds to their insights is the identification of a mechanism to account for the delay in such an engine's emergence. The new ideas that form an engine of growth emerge in environments hospitable to free inquiry and experimentation. If it is unduly costly to put forth new ideas, these will not get expressed, making it all the more risky for other potential innovators to step forward. The hallmarks of the resulting equilibrium will thus be an apparent commitment to tradition. And a by-product of the equilibrium will be a decline in analytical and critical skills, accompanied by reduced receptivity to change.

The argument of this final section does not presuppose that Islam is inherently inimical to economic development. A society's dominant interpretation of Islam can vary over time and space depending on the dynamics of public discourse. The content of public discourse can be fluid, as it was in the early centuries of Islam—a period of intercultural exchanges and intellectual vitality. It can also freeze, however, as one interpretation becomes sufficiently dominant to silence its rivals. The static worldviews promoted in the name of Islam proved remarkably durable precisely because their broad public acceptance made it risky to promote dynamic alternatives. The equilibrium in question helped keep the Islamic world from responding effectively to the challenges posed by Europe's economic ascent. Ultimately, therefore, it became self-destroying. Indeed, in helping to weaken the Islamic world militarily and economically, it invited Western intervention, which, in turn, brought Muslims in steady contact with modern European thought. The old ideological equilibrium of the Islamic world has now given way to many competing visions. No one knows where the current ideological ferment will lead. It is unlikely, however, that worldviews of the kind that Renan and Cromer found so inimical to economic progress will regain dominance.

Underlying the economic irrelevance thesis, we have seen, is the observation that widely held Islamic precepts were frequently circumvented. This well-documented divergence between word and deed is a form of preference falsification. Rodinson and Jones are correct that it limited the intended effects of economically unsound religious regulations. They overlook, however, the unintended effects of pretending to approve of such regulations. Public discourse gets corrupted, making it difficult to diagnose economic problems correctly. In Europe, the Church debated the distinctions between usury and interest and, from the twelfth century onward, the scholastic literature accepted and codified them. This recognition contributed to the growing sophistication of economic discourse. For instance, concepts such as risk and opportunity cost came to be invoked with increasing frequency.[75] Within Islamic discourse, meanwhile, interest generally continued to be equated with usury. While this did not stop individual Muslims from taking and giving what a modern economist would label interest, it undoubtedly stunted the development of economic thought within the Islamic world.

Another problem with the economic irrelevance thesis is that it ignores the logic of collective action. Unlike the circumvention of rules on personal behavior, that of social policies requires collective action, which the very availability of preference falsification can block. In practice, therefore, individuals can more easily circumvent rules on personal behavior than they can social policies. And rules on personal behavior get altered through internal pressures more readily than do social policies, which are more likely to require the assistance of external forces. In line with these implications, interest bans were regularly circumvented; rules governing the traditional curriculum were not. The impetus for changing the educational curriculum came largely from abroad.

A full-blown account of the relationship between Islam and economic development remains to be constructed. As we have seen, however, certain components of the required research have already been undertaken. The diverse insights need to be integrated more fully, of course, than has been possible here. Moreover, they need to be refined by accounting for variations across time, space, and social position in the conditions Muslims faced and the responses they made. Attention to such variations might provide additional clues to the significance of the factors highlighted in this essay—political structure, communalism, public discourse, and Islam itself. It might suggest, moreover, how the Islamic world's long economic decline could have been prevented.

Stop

Notes

PREFACE

1. Hobsbawm and Ranger, eds. (1992).
2. Udovitch (1962).
3. Kuran (2001) and Yediyıldız (1990).
4. *Islamic Economics Bulletin* (2002), p. 2. On the tensions between Pakistani rhetoric and practices, see also Shaukat Ali (2000).
5. Holden and Johns (1981), chaps. 16–18; al-Yassini (1985), esp. chap. 6.
6. Organization for Economic Co-operation and Development (1983), chap. 4.
7. On changes in the performance of the zakat system, see Kuran (2003a), and on those of Islam's commercial regulations, Kuran (2003b).
8. United Nations Development Programme (2002).
9. Huntington (1993).

CHAPTER ONE
THE ECONOMIC IMPACT OF ISLAMISM

1. For further details, see Iqbal (1984), chap. 10.
2. Moore (1988).
3. For a sympathetic survey of this literature and a useful, though dated, bibliography, see M. N. Siddiqi (1981). Among the influential contributions in English are Mannan (1970), K. Ahmad, ed. (1980b), Naqvi (1981a), Ahmed, Iqbal, and Khan, eds. (1983a), Ahmed, Iqbal, and Khan, eds. (1983b), and Khan and Mirakhor, eds. (1987).
4. "Announcement on Research Proposals" (1983).
5. For a sampling of Ibn Khaldun's writings, see Ibn Khaldun (1950/1987).
6. A representative economic work by Mawdudi is *The Economic Problem of Man and Its Islamic Solution* (1947/1975).
7. Qutb's most relevant work is *Social Justice in Islam* (1948/1970). Al-Sadr's masterwork is *Iqtisaduna: Our Economics* (1961/1982–84).
8. See, for instance, Qardawi (1966/1981), chap. 2; Mannan (1970), chap. 3; Mannan (1984b), chap. 5; and Naqvi (1981a), chap. 4.
9. Strictly speaking, only the Sunnis subscribe to this conception of the Golden Age. The Shiites believe that the Islamic social order performed ideally only during the Prophet's lifetime and the five-year tenure of the fourth caliph, Ali.
10. Hussain (1987), p. 14.
11. For the history of this period, see Hodgson (1974), pp. 187–217; and Shaban (1971), chaps. 2–4.
12. See, for example, Chapra (1985), chap. 8.

13. These themes are developed by Marty and Appleby (1991).

14. Detailed critiques of Islamic economics include Rahman (1964), Rahman (1974), Kuran (1983), Pryor (1985), Kuran (1986), Kuran (1989a), and Philipp (1990).

15. S.V.R. Nasr (1988). For references to other statements along these lines, see S.V.R. Nasr (1989), esp. n. 30.

16. M. Ahmad (1991).

17. Bakhash (1989), p. 16.

18. A detailed economic argument in favor of a pan-Islamic union is provided by Choudhury (1989).

19. This is not to say that these banks are hiring exclusively from among the non-Westernized segment of the population. Each has made a point of keeping its ranks open to Westernized bankers, even to non-Muslims from the West.

20. The Islamization of economic life was an issue even before Islamic economics achieved recognition as a discipline. Muhammad Ali Jinnah, Pakistan's founding father, spoke of creating an economy compatible with Islamic teachings. See J. Ahmad, ed. (1952), pp. 565–68.

21. These observations are based on discussions with several politically well-connected Pakistanis. Of course, the act of preference falsification is by no means unique to Pakistan. For a general analysis of the phenomenon and evidence from various times and places, see Kuran (1990).

22. Afzal-ur-Rahman (1980), vol. 3, p. 55.

23. M. N. Siddiqi (1981), p. 63.

24. Ibid.

25. Çizakça (1987).

26. Some of these countries feature only subsidiaries of Islamic banks headquartered elsewhere.

27. As cited by Khan and Mirakhor (1990), table 3.

28. Ibid., table 6.

29. Ingram (1986), pp. 58–60. Other ruses commonly employed to make interest-based loans appear like musharaka are discussed in a report prepared by a group of bank executives for the Permanent Commission on Islamisation of Economy, Pakistan (1988).

30. Çiller and Çizakça (1989), p. 76; and Moore (1990a), pp. 248–49.

31. For a detailed illustration, see Carlson (1986).

32. Ingram (1986), p. 57; and Ariff (1988b), p. 58. The existing practice of rebates is criticized in Permanent Commission on Islamisation of Economy (1988), annex A, pp. 3–4, 10. Interestingly, this report stops short of recommending a ban on rebates, proposing only that income derived from penalties be channeled into welfare activities.

33. See Permanent Commission on Islamisation of the Economy (1988), pp. 2–3. Some bankers, while admitting that Pakistani organizations continue to charge interest, point out that banks no longer earn compound interest.

34. Çiller and Çizakça (1989), p. 77.

35. Allawi (1986).

36. Ceylan (1988). My interviews with Islamic bankers suggest that this practice of risk shifting is common to Islamic banks throughout the world.

37. Islamic Development Bank (1987), pp. xviii–xix. Amazingly, few Islamic economists show an awareness of these statistics. In fact, they continue to characterize the IDB's operations as distinctly "Islamic." As a case in point, Ariff (1988b), p. 48, writes: "The IDB operations are free of interest and are explicitly based on *Shariah* principles."

38. Meenai (1989), esp. chaps. 7–10.

39. I owe this observation to Nienhaus (1986), p. 43.

40. In the early 1990s, the Islamic Development Bank established a new training center in Jeddah.

41. There are no reliable statistics on the extent of dishonesty or fraud. But anyone who has done business in, say, Pakistan, Egypt, or Morocco knows that many more transactions go unreported than in the developed economies of Europe and North America. Significantly, the first *Directory of Islamic Financial Institutions*, John R. Presley, ed. (1988), holds that "shortcomings in business ethics make it difficult to establish closer bank-client relationships." It goes on: "clients either do nor keep adequate records or keep fraudulent records of their operations" (p. 300).

42. See, for instance, W. M. Khan (1989), p. 337. In private conversations, several architects of Pakistan's Islamic banking system have suggested that genuinely Islamic banking must await a major improvement in the "moral fiber" of Pakistanis.

43. Çizakça (1986), sect. 6.

44. Udovitch (1962).

45. For further observations, see Mayer (1985), pp. 36–40.

46. Reversing this interpretation, Islamic economists now claim that although Mit Ghamr was designed according to Islamic principles, the Nasser regime's opposition to Islam forced its founder, Ahmed al-Naggar, to disguise his source of inspiration. Accordingly, the public relations ploy was to package Mit Ghamr as an Egyptian replica of Germany's local savings banks. This interpretation enjoys the endorsement of al-Naggar himself, who went on to become a prominent Islamic banker. See el-Ashker (1987), pp. 155–59.

47. Rahman (1964), pp. 30–37. Many other predominantly agricultural communities operating close to subsistence are known to have restricted interest, particularly on loans to people in distress. Invariably, the rationale has been to bolster the individual's sense of security, thus reinforcing the community's viability. For evidence and an elaborate argument, see Posner (1980).

48. Rahman (1964), esp. pp. 12–30.

49. Rodinson (1966/1973), chap. 3. For evidence on the prevalence of interest in later times, see Mandaville (1979). The Arabic term for ruse is *hīla* (plur., *hiyal*).

50. *Report of the Council of Islamic Ideology on the Elimination of Interest from the Economy* (1980), pp. 15–16. The report refers to murabaha as *bai muajjal*.

51. Presley (1988), p. 300.

52. For the pro-indexation argument, see Mannan (1984a), chap. 14a. The rationale against indexation is developed by Zaman (1985). Z. Ahmed (1989) offers additional references and a critical survey of the relevant arguments.

53. Ariff (1988a), p. 87.

54. I encountered both positions in discussions with Islamist leaders in Pakistan.

55. Uludağ (1988), esp. pp. 287–90.

56. *Economist*, September 16, 1989, p. 42. Similar positions were taken by earlier Egyptian religious leaders of this century. See Mallat (1988).

57. Patel (1986), p. 74. Influential Islamists whom I interviewed in November 1989 cited figures between 95 and 99.9 percent.

58. Moore (1990a), table 2 and pp. 235–42. For some complementary figures pertaining to the early to mid-1980s, see Nienhaus (1988), pp. 24–30.

59. For an English translation of the relevant laws and regulations in Turkey, see *Özel Finans Kurumları ve Türkiye Uygulaması Sempozyomu* (1988), pp. 73–135. An additional advantage enjoyed by Turkey's Islamic banks is that they are permitted to advertise on television, whereas most of their rivals are not. On the privileges granted to the Islamic banks, see Mumcu (1988). Islamic bankers complain that they are denied a major right that their non-Islamic rivals take for granted: a trademark of one's choice. Indeed, Turkey's Islamic banks are barred from identifying themselves as such.

60. Meenai (1989), p. 74, reports that, like the commercial Islamic banks, the Islamic Development Bank made an unusually large number of bad loans in its early years. Moreover, the losses were associated primarily with equity investments. The bank's return on equity was apparently lower even than its modest "service fee" on ordinary loans.

61. Moore (1990b), table 2.

62. M. S. Khan (1987), chap. 2; and Iqbal and Mirakhor (1987).

63. On the al-Rayan crisis, see Springborg (1989), pp. 45–61.

64. Nienhaus (1988), pp. 33–49.

65. On Iran, Iqbal and Mirakhor (1987), p. 25; on Pakistan, Khan and Mirakhor (1987), pp. 370–71.

66. For a comprehensive survey of Islam's traditional means of redistribution, see Zarqa (1988).

67. For traditional expositions, see Afzal-ur-Rahman (1980), vol. 3, chaps. 14–18; and Shad (1986).

68. See, for instance, Oran and Rashid (1989).

69. For explicit statements, see Afzal-ur-Rahman (1980), vol. 3, p. 197; and Shad (1986), p. 100.

70. Rahman (1974), p. 33.

71. For several more or less reformist positions, see Ahmed, Iqbal, and Khan, eds. (1983a), chaps. 1–4.

72. On this controversy, see Tanzil-ur-Rahman (1981), pp. 15–21.

73. Mayer (1986), esp. pp. 67–69, 73–75; and Salama (1982), esp. pp. 349–54. Pakistan's Zakat Ordinance is reproduced in Tanzil-ur-Rahman (1981), pp. 27–85. The ordinance has been amended several times.

74. Salleh and Ngah (1980), esp. pp. 81–84.

75. *Pakistan Statistical Yearbook* (1989), pp. 451–52, 507.

76. Salama (1982), table 1.

77. Ibid., p. 351.

78. Ghazali et al. (1995), p. 49.

79. Mustapha (1987), p 57. The figure excludes *zakat al-fitr*, which is paid by most practicing Muslims at the end of the month of Ramadan. It amounts to about U.S. $1 per person.

80. Salleh and Ngah (1980), pp. 86–110.

81. Scott (1987), pp. 426–27.

82. Thirteen countries have enacted zakat laws or regulations. But as a practical matter, in most of these countries the payment of zakat remains voluntary. See al-Omar (1995).

83. Schacht (1934).

84. See M.A.S. Siddiqi (1983), chaps. 4–5.

85. Sabzwari (1979).

86. Permanent Commission on Islamisation of Economy, Pakistan (1988), p. 4.

87. Hamitoğulları (1988).

88. Scott (1985), pp. 121–22, 169–78.

89. For further details, see the Zakat and ʿUshr Ordinance, reprinted in Tanzil-ur-Rahman (1981). The disbursement system is also described by Clark (1986), pp. 83–91.

90. *Pakistan Statistical Yearbook* (1989), pp. 453–59.

91. Clark (1986), p. 89.

92. Permanent Commission on Islamisation of Economy, Pakistan (1988), p. 5.

93. Ibid., pp. 5–6.

94. Various irregularities are documented in a report prepared by Zahid (1989) for the World Bank. According to a small survey included in this report, the official roster of zakat recipients includes poor people who deny having received assistance.

95. Clark (1986), p. 90.

96. *Dawn* (Karachi), November 11, 1989.

97. Scott (1987), p. 433.

98. Mustapha (1987), pp. 60–62.

99. Ibid., p. 62.

100. Ibid., pp. 63–64.

101. Scott (1987), pp. 433–34.

102. *New Straits Times* (Kuala Lumpur), March 6, 1990.

103. Mayer (1986), p. 69.

104. Official figures in the *Pakistan Statistical Yearbook* (1989), pp. 453–59, show that in the 1980–88 period 8.6 percent of the disbursements went to religious education.

105. Scott (1986), pp. 431–32.

106. See Kurin (1986), pp. 123–24.

107. Tanzil-ur-Rahman (1981), p. 9.

108. Ghazali et al. (1995), pp. 47–48 and table 13.

109. The Shiites base their objection on a precedent set by rebellious early Islamic tribes that refused to pay zakat to the first caliph, considered by Shiites a usurper. See Morad (1988), pp. 120–22.

110. Patel (1986), pp. 63–64.

111. On Pakistan, see Mayer (1986), p. 64; on Malaysia, see Scott (1987), pp. 431–35.

112. Zarqa (1988), pp. 201–2.

113. For a highly influential argument to this effect, see Weber (1922/1968). Weber's scattered remarks on Islam are synthesized and critiqued by Turner (1974).

114. These injunctions are discussed in detail by Chapra (1970), Abdul-Rauf (1979), Naqvi (1981a), and S. H. Nasr (1985).

115. Afzal-ur-Rahman (1980), p. 47.

116. For other examples, see M. N. Siddiqi (1972), pp. 57–60.

117. See, for instance, Husaini (1980), pp. 79–81.

118. Atalay (1987), p. 97.

119. K. Ahmad (1980), p. 178. For additional such statements and many more references, see Al-Buraey (1985), Ghazali (1990), and Sadeq (1990).

120. See, for instance, Naqvi (1981a), esp. p. 63. On the finer points of this view, see S.V.R. Nasr (1987).

121. Hayek (1988), pp. 45–47. The quote, recorded by Hayek, belongs to David Hume. On Hayek's views concerning the basis of modern civilization, see the remainder of this book, esp. chaps. 1–5. A more detailed presentation may be found in his 1973–79 trilogy, *Law, Legislation and Liberty*.

122. This is not to suggest the absence of countercurrents that conflict with Aristotelian perceptions. From the very beginning, Islamic philosophy has featured traditions that glorify the market, commerce, and the trader. See B. Lewis (1970), pp. 78–92. But to this day these traditions have failed to generate a sustained overt reaction against Islam's communitarian vision.

123. As an example of the former class, see Naqvi (1981b), chaps. 4–5; for the latter, see Chapra (1970), pt. 2. A detailed comparison is offered by Behdad (1989).

124. Bakhash (1987), p. 113. The debate in question took place in 1984.

125. Ibid.

126. Hirschman (1968).

127. Tawney (1926/1962).

CHAPTER TWO
ISLAMIC ECONOMICS AND THE ISLAMIC SUBECONOMY

1. For extensive bibliographies, see M. N. Siddiqi (1981) and Islamic Research and Training Institute (1993).

2. For a compilation of his most influential economic writings, see Mawdudi (1947/1975). Ahmad and Ansari (1979) have interpreted these views, and S.V.R. Nasr (1994) has studied the social and intellectual contexts in which they emerged.

3. Rahman (1964) and Rodinson (1966/1973).

4. Posner (1980).

5. See, for instance, Afzal-ur-Rahman (1980) and Chapra (1992).

6. Cowen and Kroszner (1990).

7. Ismail (1990).

8. Afzal-ur-Rahman (1980), vol. 3; and Ahmed, Iqbal, and Khan, eds. (1983b).
9. M. N. Siddiqi (1972), Naqvi (1981a), and Chapra (1992).
10. Kuran (1983).
11. Al-Sadr (1961/1982–84) and Chapra (1992).
12. The Al-Baraka group and Dār al-Māl al-Islāmī.
13. Ray (1995).
14. Moore (1990a) and R. Wilson (1990).
15. The magnitudes reflect inflation, which over the period covered hovered around 60 percent per annum.
16. Çizakça (1993).
17. Brown (1994).
18. Kahf (1995).
19. Kuran (1993b).
20. See ibid. for evidence from several countries. Novossyolov (1993) offers additional evidence from Pakistan.
21. See Sullivan (1994) for an analysis of Egyptian private associations that deliver services to the poor, including many associations that do so in the name of Islam.
22. The motives for making zakat payments have included, in addition to charity and religious duty, the encouragement of worker loyalty and the promotion of social conformity.
23. Mustapha (1987), Zahid (1989), Permanent Commission on Islamisation of Economy (1988), Kuran (1993b), and Novossyolov (1993).
24. Ghazali et al. (1995) and Mohammad (1995).
25. Kuran (1989a).
26. Erbakan (1991).
27. Behdad (1994a).
28. Qaddafi (1976–79/1980).
29. Vandewalle (1991).
30. El-Ashker (1987).
31. Rushton (1980).
32. Williamson (1985).
33. Kuran (1997).
34. A few Islamic economists, notably Naqvi (1981a), are sympathetic to this criticism. Characterizing the prevalent methodology as seriously flawed, they wish to reconstruct Islamic economics on the basis of axioms drawn from the Qur'an. The axiomatic approach enjoys little acceptance, however, partly because the diversity of opinion within Islamic economics allows both theoreticians and policy makers to adapt to virtually any exigency without stepping outside Islamic discourse. The diversity did indeed prove useful to the wider Islamic movement when, prior to the Iranian Revolution, economic controversies within the Iranian wing of Islamic thought allowed the Ayatollah Khomeini to appear at once as an egalitarian redistributionist to the poor and as a defender of property rights to the rich (Behdad 1994a).
35. Khan and Mirakhor (1987).
36. Çizakça (1993).
37. M. N. Siddiqi (1994).

CHAPTER THREE
ISLAMISM AND ECONOMICS: POLICY PRESCRIPTIONS FOR A FREE SOCIETY

1. Here I generally use the last of these terms, mainly for simplicity. The first two are just as meaningful. As al-Azm (1993), p. 97, points out, every Islamist group "is convinced that it is in the process not only of going back to the basics and fundamentals of Islam, but of reviving them as well, after a long period of, let us say, hibernation. They are reviving them as active beliefs and efficacious practices in the lives of people."

2. Mumcu (1987), pp. 171–96; and Mumcu (1988), pp. 48–50, 151–53. A militant Islamist captured by the Turkish police in early 1996 provided evidence implicating the Iranian government. Turkish-Iranian relations worsened dramatically following the revelations, and the Turkish government considered military reprisals. See *Hürriyet*, March 12, 1996, and later dates.

3. *Economist*, August 7, 1993, p. 57.

4. These ideals are defended and qualified by Hayek (1973–79).

5. See, for instance, Kuran (1986), pp. 152–54.

6. Few people without training in economics worry about the financial feasibility or desirability of Islamic banking.

7. Ayubi (1991), chap. 8, esp. p. 192.

8. Influential contributions include Mannan (1970) and Chapra (1992).

9. *Economist*, January 18, 1992, p. 33.

10. For a survey of these and related developments, see Kuran (1993b).

11. Rodinson (1966/1973).

12. The term refers to the practitioners of Islamic economics, who represent a small minority of all economists of the Muslim faith.

13. R. Ahmed (1994), pp. 688–89.

14. Mawdudi (1940/1990), p. 115 (translation edited).

15. For related points, see Kuran (1996).

16. The timing of the first practical application of Islamic banking was influenced by the restructuring of the international oil market in the early 1970s. Much of the initial capital came from oil-rich Arab states seeking politically acceptable ways to recirculate their mushrooming petrodollars.

17. Ayubi (1991), pp. 188–89.

18. For several instructive case studies, see el-Ashker (1987), chap. 11. These studies provide information on the cosmetic aspects of Islamic establishments; they provide few insights into actual practices, suggesting that el-Ashker noticed nothing unusual or worth reporting.

19. M. N. Siddiqi (1972) and Naqvi (1981a).

20. Rashwan and Gad (1993).

21. Murphy (1992).

22. A similar argument is advanced by Baker (1990), chap. 8.

23. Gürsoy-Tezcan (1991).

24. Reed (1988), pp. 2–4.

25. Based on a discussion with Mursi Saad El-Din, Cairo, August 2, 1993. For many complementary observations, see Sullivan (1994).

26. *Cumhuriyet*, July 10, 1993, pp. 1, 15; and August 7, 1993, pp. 1, 17.

27. Kuran (1993b), pp. 318–25.

28. *Cumhuriyet*, July 19, 1993, pp. 1, 15.

29. Such financing occurs largely through informal channels. See Hyman (1987), pp. 11, 19–20.

30. Roberts (1994).

31. For the underlying logic, see Kuran (1995a), chaps. 15–18.

32. M. Ahmad (1991), pp. 474–79.

33. R. Ahmed (1994), p. 687.

34. Williamson (1985) and Etzioni (1988), chap. 12.

35. For the underlying logic, see Rowley, Tollison, and Tullock, eds. (1988).

36. Such incentives arise wherever the legal system is weak. In southern Italy, Gambetta (1993) demonstrates, they fueled the rise of the Mafia.

37. On the general phenomenon, see Elster (1993), chap. 3.

38. Information provided by Tahseen Basheer, in a Cairo interview, August 3, 1993.

39. Ayubi (1991), chap. 2.

40. Saraçgil (1993) and Sullivan (1994), pp. 58–63.

41. Rahnema and Nomani (1990), chap. 3; and Behdad (1989).

42. For further examples of such divisions, see Kuran (1993b) and Kuran (1995b).

43. For a comparative overview, see Kuran (1993a).

44. Rahnema and Nomani (1990), chap. 4.

45. Ibid., p. 296.

46. Bhagwati (1988).

47. Rowley, Tollison, and Tullock, eds. (1988).

48. Chenery (1979) and Papageorgiou, Michaely, and Choksi, eds. (1991).

49. Behdad (1994b) and Amuzegar (1992).

50. Rahman (1982) and B. Lewis (1982).

51. Mokyr (1990).

52. Olson (1982) develops the underlying logic.

53. Iannaccone (1993).

54. Coulson (1969), Saleh (1986), and Kuran (1989a).

55. The logic that underlies this observation is developed at length in Kuran (1995a).

56. Moore (1990a); Kazarian (1991), p. 149; Ağaoğlu (1994).

57. For an example from Egypt, see Springborg (1989), pp. 45–61.

58. B. Lewis (1993b), esp. chaps. 8, 11.

59. Meeker (1991), p. 215; and Özel (1989), esp. pp. 149–62.

60. For instance, Bulaç (1988/1990), pp. 115–16; and Güngör (1981), pp. 11, 150, 241.

61. R. Ahmed (1994), pp. 689–95.

62. For some figures, see Mayer (1993), pp. 146–47 n. 31.

63. Roberts (1994), pp. 465–78.

64. M.S.A. Khan (1929); Rodinson (1966/1973), chap. 3; and Mandaville (1979).

65. D'Souza (1991) and Schlessinger (1991).

66. J. Q. Wilson (1993) offers much supportive evidence on the importance of norms.

67. Metcalf (1994), esp. pp. 710–17.

68. Balcı and Balcı (1986–90), Özel (1984), and Yılmaz (1990).

69. See Casanova (1992), pp. 37–43. The religious revival of our times has also been attributed to religious deregulation. In this view, religious deregulation is fueling an explosion of new religious forms and a huge increase in public religious expression, just as industrial deregulation stimulates production by allowing firms to satisfy a greater variety of needs. On this second view, see Chaves and Cann (1992). The two explanations are not mutually exclusive. Greater religious experimentation may go along with greater religious openness.

70. Such a stalemate lies at the origins of religious tolerance in the contemporary West. Persecutions inflicted by Christians trying to impose their own orthodoxies on other Christians convinced astute Europeans and Americans that it would be mutually beneficial to keep religion out of government affairs and to grant individuals broad expressive freedoms. See Dahl (1956).

CHAPTER FOUR
THE GENESIS OF ISLAMIC ECONOMICS: A CHAPTER IN THE
POLITICS OF MUSLIM IDENTITY

1. Recent expositions include Chapra (1992) and Naqvi (1994). For critiques of the literature, see Kuran (1986), Kuran (1989a), Behdad (1989), Kuran (1993b), Behdad (1994a), and Haneef (1995).

2. For critical overviews of the practice of Islamic economics, see Rahnema and Nomani (1990); Kuran (1993b); Kuran (1995b); Richards and Waterbury (1996), chap. 14; and Malik (1996), chaps. 3–4.

3. The fears were not baseless. Some Hindu politicians envisioned a centralized Hindu raj, and they considered the terms "Hindu" and "Indian" as synonymous. Moreover, certain Hindu-dominated local governments had treated Muslims as undesirable aliens. See Aziz (1967), esp. chaps. 2–3; Sayeed (1968), chaps. 3–5; and Nagarkar (1975), esp. chaps. 4–6, 14. As tensions between Muslims and Hindus mounted, certain leaders on both sides fanned hostilities by reviving memories of old grievances.

4. Darling (1947), chaps. 1, 10.

5. Ansari (1991), pp. 184–85; and Talbot (1993), pp. 239–40.

6. Mawdudi (1944/1981), p. 36.

7. M. Ahmad (1991), p. 464.

8. For examples of his writings and addresses in pre-partition India, see Mawdudi (1939/1976), Mawdudi (1940/1990), Mawdudi (1941/1976), and Mawdudi (1948/1950). Scholarly analyses of Mawdudi's thought include: S.V.R. Nasr (1996), A. Ahmad (1967), Lerman (1981), and Binder (1961), pt. 1.

9. Mawdudi (1940/1990), p. 115.

10. Mawdudi (1945/1981), pp. 38–40. See also Mawdudi (1940/1990), chaps. 2–4, 7–9.

11. Mawdudi (1945/1981), p. 40.

12. Mawdudi (1948/1981), pp. 65–68.

13. Mawdudi (1941/1976), p. 1. The essence of Mawdudi's conception of Islamic economics may be found in pp. 30–40 of this book. See also Mawdudi (1940/1990), chaps. 17–23; and Mawdudi (1951/1981).

14. Related by Brohi (1979), p. 291.

15. Quoted by A. Ahmad (1967), pp. 373–74.

16. Mawdudi (1950/1981) and Mawdudi (1952/1960).

17. Mawdudi (1940/1990), p. 56.

18. Macdonald (1909/1965), pp. 6–10.

19. Macdonald (1911/1971), pp. 254–55.

20. Said (1978).

21. K. Ahmad (1957), p. 8.

22. S.V.R. Nasr (1996), chap. 1.

23. The figures for 1931 that are reported in this paragraph and the next come from the *Census of India, 1931*, vol. 1:1, pp. 61, 328–29; and vol. 1:2, pp. 426–27. Those for 1911 are from the *Census of India, 1911*, vol. 1:1, p. 53; and vol. 1:2, pp. 322–30. Figures for 1911 are used whenever the information is lacking for 1931. For an analysis of the reported patterns, see Mishra (1962).

24. This discrepancy is reflected in census figures on occupations specializing in trade. In 1911, 3.5 percent of India's Muslims were traders, as compared with 5.1 percent of all Indians.

25. At the time, 12.3 percent of all Muslims lived in towns, as against 9.5 percent of the total population. By 1931, the differential had narrowed a bit: 13.5 percent for Muslims, as opposed to 11.1 percent for all Indians. The trend suggests that as a group Muslims were relatively unsuccessful in obtaining urban employment.

26. Luckmann (1967).

27. See also Casanova (1994), chaps. 1–2.

28. Johnson (1980).

29. Hardin (1995), chap. 4; and Hechter (1987).

30. Iannaccone (1992).

31. Aziz (1967), p. 148.

32. Denny (1989), p. 90.

33. Contemporary Islamists consider Atatürk to have attacked Islam itself by requiring the call to prayer in Turkish mosques to be in Turkish. This directive was rescinded after Atatürk's death.

34. W. C. Smith (1957), p. 20.

35. Iqbal (1909/1964), pp. 43, 54.

36. M. N. Siddiqi (1981) and Islamic Research and Training Institute (1993).

37. There is an immense literature on these leaders and the movements they directed. The major analyses include Gibb (1947), Hourani (1983), W. C. Smith (1957), and Rahman (1982).

38. Landau (1990). Modern pan-Islamism started with efforts by the Ottoman Sultan Abdülhamid II to strengthen Islamic solidarity against the European powers. After the Ottoman defeat in World War I, it attracted large numbers of Indians, who mobilized to save the caliphate, assist Muslim nations under European domination, and mediate conflicts between Turks and Arabs. When the Ottoman

Empire collapsed and the Republic of Turkey abolished the caliphate, Indian pan-Islamism entered a dormant phase, and it was soon eclipsed by Muslim nationalism. In the rest of the Islamic world, too, no major pan-Islamic initiatives were launched during the three decades following World War I.

39. Ibid., pp. 119–20.

40. During a controversy in the mid-1950s, the Jamaat-i Islami accused the nationalist-dominated government of attempting a radical reinterpretation of Islam in order to improve Pakistan's global image. An "ordinary Muslim," wrote a Jamaat publication, would greet this proposed reconstruction with a "flat rejection." The thinking behind this reaction apparently belonged to Mawdudi. See Brohi (1979), pp. 299–300.

41. Kuran (1998).

42. B. Lewis (1968), p. 267.

43. Chehabi (1993) and Banani (1961), chaps. 2–3.

44. The educational reforms of Egypt are critiqued by Heyworth-Dunne (1939); and those of the late Ottoman Empire by Berkes (1964), esp. chap. 4; and Ergin (1939–43). For a comparative critique of such efforts, see Rahman (1982), chap. 2.

45. B. Lewis (1975).

46. Mawdudi (1940/1990), pp. 125–34.

47. Mawdudi (1947/1976), esp. pp. 9–15; and Mawdudi (1940/1963), chap. 1.

48. The concept is developed by Anderson (1991).

49. This characterization applies equally to many other modern formulations of the umma. For detailed critiques, see Roy (1992/1994), chap. 4; and Al-Ahsan (1992).

50. Agwani (1986), esp. chap. 5; and M. Ahmad (1991).

51. I. Ahmad, ed. (1978).

52. Kuran (1986).

53. Mawdudi (1940/1963), chap. 1. Unlike most Islamists, Mawdudi saw some flaws in a subperiod of the Golden Age: "[the second caliph] 'Uthman . . . did not possess the qualities of leadership to the extent that his great forerunners had been endowed with. Consequently, 'Ignorance' found its way into the Islamic social system during his Caliphate" (p. 26). But even many of his close supporters objected to this qualification.

54. Ibid., pp. 26, 29, 34.

55. Kahneman and Tversky (1979) and Tversky and Kahneman (1991).

56. Lowenthal (1985), esp. pp. 21–28, 369–76.

57. Rodinson (1966/1973), pp. 28–30; and Crone (1987).

58. Shaban (1971), chaps. 1–4; and Hodgson (1974), pp. 146–217.

59. Huntington (1993), p. 23. For a fuller version of the thesis, see Huntington (1996). Its implications for Islam are critiqued by Mottahadeh (1995).

60. Jalal (1995), p. 82; and Binder (1961), chaps. 9–11.

61. Huntington (1996) contains a vast array of references. An influential contribution has been Quigley (1979). For an example pertaining specifically to the Islamic world, see B. Lewis (1993b), esp. chaps. 1, 8, 11.

62. Qutb (1948/1970), p. 90. For an analysis of this view, see Shepard (1989). See also Kepel (1984/1985), chap. 2; and Sivan (1985), chaps. 2–3.

63. Akhavi (1994).

64. Al-Sadr (1961/1982–84).

65. For critical overviews of al-Sadr's philosophy, see Katouzian (1983); and Mallat (1993), chaps. 4–5.

66. Al-Sadr (1961/1982–84), vol. 1, pt. 1.

67. Shayegan (1989/1992), p. 108.

68. Khomeini (1985), pp. 329–43.

69. Howeidi (1993).

70. This is reflected in growth rates for the Middle East and North Africa for the period 1950–1990. The average growth rate of real GNP per capita has been 2.6 percent a year in this region, as compared with 2.5 percent for developing countries as a whole. Source: Easterlin (1996), table 3.1.

71. Tibi (1993).

72. Al-e Ahmad (1964/1982).

73. See, for example, Özel (1985) and Özdenören (1990). Many additional examples are given by Çakır (1990).

74. Kısakürek (1974), pp. 68–71. The reference to Rimbaud belongs to Kısakürek himself. For insights into how the quest for a secure identity has propelled the rise of Turkish Islamism, see Mardin (1993).

CHAPTER FIVE
THE NOTION OF ECONOMIC JUSTICE IN CONTEMPORARY ISLAMIC THOUGHT

1. For a survey of the literature by a leading Islamic economist, see M. N. Siddiqi (1981). Critiques of the literature include Kuran (1983), Pryor (1985), and Kuran (1986).

2. For extensive comparisons, see Al-Qardawi (1966/1981), chap. 2; Mannan (1970), chap. 3; Mannan (1984a), chap. 5; Naqvi (1981a), chap. 4; and Ajijola (1977), esp. pt. 1.

3. For a representative works, see Mawdudi (1947/1975) and Qutb (1948/1970).

4. The most influential of these writings are by Mahmud Taleghani, Mohammed Baqir al-Sadr, and Abol-Hasan Bani-Sadr. The crucial chapters of Taleghani's leading works have appeared in English under the title Society and Economics in Islam (1982). For commentaries on the Shiite literature, and for further sources, see Bakhash (1984), chap. 7; and Katouzian (1983).

5. For some explicit statements, see Ajijola (1977), pp. 194–98; Afzal-ur-Rahman (1980), vol. 1, pp. 62–66; Chapra (1970), pp. 14–16; A. Hasan (1971), p. 211; A. Ahmad (1984), p. 1; and M. S. Khan (1987), pp. 15–16.

6. Chapra (1970), p. 11.

7. A. Ahmad (1984), p. 1. For a third such statement see M. N. Siddiqi (1972), p. 38.

8. Of the detailed surveys available, several are listed in note 1.

9. The narrow interpretation of zakat is outlined by Afzal-ur-Rahman (1980), vol. 3, chaps. 14–16. Various broad interpretations are put forth by Mannan (1970), pp. 284–302; Kahf (1982); and Choudhury (1986), chap. 5. On disagreements among the reformists, see Kahf (1982), pp. 138–44. Certain authors who subscribe to the narrow interpretation do not object to new taxes under other names. See, for example, Faridi (1980). For a critical review of the writings on zakat, see Kuran (1986), pp. 143–49.

10. Mannan (1970), p. 182. A detailed contemporary exposition of inheritance matters is contained in this source, pp. 176–86.

11. Yusuf (1971), p. 61.

12. M. N. Siddiqi (1972), p. 16. See also Mannan (1984a), pp. 300–3.

13. See Chapra (1970), pp. 9–10; Choudhury (1980), p. 514; Naqvi (1981a), p. 64; and M. N. Siddiqi (1972), pp. 61–73.

14. For extensive examples, see Abdul-Rauf (1979); M. N. Siddiqi (1972), esp. chaps. 2 and 3. For a critique of this injunction, see Kuran (1983).

15. See, for example, Chapra (1970), p. 9.

16. On just prices and wages, see Mannan (1970), chap. 8; and Yusuf (1971), pp. 77–80.

17. See M. N. Siddiqi (1972), pp. 52–54; and Mannan (1984a), pp. 256–58.

18. For a survey of the Islamic position on interest, see M. N. Siddiqi (1982). Also see Ahmed, Iqbal, and Khan, eds. (1983a), chaps. 5–8; Chapra (1985); and Khan and Mirakhor, eds. (1987). Critical reviews of the writings on interest include Karsten (1982); and Kuran (1986), pp. 149–58.

19. Yusuf (1971), p. 90.

20. The most detailed statement on insurance is by M. N. Siddiqi (1985). Other statements include Yusuf (1971), chap. 6; Mannan (1970), chap. 14; and Samiullah (1982). For a concise account of the controversies involved, see M. N. Siddiqi (1981), pp. 26–28. On the issue of regulation, see M. A. Khan (1985).

21. See Afzal-ur-Rahman (1980), vol. 2, chap. 6; M. N. Siddiqi (1972), pp. 54–57; and M. N. Siddiqi (1985), pp. 40–41.

22. See Afzal-ur-Rahman (1980), vol. 2, pp. 44–45; M. N. Siddiqi (1972), pp. 57–60; and Ajijola (1977), pp. 237–40.

23. See Chapra (1970), p. 149.

24. See M. N. Siddiqi (1981), pp. 15–16.

25. They include Yusuf (1971), pp. 23–27.

26. Afzal-ur-Rahman (1980), vol. 2, p. 173.

27. Ibid., chap. 10, esp. pp. 175–77.

28. Ibid., pp. 193–207.

29. Ajijola (1977), p. 181. Also see Yusuf (1971), p. 11; M. N. Siddiqi (1972), esp. pp. 115–35; and Mannan (1984a), chap. 11.

30. Among the opponents of the modern corporation is Yusuf (1971), pp. 34–38. The proponents include Afzal-ur-Rahman (1980), vol. 1, pp. 242–43.

31. Chapra (1970), p. 16.

32. On the question of substance versus procedure, a very illuminating discussion relating to Islamic thought can be found in Khadduri (1984), chap. 6. For general treatments, see Rawls (1971), esp. pp. 83–90; Barry (1965), chap. 6; and Brennan and Buchanan (1985), chap. 7.

33. *World Development Report* (1980), esp. chap. 4.

34. The scheme is that of Malaysia. See Salleh and Ngah (1980).

35. Witness Naqvi (1981a), p. 64: "The Islamic ethical principles not only determine individual choice and collective choice, but also provide a principle of integrating the two." A supremely optimistic argument is put forward by Afzal-ur-Rahman (1980), vol. 1, pp. 169–73.

36. There is an extensive literature on the benefits conferred by state power. See Buchanan, Tollison, and Tullock, eds. (1980).

37. Hodgson (1974) offers numerous examples.

38. Strictly speaking, the Sunni Islamic economists believe that official corruption became rampant after the death, in 661, of the fourth caliph Ali. The Shiites believe that corruption became widespread at an earlier date.

39. For the rationale behind the opposition to indexation, see Zaman (1985) and Chapra (1985), pp. 39–42. The pro-indexation argument has been put forth by Mannan (1984a), chap. 14A. The issue was addressed inconclusively at the second seminar on the "Monetary and Fiscal Economics of Islam," held in Islamabad in 1981. The proceedings of this seminar have been edited by Ahmed, Iqbal, and Khan (1983a).

40. See Chapra (1984a), p. 34.

41. See Choudhury (1986), chap. 6; and Z. Hasan (1985).

42. See M. Khan (1987), pp. 19–20. Khan also takes issue with the suggestion that profit and loss sharing would promote equality, indicating that this is not self-evident.

43. See, for example, A. Hasan (1971); Ajijola (1977), esp. pp. 208–24; and Naqvi (1981a), esp. pp. 147–50.

44. Many of those who stress individual ownership are followers of Mawdudi. They include Chapra (1970), Yusuf (1971), and Kahf (1978).

45. Chapra (1970), p. 245.

46. Yusuf (1971), p. 67 (italics removed).

47. Husaini (1980), p. 135.

48. The disagreements are discussed by A. Ahmad (1984), pp. 3–6.

49. A. Ahmad (1984), p. 5.

50. See, for instance, Kahf (1978), p. 65.

51. See Chapra (1984b), p. 84.

52. See, for example, Afzal-ur-Rahman (1980), vol. 1, pp. 145–52. Certain writers, including S. A. Ali (1983), favor variable wages.

53. See Barzel (1982).

54. See Udovitch (1985).

55. Saleh (1986).

56. Ibid., p. 59.

57. Ibid., p. 60.

58. Ibid., pp. 1–7.

59. See, for instance, M. N. Siddiqi (1972), pp. 56–57.

60. Naqvi (1981b), p. 23. The same point is made by Chapra (1970), pp. 8, 94.

61. Naqvi (1981b), p. 30.

62. Mannan (1982). See also Mannan (1984b), pp. 10–11.

63. Chapra (1985), pp. 38–39.
64. On intuitionism, see Rawls (1971), pp. 34–45.
65. Mannan (1984b), p. 11.
66. Mannan (1984b). The quote is from p. xii, and the same point is made on p. 1 and again, following the remarks on intuitionism, on p. 11.
67. See Simon (1983) and Polanyi (1966/1983).
68. The argument that the role of judges and social thinkers is to bring order over doctrine is developed by Dworkin (1986).
69. Afzal-ur-Rahman (1980), vol. 3, p. 217.
70. See Wilson (1985), p. 17.
71. See Husaini (1980), esp. pp. 79–81; and Mannan (1970), pp. 23–26.
72. See Rahman (1979), pp. 71–79.
73. On the biases that inevitably afflict analogical reasoning, see Holland, Holyoak, Nisbett, and Thagard (1986), chap. 10.
74. See Husaini (1980), p. 81 and chap. 5; and Mannan (1970), pp. 21–23.
75. Mannan (1970), p. 22.
76. The main reason for doubting the saying's authenticity is that it emerged several generations after the Prophet's death, at a time when many Muslims were becoming acutely aware that their institutions were not based on scripture alone. See Hurgronje (1882/1975), p. 275.
77. See Chapra (1970), esp. pp. 143–45; Afzal-ur-Rahman (1980), vol. 1, chaps. 2–5; and Choudhury (1980), chap. 1.
78. See Brennan and Buchanan (1985) and Ullmann-Margalit (1977).
79. On the evolution of people's perceptions there is an extensive literature to which researchers in several disciplines have contributed. For two broad statements, both by anthropologists, see White (1975) and Douglas (1986). The pertinent dynamics have been explored by Kuran (1987).
80. Hourani (1964) and Hallaq (1986).
81. Esposito (1984), pp. 71–75.
82. See B. Lewis (1971).
83. See Afzal-ur-Rahman (1980), vol. 3, pp. 237–38; and Choudhury (1986), p. 56.

CHAPTER SIX
ISLAM AND UNDERDEVELOPMENT: AN OLD PUZZLE REVISITED

1. Atatürk (1923/1990), p. 68.
2. See, for example, Todaro (1985) and Gillis et al. (1992). In passing, Todaro notes that the meaning of development incorporates freedom from "dogmatic beliefs" and also that wealth offers the choice to "live a life of spiritual contemplation" (p. 87). He does not elaborate, leaving the economic role of religion unspecified.
3. Edward Said's *Orientalism* (1978) offers an influential case for thinking twice before publicizing shortcomings of the Muslim East. For the counterargument, see B. Lewis (1993b), chap. 6.

4. For five of the countries, including three with heavily Muslim populations, the *Report* omits income data. I assigned these countries incomes that placed them at the top of their income groups. For example, Saudi Arabia and Turkmenistan, which the *Report* treats as upper-middle income countries, were assumed to have per capita incomes at the top of the upper-middle bracket.

5. No distinction is made between practicing and nonpracticing Muslims. The population shares would be lower if account were taken only of the former.

6. Most of the figures come from the "Nations of the World" section, with adjustments to those of Armenia, Azerbaijan, the Russian Federation, Ukraine, and the United Kingdom, to correct either typographical errors or official misclassifications. Where the Muslim share of the population was not reported, it was computed on the basis of information in the "Comparative National Statistics, Religion" section.

7. Adding to the independent variables the logarithm of population improves the fit slightly, but the new coefficient turns out insignificant.

8. The term "West" is defined to include Western Europe as well as places, like North America, settled largely by West Europeans. It excludes Latin America.

9. The poem is reproduced in Akyüz, ed. (1953), p. 29.

10. A forceful variant of this argument belongs to Hodgson (1974).

11. For the full argument see Issawi (1970) and Issawi (1980).

12. Döğen (1987).

13. The temporal breakdown comes from Ölçen (1991), pp. 69–70, who observes also that science was defined more liberally for later centuries than for earlier ones. In sharp contrast to the period before 1250, the pathbreakers who came after 1400 made no contributions to physics, chemistry, biology, or mathematics.

14. Hoodbhoy (1991), p. 34.

15. Cook (1974) and Owen (1981).

16. For fuller definitions, see Jones (1988).

17. Rodinson (1966/1973).

18. Jomo (1977).

19. Jones (1988).

20. Ibid., p. 97.

21. For a recent contribution to Islamic economics, see Chapra (1992). Kuran (1993b) critiques the literature and evaluates its practical impact.

22. For instance: "When the service of prayer is over, spread out in the land, and look for the bounty of God" (62:10), and "Do not forget your part in this world" (28:77).

23. Udovitch (1970).

24. Udovitch (1962).

25. Haffar (1975).

26. Cromer (1909), vol. 2, pp. 228–29.

27. Renan (1883).

28. Said (1978), chap. 2.

29. Example: "Believing men and women have no choice in a matter after God and his Apostle have decided it" (33:36).

30. An empirical test of their proposition, conducted much later in rural Jordan (Sutcliffe 1975), found that religious commitment, as measured by frequency of prayers, bears no statistical relationship to productivity or receptivity to technological change. But this test has not been replicated elsewhere. In any case, its measure of religious commitment is unduly simplistic.

31. Lerner (1958), p. 105.

32. W. A. Lewis (1955), p. 105.

33. Adelman and Morris (1973), pp. 38–39.

34. Stark, Iannaccone, and Finke (1995) offer a critical survey of these trends, to which Compte, Marx, and Freud made major contributions.

35. In the rating scheme used by Adelman and Morris, Hinduism and Buddhism get a C.

36. Berkes (1964).

37. See, for example, B. Lewis (1968).

38. Berkes (1964), pp. 36–41.

39. Berkes (1978), pp. 57–65.

40. Berkes (1964), esp. pp. 115–17.

41. İnalcık (1970); and İnalcık (1994), esp. pp. 44–54.

42. Cahen and Talbi (1971).

43. Ibn Khaldun (1379/1958), vol. 1, esp. pp. 311–19.

44. See ibid., vol. 3, pp. 1117–18. The territories to which he refers are the Christian-ruled states of the northern Mediterranean.

45. Accounts of these revolts are given by Akdağ (1975) and Griswold (1981).

46. Ülgener (1981, 1984).

47. Goldstone (1987), p. 123.

48. Jones (1987), pp. 98–103.

49. Chapra (1992), chap. 5, offers details. For critical surveys, see Kuran (1986) and Kuran (1993b).

50. Rosenberg and Birdzell (1986), chap. 4; and Hirschman (1977) describe the transformation. They show that the new morality helped convince people that personal economic success does not signify character flaws inimical to salvation.

51. B. Lewis (1982); and B. Lewis (1993a), chaps. 16, 27. In 1625, the Ottoman observer Ömer Talib saw Europe's growing success in international trade as a threat to the Ottoman Empire. "The Ottoman Empire must seize the shores of Yemen and the trade passing that way," he wrote. "Otherwise before very long, the Europeans will rule over the lands of Islam" (B. Lewis [1968], p. 28).

52. B. Lewis (1982), p. 196.

53. For further insights on the last point, see Goldstone (1987), pp. 129–32.

54. B. Lewis (1993a), p. 347.

55. Ibid., pp. 354–57.

56. B. Lewis (1982), p. 296.

57. Ibid., pp. 229–30.

58. Watt (1988), chap. 1, offers a similar assessment of how the closure of the gate of *ijtihād* bred complacency with the status quo.

59. Mokyr (1990), esp. pp. 170–76.

60. As cited by Berkes (1964), p. 302. Chaps. 9–10 of this book contain many additional quotations in the same vein.

61. These definitions belong to Oakeshott (1958/1993), pp. 18–21, who uses the terms "morality of individuality" and "morality of communal ties." The distinction mirrors that which Ferdinand Tönnies (1887/1957) draws between *Gemeinschaft* and *Gesellschaft*. The former concept refers to the solidarity of the face-to-face society, the latter to the modern, largely impersonal society where ties are rooted in self-interest.

62. Triandis (1990).

63. Greif (1994).

64. Along with Triandis (1990), Greif uses the term "collectivism" to characterize what I am calling "communalism." The former term is best reserved, as Oakeshott (1958/1993), pp. 24–28 and pt. 3, explains, for a class of moralities that assign an important role to government.

65. Kaufmann (1997).

66. See, for instance, Issawi (1955/1981), pp. 331–32; and İnalcık (1994), pp. 48–54.

67. See, in particular, Kafadar (1986), who demonstrates that some Turkish traders were active in Ancona and Venice until the seventeenth century.

68. İnalcık (1970), pp. 214–15; and İnalcık (1971), p. 1179. The latter source also cites the opportunity of obtaining "scarce goods and raw materials" and "customs revenues, the principal source of hard cash for the Treasury." It is unclear why such objectives could not have been met through trade conducted by Muslims.

69. Weber (1904–5/1958).

70. Tawney (1926/1962).

71. Abu-Lughod (1989), esp. chaps. 5–10, provides evidence on the stimulus to trade that Muslims gave to regions from China to the shores of Africa. See also Risso (1989), who focuses on Asian maritime trade in the eighteenth century, and Ensminger (1997), who shows that, even in recent times, Islamization has been a boon to East African trade.

72. Putnam (1993).

73. Kuran (1995a).

74. Kuran (1989b).

75. Kaufmann (1997), sect. 6.

References

Abdul-Rauf, Muhammad (1979). "The Islamic Doctrine of Economics and Contemporary Economic Thought." Pp. 4–12 in *Capitalism and Socialism: A Theological Inquiry*, edited by Michael Novak. Washington, D.C.: American Enterprise Institute.

Abu-Lughod, Janet L. (1989). *Before European Hegemony: The World System A.D. 1250–1350.* New York: Oxford University Press.

Adelman, Irma, and Cynthia Taft Morris (1973). *Economic Growth and Social Equity in Developing Countries.* Stanford: Stanford University Press.

Afzal-ur-Rahman (1980). *Economic Doctrines of Islam.* 2nd ed. 3 vols. Lahore: Islamic Publications.

Agwani, M. S. (1986). *Islamic Fundamentalism in India.* Chandigarh: Twenty-First Century India Society.

Ağaoğlu, E. Abdülgaffar (1994). "A Camel-wise Comparative Financial and Market Share Analysis of the Islamic Banks Currently Operating in Turkey." *METU Studies in Development* 21: 475–500.

Ahmad, Ausaf (1984). "A Macro Model of Distribution in an Islamic Economy." *Journal of Research in Islamic Economics* 2 (1): 1–20.

Ahmad, Aziz (1967). "Mawdudi and Orthodox Fundamentalism in Pakistan." *Middle East Journal* 21: 369–80.

Ahmad, Imtiaz, ed. (1978). *Caste and Stratification among Muslims in India.* New Delhi: Manohar.

Ahmad, Jamil-ud-din, ed. (1952). *Speeches and Writings of Mr. Jinnah.* Vol. 2. Lahore: Sh. Muhammad Ashraf.

Ahmad, Khurshid (1957). *Islam and the West.* Lahore: Jamaat-i Islami Pakistan.
––––––– (1980a). "Economic Development in an Islamic Framework." Pp. 171–88 in *Studies in Islamic Economics*, edited by K. Ahmad. Jeddah: International Center for Research in Islamic Economics.
––––––– ed. (1980b). *Studies in Islamic Economics.* Jeddah: International Center for Research in Islamic Economics.

Ahmad, Khurshid, and Zafar Ishaq Ansari (1979). "Mawlana Sayyid Abul A'la Mawdudi: An Introduction to His Vision of Islam and Islamic Revival." Pp. 359–84 in *Islamic Perspectives: Studies in Honour of Mawlana Sayyid Abul A'la Mawdudi*, edited by Khurshid Ahmad and Zafar Ishaq Ansari. Leicester: Islamic Foundation.

Ahmad, Mumtaz (1991). "Islamic Fundamentalism in South Asia: The Jama'at-i-Islami and the Tablighi Jamaat of South Asia." Pp. 457–530 in *Fundamentalisms Observed*, edited by Martin E. Marty and R. Scott Appleby. Chicago: University of Chicago Press.

Ahmed, Rafiuddin (1994). "Redefining Muslim Identity in South Asia: The Transformation of the Jama'at-i-Islami." Pp. 669–705 in *Accounting for Fundamen-*

talisms: *The Dynamic Character of Movements*, edited by Martin E. Marty and R. Scott Appleby. Chicago: University of Chicago Press.

Ahmed, Ziauddin (1989). "Currency Notes and Loan Indexation." *Islamic Studies* 28: 39–53.

Ahmed, Ziauddin, Munawar Iqbal, and M. Fahim Khan, eds. (1983a). *Money and Banking in Islam*. Jeddah: International Center for Research in Islamic Economics.

——— (1983b). *Fiscal Policy and Resource Allocation in Islam*. Islamabad: Institute of Policy Studies.

Ajijola, Alhaji Adeleke Dirisu (1977). *The Islamic Concept of Social Justice*. Lahore: Islamic Publications.

Akdağ, Mustafa (1975). *Türk Halkının Dirlik ve Düzenlik Kavgası*. Ankara: Bilgi Yayınevi.

Akhavi, Shahrough (1994). "Sayyid Qutb: The Poverty of Philosophy and the Vindication of Islamic Tradition." Pp. 130–52 in *Cultural Transitions in the Middle East*, edited by Şerif Mardin. Leiden: E. J. Brill.

Akyüz, Kenan, ed. (1953). *Batı Tesirinde Türk Şiiri Antolojisi*. Ankara: Dil ve Tarih-Coğrafya Fakültesi.

Al-Ahram Weekly (Cairo), July 1–7, 1993.

Al-Ahsan, Abdullah (1992). *Ummah or Nation? Identity Crisis in Contemporary Muslim Society*. Leicester: Islamic Foundation.

Al-Azm, Sadik J. (1993). "Islamic Fundamentalism Reconsidered: A Critical Outline of Problems, Ideas, and Approaches." *South Asia Bulletin* 13: 93–121.

Al-Buraey, Muhammad A. (1985). *Administrative Development: An Islamic Perspective*. London: Kegan Paul International.

Al-e Ahmad, Jalal (1964/1982). *Plagued by the West (Gharbzadegi)*, translated by Paul Sprachman. Delmar, N.Y.: Caravan Books.

Ali, Shaukat (2000). "Islamic Law and Modernity: Pakistan on Legal Crossroads." *Pakistan Journal of History and Culture* 21: 1–32.

Ali, Syed Aftab (1983). "Risk-Bearing and Profit-Sharing in an Islamic Framework: Some Allocational Considerations." Pp. 253–70 in *Fiscal Policy and Resource Allocation in Islam*, edited by Ziauddin Ahmed, Munawar Iqbal, and M. Fahim Khan. Jeddah: International Center for Research in Islamic Economics.

Allawi, Luay (1986). "Leasing: An Islamic Financial Instrument." Pp. 120–27 in *Islamic Banking and Finance*, edited by Butterworths Editorial Board. London: Butterworths.

Al-Omar, Fouad Abdullah (1995). "A Comparative Study of *Zakah* Administration System in Muslim Countries: General, Administrative, and Organizational Aspects." Pp. 21–64 in *Institutional Framework of* Zakah: *Dimensions and Implications*, edited by Ahmed Abdel-Fattah El-Ashker and Muhammad Sirajul Haq. Jeddah: Islamic Development Bank.

Al-Qardawi, Yusuf (1966/1981). *Economic Security in Islam*, translated by Muhammad Iqbal Siddiqi. Lahore: Kazi Publications.

Al-Sadr, Muhammad Baqir (1961/1982–84). *Iqtisaduna: Our Economics*. 4 vols. Tehran: World Organization for Islamic Services.

Al-Yassini, Ayman (1985). *Religion and State in the Kingdom of Saudi Arabia*. Boulder: Westview.

Amuzegar, Jahangir (1992). "The Iranian Economy before and after the Revolution." *Middle East Journal* 46: 413–25.

Anderson, Benedict (1991). *Imagined Communities.* Rev. ed. London: Verso.

"Announcement on Research Proposals" (1983). 4th. ed. Jeddah: International Center for Research in Islamic Economics.

Ansari, Sarah (1991). "Political Legacies of Pre-1947 Sind." Pp. 173–93 in *The Political Inheritance of Pakistan,* edited by D. A. Low. New York: St. Martin's.

Ariff, Muhammad (1988a). "Islamic Economics: Challenges and Potentials." Pp. 73–93 in *Today's Problems, Tomorrow's Solutions: The Future Structure of Muslim Societies,* edited by Abdullah Omar Naseef. London: Mansell Publishing.

——— (1988b). "Islamic Banking." *Asian-Pacific Economic Literature* 2: 48–64.

Atalay, Beşir (1987). "İktisadî Kalkınmada Geleneksel Değerlerin Yeri (Japon Örneği)." Pp. 65–111 in *İktisadî Kalkınma ve İslâm,* edited by Ahmet Tabakoğlu and İsmail Kurt. Istanbul: İslâmi İlimler Araştırma Vakfı.

Atatürk, Mustafa Kemal (1923/1990). "Maurice Pernot ile mülâkat." Pp. 65–68 in *Atatürk'ün Kültür ve Medeniyet Konusundaki Sözleri,* edited by Atatürk Kültür, Dil ve Tarih Yüksek Kurumu. Ankara: Atatürk Kültür Merkezi.

Ayubi, Nazih (1991). *Political Islam: Religion and Politics in the Arab World.* London: Routledge.

Aziz, K. K. (1967). *The Making of Pakistan: A Study in Nationalism.* London: Chatto and Windus.

Baker, Raymond William (1990). *Sadat and After: Struggles for Egypt's Political Soul.* Cambridge: Harvard University Press.

Bakhash, Shaul (1984). *Reign of the Ayatollahs: Iran and the Islamic Revolution.* New York: Basic Books.

——— (1987). "Islam and Social Justice in Iran." Pp. 95–115 in *Shi'ism, Resistance, and Revolution,* edited by Martin Kramer. Boulder: Westview.

——— (1989). "What Khomeini Did." *New York Review of Books,* July 20, pp. 16–19.

Balcı, İbrahim, and M. Balcı (1986–90). *Ertelenen İslami Hayat.* 4 vols. Istanbul: İklim Yayınları.

Banani, Amin (1961). *The Modernization of Iran, 1921–1941.* Stanford: Stanford University Press.

Barry, Brian (1965). *Political Argument.* London: Routledge and Keagan Paul.

Barzel, Yoram (1982). "Measurement Costs and the Organization of Markets." *Journal of Law and Economics* 25: 27–48.

Behdad, Sohrab (1989). "Property Rights in Contemporary Islamic Economic Thought: A Critical Perspective." *Review of Social Economy* 47: 185–211.

——— (1994a). "A Disputed Utopia: Islamic Economics in Revolutionary Iran." *Comparative Studies in Society and History* 36: 775–813.

——— (1994b). "Production and Employment in Iran: Involution and De-Industrialization Thesis." Pp. 85–111 in *The Economy of Islamic Iran: Between State and Market,* edited by Thierry Coville. Tehran: Institut Français de Recherche en Iran.

Berkes, Niyazi (1964). *The Development of Secularism in Turkey*. Montreal: McGill University Press.

—— (1978). *Türkiye'de Çağdaşlaşma*. Istanbul: Doğu-Batı Yayınları.

Bhagwati, Jagdish (1988). *Protectionism*. Cambridge: MIT Press.

Binder, Leonard (1961). *Religion and Politics in Pakistan*. Berkeley: University of California Press.

Brennan, Geoffrey, and James M. Buchanan (1985). *The Reason of Rules*. Cambridge: Cambridge University Press.

Brohi, Allahbukhsh K. (1979). "Mawlana Abul A'la Mawdudi: The Man, the Scholar, the Reformer." Pp. 289–312 in *Studies in Honour of Mawlana Sayyid Abul A'la Mawdudi*, edited by Khurshid Ahmad and Zafar Ishaq Ansari. Leicester: Islamic Foundation.

Brown, Ken (1994). "Islamic Banking: Faith and Creativity." *Los Angeles Times*, April 8, pp. C1, C6.

Buchanan, James M., Robert D. Tollison, and Gordon Tullock, eds. (1980). *Toward a Theory of the Rent-Seeking Society*. College Station: Texas A&M University Press.

Bulaç, Ali (1988/1990). *İnsanın Özgürlük Arayışı*. Istanbul: Endülüs Yayınları.

Cahen, Claude, and Mohamed Talbi (1971). "Hisba." *Encyclopaedia of Islam*. 2nd ed. 3: 485–89.

Carlson, Terrence L. (1986). "Trade Finance under Islamic Principles: A Case Study." *Middle East Executive Reports* 9 (December): 9, 15–16.

Casanova, José (1992). "Private and Public Religions." *Social Research* 59: 17–57.

—— (1994). *Public Religions in the Modern World*. Chicago: University of Chicago Press.

Census of India, 1911 (1913). Calcutta: Superintendent Government Printing.

Census of India, 1931 (1933). Delhi: Manager of Publications.

Ceylan, Barbaros (1988). "Finansal Kiralama ve Uygulamaya İlişkin Sorunlar." Pp. 212–28 in *Özel Finans Kurumları ve Türkiye Uygulaması Sempozyumu*. Istanbul: Marmara Üniversitesi Ortadoğu ve İslâm Ülkeleri Ekonomik Araştırma Merkezi.

Chapra, Umar (1970). "The Economic System of Islam: A Discussion of Its Goals and Nature." 3 parts. *Islamic Quarterly* 14: 3–18, 91–96, 143–56.

—— (1984a). "The Prohibition of *Riba* in Islam: An Evaluation of Some Objections." *American Journal of Islamic Social Sciences* 1 (2): 23–42.

—— (1984b). "Review of Kahf's *The Islamic Economy*." *Journal of Research in Islamic Economics* 1 (Winter): 83–86.

—— (1985). *Towards a Just Monetary System: A Discussion of Money, Banking and Monetary Policy in the Light of Islamic Teachings*. Leicester: Islamic Foundation.

—— (1992). *Islam and the Economic Challenge*. Leicester: Islamic Foundation.

Chaves, Mark, and David E. Cann (1992). "Regulation, Pluralism, and Religious Market Structure: Explaining Religion's Vitality." *Rationality and Society* 4: 272–90.

Chehabi, Houchang E. (1993). "Staging the Emperor's New Clothes: Dress Codes and Nation-Building under Reza Shah." *Iranian Studies* 26: 209–23.

Chenery, Hollis B. (1979). *Structural Change and Development Policy.* New York: Oxford University Press.

Choudhury, Masudul Alam (1980). *An Islamic Social Welfare Function.* Indianapolis: American Trust Publications.

—— (1986). *Contributions to Islamic Theory: A Study in Social Economics.* New York: Macmillan.

—— (1989). *Islamic Economic Co-operation.* New York: St. Martin's.

Clark, Grace (1986). "Pakistan's Zakat and 'Ushr as a Welfare System." Pp. 79–95 in *Islamic Reassertion in Pakistan: The Application of Islamic Laws in a Modern State,* edited by Anita M. Weiss. Syracuse: Syracuse University Press.

Cook, Michael A. (1974). "Economic Developments." Pp. 210–43 in *The Legacy of Islam.* 2nd ed., edited by Joseph Schacht and C. E. Bosworth. Oxford: Clarendon Press.

Coulson, Noel J. (1969). *Conflicts and Tensions in Islamic Jurisprudence.* Chicago: University of Chicago Press.

Cowen, Tyler, and Randall Kroszner (1990). "Mutual Fund Banking: A Market Approach." *Cato Journal* 10: 223–37.

Cromer, Evelyn Baring (1909). *Modern Egypt.* 2 vols. New York: Macmillan.

Crone, Patricia (1987). *Meccan Trade and the Rise of Islam.* Princeton: Princeton University Press.

Cumhuriyet, July 1, 1993.

Cumhuriyet, July 10, 1993.

Cumhuriyet, July 19, 1993.

Cumhuriyet, August 7, 1993.

Çakır, Ruşen (1990). *Ayet ve Slogan.* Istanbul: Metis Yayınları.

Çiller, Tansu, and Çizakça, Murat (1989). *Türk Finans Kesiminde Sorunlar ve Reform Önerileri.* Istanbul: İstanbul Sanayi Odası.

Çizakça, Murat (1986). "Origins and Evolution of Islamic Banks." Boğaziçi University Research Paper ISS/E-86-11.

—— (1987). "Rise of Islamic Banks and the Potential for Venture Capital in the Middle East." Pp. 74–90 in *The Middle East and Eastern Mediterranean: Recent Economic and Political Developments,* edited by Erol Manisalı. Istanbul: Middle East Business and Banking.

—— (1993). *Risk Sermayesi, Özel Finans Kurumları, ve Para Vakıfları.* Istanbul: İlmi Neşriyat.

Dahl, Robert A. (1956). *A Preface to Democratic Theory.* Chicago: University of Chicago Press.

Darling, Malcolm (1947). *The Punjab Peasant in Prosperity and Debt.* 4th ed. New Delhi: Manohar.

Dawn (Karachi), November 11, 1989.

Denny, Frederick M. (1989). "Orthopraxy in Islam and Judaism: Convictions and Categories." Pp. 83–95 in *Studies in Islamic and Judaic Traditions II,* edited by William M. Brinner and Stephen D. Ricks. Atlanta: Scholars Press.

Douglas, Mary (1986). *How Institutions Think.* Syracuse: Syracuse University Press.

Döğen, Şaban (1987). *Müslüman İlim Öncüleri Ansiklopedisi.* Istanbul: Yeni Asya Yayınevi.

D'Souza, Dinesh (1991). *Illiberal Education: The Politics of Race and Sex on Campus*. New York: Free Press.

Dworkin, Ronald (1986). *Law's Empire*. Cambridge: Harvard University Press.

Easterlin, Richard A. (1996). *Growth Triumphant: The Twenty-first Century in Historical Perspective*. Ann Arbor: University of Michigan Press.

Economist (London), September 16, 1989.

Economist (London), January 18, 1992.

Economist (London), August 7, 1993.

El-Ashker, Ahmed Abdel-Fattah (1987). *The Islamic Business Enterprise*. London: Croom Helm.

Elster, Jon (1983). *Sour Grapes: Studies in the Subversion of Rationality*. Cambridge: Cambridge University Press.

Ensminger, Jean (1997). "Transaction Costs and Islam: Explaining Conversion in Africa." *Journal of Institutional and Theoretical Economics* 153: 4–29.

Erbakan, Necmettin (1991). *Adil Ekonomik Düzen*. Ankara: Refah Partisi.

Ergin, Osman (1939–43). *Türkiye Maarif Tarihi*. 5 vols. Istanbul: Osmanbey Matbaası.

Esposito, John L. (1984). "Law in Islam." Pp. 69–88 in *The Islamic Impact*, edited by Yvonne Yazbeck Haddad, Byron Haines, and Ellison Findly Haines. Syracuse: Syracuse University Press.

Etzioni, Amitai (1988). *The Moral Dimension: Toward a New Economics*. New York: Free Press.

Faridi, F. R. (1980). "*Zakāt* and Fiscal Policy." Pp. 119–30 in *Studies in Islamic Economics*, edited by Khurshid Ahmad. Jeddah: International Center for Research in Islamic Economics.

Gambetta, Diego (1993). *The Sicilian Mafia: The Business of Protection*. Cambridge: Harvard University Press.

Ghazali, Aidit (1990). *Development: An Islamic Perspective*. Petaling Jaya, Malaysia: Pelanduk Publications.

Ghazali, Aidit bin, et al. (1995). "Zakat: A Case Study of Malaysia." Pp. 297–378 in *Institutional Framework of Zakah: Dimensions and Implications*, edited by Ahmed Abdel-Fattah El-Ashker and Muhammad Sirajul Haq. Jeddah: Islamic Development Bank.

Gibb, H.A.R. (1947). *Modern Trends in Islam*. Chicago: University of Chicago Press.

Gillis, Malcolm, Dwight H. Perkins, Michael Roemer, and Donald Snodgrass (1992). *Economics of Development*. 3rd ed. New York: W. W. Norton.

Goldstone, Jack A. (1987). "Cultural Orthodoxy, Risk, and Innovation: The Divergence of East and West in the Early Modern World." *Sociological Theory* 5: 119–35.

Greif, Avner (1994). "Cultural Beliefs and the Organization of Society: A Historical and Theoretical Reflection on Collectivist and Individualist Societies." *Journal of Political Economy* 102: 912–50.

Griswold, W. J. (1981). "Djalali." *Encyclopedia of Islam*. 2nd ed. 5: 238–39.

Güngör, Erol (1981). *İslamın Bugünkü Meseleleri*. Istanbul: Ötüken Neşriyat.

Gürsoy-Tezcan, Akile (1991). "Mosque or Health Centre? A Dispute in a *Gece-kondu.*" Pp. 84–101 in *Islam in Modern Turkey: Religion, Politics, and Literature in a Secular State*, edited by Richard Tapper. London: I. B. Tauris.

Haffar, Ahmad R. (1975). "Economic Development in Islam in Western Scholarship." 2 parts. *Islam and the Modern Age* 6 (2): 5–22 and 6 (3): 5–29.

Hallaq, Wael B. (1986). "On the Authoritativeness of Sunni Consensus." *International Journal of Middle East Studies* 18: 427–54.

Hamitoğulları, Beşir (1988). "Türkiye'de Altın-Gümüş Gibi Varlıklarda Zekât Potansiyeli." Pp. 27–51 in *Türkiye'de Zekât Potansiyeli*. Istanbul: İslâmi İlimler Araştırma Vakfı.

Haneef, Mohamed Aslam (1995). *Contemporary Islamic Economic Thought: A Selected Comparative Analysis*. Kuala Lumpur: Ikraq.

Hardin, Russell (1995). *One for All: The Logic of Group Conflict*. Princeton: Princeton University Press.

Hasan, Ahmad (1971). "Social Justice in Islam." *Islamic Studies* 10: 209–19.

Hasan, Zubair (1985). "Determination of Profit and Loss Sharing Ratios in Interest-Free Business Finance." *Journal of Research in Islamic Economics* 3 (Summer): 13–29.

Hayek, Friedrich A. (1973–79). *Law, Legislation, and Liberty*. 3 vols. Chicago: University of Chicago Press.

——— (1988). *The Fatal Conceit: The Errors of Socialism*. Chicago: University of Chicago Press.

Hechter, Michael (1987). *Principles of Group Solidarity*. Berkeley: University of California Press.

Heyworth-Dunne, J. (1939). *An Introduction to the History of Education in Modern Egypt*. London: Luzac.

Hirschman, Albert O. (1968). "Underdevelopment, Obstacles to the Perception of Change, and Leadership." *Daedalus* 97: 925–37.

——— (1977). *The Passions and the Interests: Political Arguments for Capitalism before Its Triumph*. Princeton: Princeton University Press.

Hobsbawm, Eric, and Terence Ranger, eds. (1992). *The Invention of Tradition*. Cambridge: Cambridge University Press.

Hodgson, Marshall G. S. (1974). *The Venture of Islam: Conscience and History in a World Civilization*. Vol. 1. Chicago: University of Chicago Press.

Holden, David, and Richard Johns (1981). *The House of Saud: The Rise and Rule of the Most Powerful Dynasty in the Arab World*. New York: Holt, Rinehart and Winston.

Holland, John H., Keith J. Holyoak, Richard E. Nisbett, and Paul Thagard (1986). *Induction: Processes of Inference, Learning, and Discovery*. Cambridge: MIT Press.

Hoodbhoy, Pervez (1991). *Islam and Science: Religious Orthodoxy and the Battle for Rationality*. London: Zed Books.

Hourani, Albert (1983). *Arabic Thought in the Liberal Age, 1789–1939*. Rev. ed. Cambridge: Cambridge University Press.

Hourani, George F. (1964). "The Basis of Authority of Consensus in Sunnite Islam." *Studia Islamica* 21: 13–60.

Howeidi, Fahmi (1993). "Intellectual's Civil War." *Al-Ahram Weekly* no. 123, July 1–7, 1993, p. 7.

Huntington, Samuel P. (1993). "The Clash of Civilizations?" *Foreign Affairs* 72: 22–49.

——— (1996). *The Clash of Civilizations and the Remaking of World Order.* New York: Simon and Schuster.

Hurgronge, C. Snouck (1882/1975). "The 'Foundations' of Islamic Law." Pp. 268–89 in *Œuvres Choisies—Selected Works*, edited by G.-H. Bousquet and J. Schacht. Leiden: E. J. Brill.

Husaini, S. Waqar Ahmed (1980). *Islamic Environmental Systems Engineering.* London: Macmillan.

Hussain, Muhammad (1987). *Development Planning in an Islamic State.* Karachi: Royal Book Company.

Hürriyet, March 12, 1996.

Hyman, Anthony (1987). *Muslim Fundamentalism.* London: Institute for the Study of Conflict.

Iannaccone, Laurence R. (1992). "Sacrifice and Stigma: Reducing Free-Riding in Cults, Communes, and Other Collectives." *Journal of Political Economy* 100: 271–91.

——— (1993). "Heirs to the Protestant Ethic? The Economics of American Fundamentalists." Pp. 342–66 in *Fundamentalisms and the State: Remaking Polities, Economies, and Militance*, edited by Martin E. Marty and R. Scott Appleby. Chicago: University of Chicago Press.

Ibn Khaldun (1379/1958). *The Muqaddimah: An Introduction to History*, translated by Franz Rosenthal. 3 vols. New York: Pantheon Books.

——— (1950/1987). *An Arab Philosophy of History: Selections from the "Prolegomena" of Ibn Khaldun of Tunis (1332–1406)*, translated and edited by Charles Issawi. Princeton: Darwin Press.

Ingram, Tim (1986). "Islamic Banking: A Foreign Bank's View." Pp. 53–68 in *Islamic Banking and Finance*, edited by Butterworths Publication Staff. London: Butterworths.

Iqbal, Afzal (1984). *Islamisation of Pakistan.* Delhi: Idarah-i Adabiyat-i Delli.

Iqbal, Mohammad (1909/1964). "Islam as a Moral and Political Ideal." Pp. 29–55 in *Thoughts and Reflections of Iqbal*, edited by Syed Abdul Vahid. Lahore: Sh. Muhammad Ashraf.

Iqbal, Zubair, and Abbas Mirakhor (1987). "Islamic Banking." International Monetary Fund Occasional Paper no. 49.

Islamic Development Bank (1987). *Eleventh Annual Report (1985–1986).* Jeddah: Islamic Development Bank.

Islamic Economics Bulletin 12 (5) (September-October, 2002).

Islamic Research and Training Institute (1993). *A Bibliography of Islamic Economics.* Jeddah: Islamic Development Bank.

Ismail, Abdul Halim (1990). "The Teaching of Islamic Economics: The Practitioner's Point of View." Paper presented to the Seminar on the Teaching of Islamic Economics, International Islamic University, Malaysia, July.

Issawi, Charles (1955/1981). "The Entrepreneurial Class." Pp. 331–47 in the author's *The Arab World's Legacy.* Princeton: Darwin Press.

———— (1970). "The Decline of Middle Eastern Trade, 1100–1850." Pp. 245–66 in *Islam and the Trade of Asia*, edited by D. S. Richards. Oxford: Bruno Cassirer.

———— (1980). "Europe, the Middle East, and the Shift in Power: Reflections on a Theme by Marshall Hodgson." *Comparative Studies in Society and History* 22: 487–504.

İnalcık, Halil (1970). "The Ottoman Economic Mind and Aspects of the Ottoman Economy." Pp. 207–18 in *Studies in the Economic History of the Middle East*, edited by M. A. Cook. London: Oxford University Press.

———— (1971). "Imtiyāzāt, Ottoman Empire." *Encyclopaedia of Islam*. 2nd ed. 3: 1179–89.

———— (1994). "The Ottoman State: Economy and Society, 1300–1600." Pp. 9–409 in *An Economic and Social History of the Ottoman Empire, 1300–1914*, edited by Halil İnalcık with Donald Quataert. Cambridge: Cambridge University Press.

Jalal, Ayesha (1995). "Conjuring Pakistan: History as Official Imagining." *International Journal of Middle East Studies* 27: 73–89.

Johnson, Robert Alan (1980). *Religious Assortative Marriage in the United States*. New York: Academic Press.

Jomo, K. S. (1977). "Islam and Weber: Rodinson on the Implications of Religion for Capitalist Development." *Developing Economies* 15: 240–50.

Jones, E. L. (1987). *The European Miracle: Environments, Economies, and Geopolitics in the History of Europe and Asia*. 2nd ed. Cambridge: Cambridge University Press.

———— (1988). *Growth Recurring: Economic Change in World History*. Oxford: Clarendon Press.

Kafadar, Cemal (1986). "A Death in Venice (1575): Anatolian Muslim Merchants Trading in the Serenissima." *Journal of Turkish Studies* 10: 191–218.

Kahf, Monzer (1978). *The Islamic Economy: Analytical Study of the Functioning of the Islamic Economic System*. Plainfield, Ind.: Muslim Students' Association of the United States and Canada.

———— (1982). "Fiscal and Monetary Policies in an Islamic Economy." Pp. 125–44 in *Monetary and Fiscal Economics of Islam*, edited by Mohammad Ariff. Jeddah: International Center for Research in Islamic Economics.

———— (1995). "Applied Institutional Models for *Zakah* Collection and Distribution in Islamic Countries and Communities." Pp. 197–228 in *Institutional Framework of Zakah: Dimensions and Implications*, edited by Ahmed Abdel-Fattah El-Ashker and Muhammad Sirajul Haq. Jeddah: Islamic Development Bank.

Kahneman, Daniel, and Amos Tversky (1979). "Prospect Theory: An Analysis of Decision under Risk." *Econometrica* 47: 263–91.

Karsten, Ingo (1982). "Islam and Financial Intermediation." *International Monetary Fund Staff Papers* 29: 108–42.

Katouzian, Homa (1983). "Shi'ism and Islamic Economics: Sadr and Bani Sadr." Pp. 145–65 in *Religion and Politics in Iran: Shi'ism from Quietism to Revolution*, edited by Nikki R. Keddie. New Haven: Yale University Press.

Kaufmann, Franz-Xaver (1997). "Religion and Modernization in Europe." *Journal of Institutional and Theoretical Economics* 153: 80–96.

Kazarian, Elias (1991). *Islamic Banking in Egypt.* Lund, Sweden: Lund Economic Studies.

Kepel, Gilles (1984/1985). *The Prophet and the Pharaoh: Muslim Extremism in Egypt,* translated by Jon Rothschild. London: Al Saqi.

Khadduri, Majid (1984). *The Islamic Conception of Justice.* Baltimore: Johns Hopkins University Press.

Khan, Mir Siadat Ali (1929). "The Mohammadan Laws against Usury and How They Are Evaded." *Journal of Comparative Legislation and International Law* 11: 233–44.

Khan, Mohsin S. (1987). "Islamic Interest-Free Banking: A Theoretical Analysis." Pp. 15–35 in *Theoretical Studies in Islamic Banking and Finance,* edited by M. S. Khan and Abbas Mirakhor. Houston: Institute for Research and Islamic Studies.

Khan, Mohsin S., and Abbas Mirakhor (1990). "Islamic Banking: Experiences in the Islamic Republic of Iran and Pakistan." *Economic Development and Cultural Change* 38: 353–76.

——— eds. (1987). *Theoretical Studies in Islamic Banking and Finance.* Houston: Institute for Research and Islamic Studies.

Khan, Muhammad Akram (1985). "Role of the Auditor in an Islamic Economy." *Journal of Research in Islamic Economics* 3 (1): 31–42.

Khan, Waqar Masood (1989). "Towards an Interest-Free Islamic Economic System." *Journal of King Abdulaziz University: Islamic Economics* 1: 3–37.

Khomeini, Imam Ruhollah (1985). *Islam and Revolution: Writings and Declarations,* translated by Hamid Algar. London: KPI.

Khurshid, Ahmad, ed. (1985). *Studies in Islamic Economics.* Jeddah: International Center for Research in Islamic Economics.

Kısakürek, Necip Fazıl (1974). *O ve Ben.* Istanbul: Büyük Doğu.

Köfteoğlu, Fehmi (1994). "Kapitalist Sisteme Ahlakî Kılıf: İslam Ekonomisi." *İktisat Dergisi* 30 (July): 26–35.

Kuran, Timur (1983). "Behavioral Norms in the Islamic Doctrine of Economics: A Critique." *Journal of Economic Behavior and Organization* 4: 353–79.

——— (1986). "The Economic System in Contemporary Islamic Thought: Interpretation and Assessment." *International Journal of Middle East Studies* 18: 135–64.

——— (1987). "Preference Falsification, Policy Continuity, and Collective Conservatism." *Economic Journal* 97: 642–65

——— (1989a). "On the Notion of Economic Justice in Contemporary Islamic Thought." *International Journal of Middle East Studies* 21: 171–91. Chapter 5 of this volume.

——— (1989b). "The Craft Guilds of Tunis and Their Amins: A Study in Institutional Atrophy." Pp. 236–64 in *The New Institutional Economics and Development: Theory and Applications to Tunisia,* edited by Mustapha K. Nabli and Jeffrey B. Nugent. Amsterdam: North-Holland.

——— (1990). "Private and Public Preferences." *Economics and Philosophy* 6: 1–26.

——— (1993a). "Fundamentalisms and the Economy." Pp. 289–301 in *Fundamentalisms and the State: Remaking Polities, Economies, and Militance*, edited by Martin E. Marty and R. Scott Appleby. Chicago: University of Chicago Press.

——— (1993b). "The Economic Impact of Islamic Fundamentalism." Pp. 302–41 in *Fundamentalisms and the State: Remaking Polities, Economies, and Militance*, edited by Martin E. Marty and R. Scott Appleby. Chicago: University of Chicago Press. Chapter 1 of this volume.

——— (1995a). *Private Truths, Public Lies: The Social Consequences of Preference Falsification*. Cambridge: Harvard University Press.

——— (1995b). "Islamic Economics and the Islamic Subeconomy." *Journal of Economic Perspectives* 9: 155–73. Chapter 2 of this volume.

——— (1996). "The Discontents of Islamic Economic Morality." *American Economic Review* 86: 438–42.

——— (1997). "Islamism and Economics: Policy Implications for a Free Society." *International Review for Comparative Public Policy* 9: 71–102. Chapter 3 of this volume.

———(1998). "Moral Overload and Its Alleviation." Pp. 231–66 in *Economics, Values, and Organization*, edited by Avner Ben-Ner and Louis Putterman. New York: Cambridge University Press.

——— (2001). "The Provision of Public Goods under Islamic Law: Origins, Impact and Limitations of the Waqf System." *Law and Society Review* 35: 841–97.

——— (2003a). "Islamic Redistribution through *Zakat*: Historical Record and Modern Realities." Pp. 275–93 in *Poverty and Charity in Middle Eastern Contexts*, edited by Michael Bonner, Mine Ener, and Amy Singer. Albany: State University of New York Press.

——— (2003b). "The Islamic Commercial Crisis: Institutional Roots of Economic Underdevelopment in the Middle East." *Journal of Economic History* 63: 414–46.

Kurin, Richard (1986). "Islamization: A View from the Countryside." Pp. 115–28 in *Islamic Reassertion in Pakistan: The Application of Islamic Laws in a Modern State*, edited by Anita M. Weiss. Syracuse: Syracuse University Press.

Landau, Jacob (1990). *The Politics of Pan-Islam: Ideology and Organization*. Oxford: Clarendon Press.

Lerman, Eran (1981). "Mawdudi's Concept of Islam." *Middle Eastern Studies* 17: 492–509.

Lerner, Daniel (1958). *The Passing of Traditional Society: Modernizing the Middle East*. Glencoe, Ill.: Free Press.

Lewis, Bernard (1968). *The Emergence of Modern Turkey*. 2nd ed. London: Oxford University Press.

——— (1970). "Sources for the Economic History of the Middle East." Pp. 78–92 in *Studies in the Economic History of the Middle East*, edited by M. A. Cook. London: Oxford University Press.

——— (1971). *Race and Color in Islam*. New York: Harper and Row.

——— (1975). *History Remembered, Recovered, Invented*. Princeton: Princeton University Press.

——— (1982). *The Muslim Discovery of Europe*. New York: W. W. Norton.

Lewis, Bernard (1993a). *Islam in History: Ideas, People, and Events in the Middle East.* 2nd ed. Chicago: Open Court.

—— (1993b). *Islam and the West.* New York: Oxford University Press.

Lewis, W. Arthur (1955). *The Theory of Economic Growth.* London: George Allen and Unwin.

Lowenthal, David (1985). *The Past Is a Foreign Country.* New York: Cambridge University Press.

Luckmann, Thomas (1967). *The Invisible Religion: The Problem of Religion in Modern Society.* New York: Macmillan.

Macdonald, Duncan Black (1909/1965). *The Religious Attitude and Life in Islam.* Beirut: Khayats.

—— (1911/1971). *Aspects of Islam.* New York: Books for Libraries Press.

Malik, Jamal (1996). *Colonialization of Islam: Dissolution of Traditional Institutions in Pakistan.* New Delhi: Manohar.

Mallat, Chibli (1988). "The Debate on Ribā and Interest in Twentieth Century Jurisprudence." Pp. 69–88 in *Islamic Law and Finance*, edited by Mallat. London: Graham and Totman.

—— (1993). *The Renewal of Islamic Law: Muhammad Baqer as-Sadr, Najaf and the Shiʾi International.* Cambridge: Cambridge University Press.

Mandaville, Jon E. (1979). "Usurious Piety: The Cash Waqf Controversy in the Ottoman Empire." *International Journal of Middle East Studies* 10: 289–308.

Mannan, Muhammad Abdul (1970). *Islamic Economics: Theory and Practice.* Lahore: Sh. Muhammad Ashraf.

—— (1982). "Allocative Efficiency, Decision and Welfare Criteria in an Interest-Free Islamic Economy: A Comparative Policy Approach." Pp. 43–62 in *Monetary and Fiscal Economics of Islam*, edited by Mohammad Ariff. Jeddah: International Center for Research in Islamic Economics.

—— (1984a). *The Making of an Islamic Economic Society: Islamic Dimensions in Economic Analysis.* Cairo: International Association of Islamic Banks.

—— (1984b). *The Frontiers of Islamic Economics: Theory and Practice.* Delhi: Idarah-i Adabiyat-i Delli.

Mardin, Şerif (1993). "The Nakshibendi Order in Modern Turkey." Pp. 204–32 in *Fundamentalisms and the State: Remaking Polities, Economies, Militance*, edited by Martin E. Marty and R. Scott Appleby. Chicago: University of Chicago Press.

Marty, Martin E., and R. Scott Appleby (1991). "Conclusion: An Interim Report on a Hypothetical Family." Pp. 814–42 in *Fundamentalisms Observed.*, edited by Martin E. Marty and R. Scott Appleby. Chicago: University of Chicago Press.

—— eds. (1993). *Fundamentalisms and the State: Remaking Polities, Economies, and Militance.* Chicago: University of Chicago Press.

Mawdudi, Sayyid Abul-Ala (1939/1976). *Jihad in Islam*, translated from Urdu. Lahore: Islamic Publications.

—— (1939–60/1981). *Selected Speeches and Writings of Mawlana Mawdudi.* Vol. 1, translated by S. Zakir Aijaz. Karachi: International Islamic Publishers.

—— (1940/1963). *Short History of the Revivalist Movement in Islam*, translated by Al-Ash'ari. Lahore: Islamic Publications.

———— (1940/1990). *Let Us Be Muslims*, translated from Urdu. Kuala Lumpur: Noordeen.

———— (1941/1976). *Islam and Ignorance*, translated from Urdu. Lahore: Islamic Publications.

———— (1944/1981). "Pakistan versus Jewish State." Pp. 35–36 in *Selected Speeches and Writings of Mawlana Mawdudi*. Vol. 1, translated by S. Zakir Aijaz. Karachi: International Islamic Publishers.

———— (1945/1981). "Formal and Real Islam Differentiated." Pp. 37–42 in *Selected Speeches and Writings of Mawlana Mawdudi*. Vol. 1, translated by S. Zakir Aijaz. Karachi: International Islamic Publishers.

———— (1947/1975). *The Economic Problem of Man and Its Islamic Solution*, translated from Urdu. Lahore: Islamic Publications.

———— (1947/1976). *Nations Rise and Decline—Why?*, translated from Urdu. Lahore: Islamic Publications.

———— (1948/1950). *Islamic Way of Life*, translated from Urdu. Lahore: Islamic Publications.

———— (1948/1981). "Speech Delivered in a Gathering of Ladies at Lahore." Pp. 58–75 in *Selected Speeches and Writings of Mawlana Mawdudi*. Vol. 1, translated by S. Zakir Aijaz. Karachi: International Islamic Publishers.

———— (1950/1981). "A Critique of Constitutional Proposals." Pp. 140–70 in *Selected Speeches and Writings of Mawlana Mawdudi*. Vol. 1, translated by S. Zakir Aijaz. Karachi: International Islamic Publishers.

———— (1951/1981). "The Rudiments of Islamic Philosophy of Economics." Pp. 173–82 in *Selected Speeches and Writings of Mawlana Mawdudi*. Vol. 1, translated by S. Zakir Aijaz. Karachi: International Islamic Publishers.

———— (1952/1960). *First Principles of the Islamic State*, translated from Urdu. Lahore: Islamic Publications.

Mayer, Ann Elizabeth (1985). "Islamic Banking and Credit Policies in the Sadat Era: The Social Origins of Islamic Banking in Egypt." *Arab Law Quarterly* 1: 32–50.

———— (1986). "Islamization and Taxation in Pakistan." Pp. 59–77 in *Islamic Reassertion in Pakistan: The Application of Islamic Laws in a Modern State*, edited by Anita M. Weiss. Syracuse: Syracuse University Press.

———— (1993). "The Fundamentalist Impact on Law, Politics, and Constitutions in Iran, Pakistan, and the Sudan." Pp. 110–51 in *Fundamentalisms and the State: Remaking Polities, Economies, and Militance*, edited by Martin E. Marty and R. Scott Appleby. Chicago: University of Chicago Press.

Meeker, Michael E. (1991). "The New Muslim Intellectuals in the Republic of Turkey." Pp. 189–219 in *Islam in Modern Turkey: Religion, Politics, and Literature in a Secular State*, edited by Richard Tapper. London: I. B. Tauris.

Meenai, S. A. (1989). *The Islamic Development Bank: A Case Study of Islamic Co-operation*. London: Kegan Paul International.

Metcalf, Barbara D. (1994). "'Remaking Ourselves': Islamic Self-Fashioning in a Global Movement of Spiritual Renewal." Pp. 706–25 in *Accounting for Fundamentalisms: The Dynamic Character of Movements*, edited by Martin E. Marty and R. Scott Appleby. Chicago: University of Chicago Press.

Mishra, Vikas (1962). *Hinduism and Economic Growth*. London: Oxford University Press.

Mohammad, Faiz (1995). "Relationship between Obligatory Official *Zakah* Collection and Voluntary *Zakah* Collection by Charitable Organizations." Pp. 163–95 in *Institutional Framework of Zakah: Dimensions and Implications*, edited by Ahmed Abdel-Fattah el-Ashker and Muhammad Sirajul Haq. Jeddah: Islamic Development Bank.

Mokyr, Joel (1990). *The Lever of Riches: Technological Creativity and Economic Progress*. New York: Oxford University Press.

Moore, Clement Henry (1988). "Islamic Banks: Financial and Political Intermediation in Arab Countries." *Orient* 29: 45–57.

——— (1990a). "Islamic Banks and Competitive Politics in the Arab World and Turkey." *Middle East Journal* 44: 234–55.

——— (1990b). "La place des banques Islamiques dans un système politique d'ouverture: Comparison des cas turc et égyptien." Unpublished paper presented at the National Political Science Foundation (Fondation Nationale des Sciences Politiques), Paris, March.

Morad, Munir (1988). "Current Thought on Islamic Taxation: A Critical Synthesis." Pp. 117–27 in *Islamic Law and Finance*, edited by Chibli Mallat. London: Graham and Totman.

Mottahadeh, Roy P. (1995). "The Clash of Civilizations: An Islamicist's Critique." *Harvard Middle Eastern and Islamic Review* 2: 1–26.

Mumcu, Uğur (1987). *Rabıta*. Istanbul: Tekin Yayınevi.

——— (1988). *Tarikat, Siyaset, Ticaret*. Istanbul: Tekin Yayınevi.

Murphy, Kim (1992). "Islamic Extremists Declaring War on Egypt's Tourist Industry." *Los Angeles Times*, October 23, A6.

Mustapha, Nik, Bin Hj. Nik Hasan (1987). "Zakat in Malaysia—Present and Future Status." *Journal of Islamic Economics* 1 (August-September): 47–75.

Nagarkar, V. V. (1975). *Genesis of Pakistan*. Bombay: Allied Publishers.

Naqvi, Syed Nawab Haider (1981a). *Ethics and Economics: An Islamic Synthesis*. Leicester: Islamic Foundation.

——— (1981b). *Individual Freedom, Social Welfare and Islamic Economic Order*. Islamabad: Pakistan Institute of Development Economics.

——— (1994). *Islam, Economics, and Society*. London: Kegan Paul International.

Nasr, Seyyed Hossein (1985). "Islamic Work Ethics." Pp. 49–62 in *Comparative Work Ethics: Judeo-Christian, Islamic, and Eastern*, edited by Jaroslav Pelikan, Joseph Kitagawa, and Seyyed Hossein Nasr. Washington, D.C.: Library of Congress.

Nasr, Seyyed Vali Reza (1987). "Toward a Philosophy of Islamic Economics." *Muslim World* 77: 175–96.

——— (1988). "Whither Islamic Economics?" *Islamic Quarterly* 30: 211–20.

——— (1989). "Islamic Economics: Novel Perspectives." *Middle Eastern Studies* 25: 516–30.

——— (1994). *The Vanguard of the Islamic Revolution: The Jama'at-i Islami of Pakistan*. Berkeley: University of California Press.

——— (1996). *Mawdudi and the Making of Islamic Revivalism*. New York: Oxford University Press.

New Straits Times (Kuala Lumpur), March 6, 1990.

Nienhaus, Volker (1986). "Islamic Economics, Finance and Banking: Theory and Practice." *Journal of Islamic Banking and Finance* (London) 3: 1–17.

—— (1988). "Lectures on Islamic Economics and Banking." Faculty of Economics Discussion Paper no. 6. University of Bochum, West Germany, December.

Novossyolov, Dimitri B. (1993). "The Islamization of Welfare in Pakistan." Pp. 160–74 in *Russia's Muslim Frontiers: New Directions in Cross-Cultural Analysis*, edited by Dale F. Eickelman. Bloomington: Indiana University Press.

Oakeshott, Michael (1958/1993). *Morality and Politics in Modern Europe: The Harvard Lectures*, edited by Shirley Robin Letwin. New Haven: Yale University Press.

Olson, Mancur (1982). *The Rise and Decline of Nations: Economic Growth, Stagflation, and Social Rigidities*. New Haven: Yale University Press.

Oran, Ahmad, and Salim Rashid (1989). "Fiscal Policy in Early Islam." *Public Finance* 44: 75–101.

Organization for Economic Co-operation and Development (1983). *Aid from OPEC Countries*. Paris: OECD.

Owen, Roger (1981). *The Middle East in the World Economy, 1800–1914*. London: Methuen.

Ölçen, Ali Nejat (1991). *İslâmda Karanlığın Başlangıcı ve Türk-İslâm Sentezi*. Ankara: Ekin Yayınevi.

Özdenören, Rasim (1990). *Müslümanca Yaşamak*. Istanbul: İz Yayıncılık.

Özel Finans Kurumları ve Türkiye Uygulaması Sempozyumu (1988). Istanbul: Marmara Üniversitesi Ortadoğu ve İslâm Ülkeleri Ekonomik Araştırma Merkezi.

Özel, İsmet (1984). *Zor Zamanda Konuşmak*. Istanbul: Çıdam Yayınları.

—— (1985). *Bakanlar ve Görenler*. Istanbul: Çıdam Yayınları.

—— (1989). *Sorulunca Söylenen*. Istanbul: Çıdam Yayınları.

Pakistan Statistical Yearbook (1989). Karachi: Manager of Publications.

Papageorgiou, Demetris, Michael Michaely, and Armeane Choksi, eds. (1991). *Liberalizing Foreign Trade*. 7 vols. Cambridge, Mass.: Basil Blackwell.

Patel, Rashida (1986). *Islamisation of Laws in Pakistan?* Karachi: Faiza Publishers.

Permanent Commission on Islamisation of Economy, Pakistan (1988). "Improvement in the Nizam-e Zakat and Ushr for Achieving Its Declared Objectives of Removing Abject Poverty and Eradication of Beggary from the Country." Mimeographed report, February.

Philipp, Thomas (1990). "The Idea of Islamic Economics." *Die Welt des Islams* 30: 117–39.

Polanyi, Michael (1966/1983). *The Tacit Dimension*. Gloucester, Mass.: Peter Smith.

Posner, Richard A. (1980). "A Theory of Primitive Society with Special Reference to Law." *Journal of Law and Economics* 23: 1–53.

Presley, John R., ed. (1988). *Directory of Islamic Financial Institutions*. London: Croom Helm for the International Center for Islamic Studies.

Pryor, Frederic L. (1985). "The Islamic Economic System." *Journal of Comparative Economics* 9: 197–223.

Putnam, Robert D. (1993). *Making Democracy Work: Civic Traditions in Modern Italy*. Princeton: Princeton University Press.

Qaddafi, Muammar (1976–79/1980). *The Green Book*, translated from Arabic. Tripoli: Green Book World Center for Research and Study.

Qardawi, Yusuf (1966/1981). *Economic Security in Islam*, translated by Muhammad Iqbal Siddiqi. Lahore: Kazi Publications.

Quigley, Carroll (1979). *The Evolution of Civilizations: An Introduction to Historical Analysis*. 2nd ed. Indianapolis: Liberty Press.

Qutb, Sayyid (1948/1970). *Social Justice in Islam*, translated by John D. Hardie. New York: American Council of Learned Societies.

Rahman, Fazlur (1964). "*Ribā* and Interest." *Islamic Studies* 3: 1–43.

——— (1974). "Islam and the Problem of Economic Justice." *Pakistan Economist* 14 (August 24): 14–39.

——— (1979). *Islam*. 2nd ed. Chicago: University of Chicago Press.

——— (1982). *Islam and Modernity: Transformation of an Intellectual Tradition*. Chicago: University of Chicago Press.

Rahnema, Ali, and Farhad Nomani (1990). *The Secular Miracle: Religion, Politics, and Economic Policy in Iran*. London: Zed Books.

Rashwan, Diaa, and Emad Gad (1993). "The Marriage of Militancy and Tradition." *Al-Ahram Weekly* (Cairo), July 8–14, p. 3.

Rawls, John (1971). *A Theory of Justice*. Cambridge: Harvard University Press.

Ray, Nicholas D. (1995) *Arab Islamic Banking and the Renewal of Islamic Law*. London: Graham and Trotman.

Reed, Howard A. (1988). "Islam and Education in Turkey." *Turkish Studies Association Bulletin* 12: 1–5.

Renan, Ernest (1883). *L'Islamisme et la science* (Sorbonne conference, March 29). Paris: Calmann Lévy.

Report of the Council of Islamic Ideology on the Elimination of Interest from the Economy (1980). Islamabad: Council of Islamic Ideology.

Richards, Alan, and John Waterbury (1996). *A Political Economy of the Middle East*. 2nd ed. Boulder: Westview.

Risso, Patricia (1989). "Muslim Identity in Maritime Trade: General Observations and Some Evidence from the 18th-Century Persian Gulf/Indian Ocean Region." *International Journal of Middle East Studies* 21: 381–92.

Roberts, Hugh (1994). "From Radical Mission to Equivocal Ambition: The Expansion and Manipulation of Algerian Islamism, 1979–1992." Pp. 428–89 in *Accounting for Fundamentalisms: The Dynamic Character of Movements*, edited by Martin E. Marty and R. Scott Appleby. Chicago: University of Chicago Press.

Rodinson, Maxime (1966/1973). *Islam and Capitalism*, translated by Brian Pearce. New York: Pantheon.

Rosenberg, Nathan, and Luther E. Birdzell, Jr. (1986). *How the West Grew Rich: The Economic Transformation of the Industrial World*. New York: Basic Books.

Roy, Olivier (1992/1994). *The Failure of Political Islam*, translated by Carol Volk. Cambridge: Harvard University Press.

Rowley, Charles K., Robert D. Tollison, and Gordon Tullock, eds. (1988). *The Political Economy of Rent-Seeking*. Boston: Kluwer.

Rushton, J. Philippe (1980). *Altruism, Socialization, and Society*. Englewood Cliffs, N.J.: Prentice-Hall.

Sabzwari, M. A. (1979). *A Study of Zakat and 'Ushr with Special Reference to Pakistan*. Karachi: Industries Printing Press.

Sadeq, Abul Hasan Muhammad (1990). *Economic Development in Islam*. Petaling Jaya, Malaysia: Pelanduk Publications.

Said, Edward W. (1978). *Orientalism*. New York: Pantheon Books.

Salama, Abdin Ahmed (1982). "Fiscal Analysis of Zakah with Special Reference to Saudi Arabia's Experience in Zakah." Pp. 341–71 in *Monetary and Fiscal Economics of Islam*, edited by Mohammad Ariff. Jeddah: International Center for Research in Islamic Economics.

Saleh, Nabil A. (1986). *Unlawful Gain and Legitimate Profit in Islamic Law*. Cambridge: Cambridge University Press.

Salleh, Ismail Muhd, and Rogayah Ngah (1980). "Distribution of the Zakat Burden on Padi Producers in Malaysia." Pp. 80–153 in *Some Aspects of the Economics of Zakah*, edited by M. Raqibuz Zaman. Plainfield, Ind.: Association of Muslim Social Scientists.

Samiullah, Muhammad (1982). "Prohibition of Riba (Interest) and Insurance in the Light of Islam." *Islamic Studies* 21: 53–76.

Saraçgil, Bahadır (1993). "İslamî Giyimde Moda ve Tüketim." *Yeni Zemin*, August: 74–76.

Sayeed, Khalid B. (1968). *Pakistan: The Formative Phase, 1857–1948*. 2nd ed. London: Oxford University Press.

Schacht, Joseph (1934). "Zakāt." *Encyclopaedia of Islam*. Vol. 3: 1202–4.

Schlessinger, Arthur M., Jr. (1991). *The Disuniting of America: Reflections on a Multicultural Society*. Knoxville, Tenn.: Whittle Books.

Scott, James C. (1985). *Weapons of the Weak: Everyday Forms of Peasant Resistance*. New Haven: Yale University Press.

——— (1987). "Resistance without Protest and without Organization: Peasant Opposition to the Islamic Zakat and the Christian Tithe." *Comparative Studies in Society and History* 29: 417–52.

Shaban, M. A. (1971). *Islamic History: A New Interpretation*. Vol. 1. Cambridge: Cambridge University Press.

Shad, Abdur Rahman (1986). *Zakat and Ushr*. Lahore: Kazi Publications.

Shayegan, Daryush (1989/1992). *Cultural Schizophrenia: Islamic Societies Confronting the West*, translated by John Howe. London: Saqi Books.

Shepard, William E. (1989). "Islam as a 'System' in the Later Writings of Sayyid Qutb." *Middle Eastern Studies* 25: 31–50.

Siddiqi, Mohammad Akhtar Saeed (1983). *Early Development of Zakat Law and Ijtihad*. Karachi: Islamic Research Academy.

Siddiqi, Muhammad Nejatullah (1972). *The Economic Enterprise in Islam*. Lahore: Islamic Publications.

Siddiqi, Muhammad Nejatullah (1981). *Muslim Economic Thinking: A Survey of Contemporary Literature.* Leicester: Islamic Foundation.

———— (1982). "Islamic Approaches to Money, Banking and Monetary Policy: A Review." Pp. 25–38 in *Monetary and Fiscal Economics of Islam,* edited by Mohammad Ariff. Jeddah: International Center for Research in Islamic Economics.

———— (1985). *Insurance in an Islamic Economy.* Leicester: Islamic Foundation.

———— (1994). "Nature and Methodology of Islamic Political Economy." Paper presented at the seminar on Islamic Political Economy in the Age of Capitalist Globalization, Universiti Sains Malaysia, Penang, December.

Simon, Herbert A. (1983). *Reason in Human Affairs.* Stanford: Stanford University Press.

Sivan, Emmanuel (1985). *Radical Islam: Medieval Theology and Modern Politics.* New Haven: Yale University Press.

Smith, Adam (1759/1976). *The Theory of Moral Sentiments.* Oxford: Clarendon Press.

———— (1776/1937). *The Wealth of Nations.* New York: Modern Library.

Smith, Wilfred Cantwell (1957). *Islam in Modern History.* Princeton: Princeton University Press.

Springborg, Robert (1989). *Mubarak's Egypt: Fragmentation of the Political Order.* Boulder: Westview.

Stark, Rodney, Laurence Iannaccone, and Roger Finke (1998). "Rationality and the 'Religious Mind.' " *Economic Inquiry* 36: 373–89.

Sullivan, Denis (1994). *Private Voluntary Organizations in Egypt: Islamic Development, Private Initiative, and State Control.* Gainesville: University Press of Florida.

Sutcliffe, Claud R. (1975). "Is Islam an Obstacle to Development? Ideal Patterns of Belief versus Actual Patterns of Behavior." *Journal of Developing Areas* 10: 77–82.

Talbot, Ian (1993). "The Growth of the Muslim League in the Punjab, 1937–46." Pp. 230–53 in *India's Partition: Process, Strategy, and Mobilization,* edited by Mushirul Hasan. Delhi: Oxford University Press.

Taleghani, Sayyid Mahmud (1982). *Society and Economics in Islam,* translated by R. Campbell. Berkeley: Mizan Press.

Tanzil-ur-Rahman (1981). *Introduction of Zakat in Pakistan.* Islamabad: Council of Islamic Ideology.

Tawney, R. H. (1926/1962). *Religion and the Rise of Capitalism.* Gloucester, Mass: Peter Smith.

Tibi, Bassam (1993). "The Worldview of Sunni Arab Fundamentalists: Attitudes toward Modern Science and Technology." Pp. 73–102 in *Fundamentalisms and Society: Reclaiming the Sciences, the Family, and Education,* edited by Martin E. Marty and R. Scott Appleby. Chicago: University of Chicago Press.

Todaro, Michael P. (1985). *Economic Development in the Third World.* 3rd ed. New York: Longman.

Tönnies, Ferdinand (1887/1957). *Community and Society (Gemeinschaft and Gesellschaft),* translated by Charles P. Loomis. East Lansing: Michigan State University Press.

Triandis, Harry C. (1990). "Cross-cultural Studies of Individualism and Collectivism." Pp. 41–133 in *Nebraska Symposium on Motivation 1989*, edited by John J. Berman. Lincoln: University of Nebraska Press.

Turner, Bryan S. (1974). *Weber and Islam: A Critical Study*. London: Routledge and Kegan Paul.

Tversky, Amos, and Daniel Kahneman (1991). "Loss Aversion and Riskless Choice: A Reference Dependent Model." *Quarterly Journal of Economics* 106: 1039–61.

Udovitch, Abraham L. (1962). "At the Origins of the Western *Commenda*: Islam, Israel, Byzantium?" *Speculum* 37: 198–207.

────── (1970). *Partnership and Profit in Medieval Islam*. Princeton: Princeton University Press.

────── (1985). "Islamic Law and the Social Context of Exchange in the Medieval Middle East." *History and Anthropology* 1: 445–65.

Ullmann-Margalit, Edna (1977). *The Emergence of Norms*. Oxford: Clarendon Press.

Uludağ, Süleyman (1988). *İslâm'da Faiz Meselesine Yeni Bir Bakış*. Istanbul: Dergâh Yayınları.

United Nations Development Programme (2002). *Arab Human Development Report 2002: Creating Opportunities for Future Generations*. New York: UNDP.

Ülgener, Sabri F. (1981). *İktisadi Çözülmenin Ahlak ve Zihniyet Dünyası*. 2nd ed. Istanbul: Der Yayınları.

────── (1984). *Darlık Buhranları ve İslâm İktisat Siyaseti*. Ankara: Mayaş Yayınları.

Vandewalle, Dirk (1991). "Qadhafi's 'Perestroika': Economic and Political Liberalization in Libya." *Middle East Journal* 45: 216–31.

Watt, W. Montgomery (1988). *Islamic Fundamentalism and Modernity*. London: Routledge.

Weber, Max (1904–5/1958). *The Protestant Ethic and the Spirit of Capitalism*, translated by A. M. Henderson and Talcott Parsons. New York: Charles Scribner's Sons.

────── (1922/1968). *Economy and Society: An Outline of Interpretive Sociology*. 3 vols., edited by Guenther Roth and Claus Wittich. New York: Bedminster Press.

White, Leslie (1975). *The Concept of Cultural Systems: A Key to Understanding Tribes and Nations*. New York: Columbia University Press.

Williamson, Oliver E. (1985). *The Economic Institutions of Capitalism*. New York: Free Press.

Wilson, James Q. (1993). *The Moral Sense*. New York: Free Press.

Wilson, Rodney (1985). *Islamic Business. Theory and Practice*. Rev. ed. London: Economist Intelligence Unit.

────── (1990). "Retail Development and Wholesale Possibilities." Pp. 7–18 in *Islamic Financial Markets*, edited by Rodney Wilson. London: Routledge.

World Development Report (1980). Washington, D.C.: World Bank.

Yediyıldız, Bahaeddin (1990). *Institution du vakf au XVIIIe siècle en Turquie*. Ankara: Éditions Ministère de la Culture.

Yılmaz, Hüseyin (1990). *Öldükten Sonra "Allah" Diyen Bakan*. Istanbul: Timaş Yayınları.

Yusuf, S. M. (1971). *Economic Justice in Islam*. Lahore: Sh. Muhammad Ashraf.

Zahid, Shahid N. (1989). "The Zakat and Ushr System in Pakistan." Report prepared for the World Bank, Karachi, August.

Zaman, S. M. Hasanuz (1985). "Indexation—An Islamic Evaluation." *Journal of Research in Islamic Economics* 2: 31–53.

Zarqa, Muhammad Anas (1988). "Islamic Distributive Schemes." Pp. 163–216 in *Distributive Justice and Need Fulfilment in an Islamic Economy*, edited by Munawar Iqbal. Leicester: Islamic Foundation.

Index

Printed in the United States
154457LV00003B/20/P